Judges and Legislators

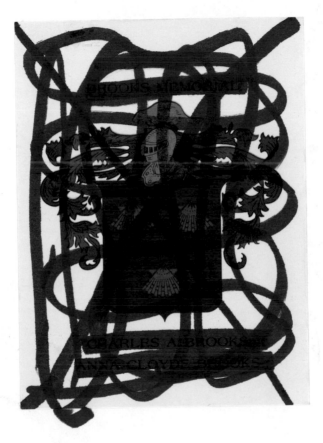

Judges and Legislators: Toward Institutional Comity

Robert A. Katzmann
editor

THE BROOKINGS INSTITUTION
WASHINGTON, D.C.

Copyright © 1988 by
THE BROOKINGS INSTITUTION
1775 Massachusetts Avenue, N.W., Washington, D.C. 20036

Library of Congress Cataloging-in-Publication Data

Judges and legislators : toward institutional comity / Robert A.
  Katzmann, editor.
     p.   cm.
  Includes index.
  ISBN 0-8157-4862-0   ISBN 0-8157-4861-2 (pbk.)
  1. Separation of powers—United States.   2. Legislative power—
United States.   3. Judicial power—United States.   I. Katzmann,
Robert A.
KF4565.J83   1988
342.73′052—dc19
[347.30252]
                                                           88-19422
                                                              CIP

9 8 7 6 5 4 3 2 1

Set in Linotron Berkeley Old Style
Composition by Monotype Composition Co.
Baltimore, Maryland
Printed by R.R. Donnelley and Sons, Co.
Harrisonburg, Virginia

THE BROOKINGS INSTITUTION

The Brookings Institution is an independent organization devoted to nonpartisan research, education, and publication in economics, government, foreign policy, and the social sciences generally. Its principal purposes are to aid in the development of sound public policies and to promote public understanding of issues of national importance.

The Institution was founded on December 8, 1927, to merge the activities of the Institute for Government Research, founded in 1916, the Institute of Economics, founded in 1922, and the Robert Brookings Graduate School of Economics and Government, founded in 1924.

The Board of Trustees is responsible for the general administration of the Institution, while the immediate direction of the policies, program, and staff is vested in the President, assisted by an advisory committee of the officers and staff. The by-laws of the Institution state: "It is the function of the Trustees to make possible the conduct of scientific research, and publication, under the most favorable conditions, and to safeguard the independence of the research staff in the pursuit of their studies and in the publication of the results of such studies. It is not a part of their function to determine, control, or influence the conduct of particular investigations or the conclusions reached."

The President bears final responsibility for the decision to publish a manuscript as a Brookings book. In reaching his judgment on the competence, accuracy, and objectivity of each study, the President is advised by the director of the appropriate research program and weighs the views of a panel of expert outside readers who report to him in confidence on the quality of the work. Publication of a work signifies that it is deemed a competent treatment worthy of public consideration but does not imply endorsement of conclusions or recommendations.

The Institution maintains its position of neutrality on issues of public policy in order to safeguard the intellectual freedom of the staff. Hence interpretations or conclusions in Brookings publications should be understood to be solely those of the authors and should not be attributed to the Institution, to its trustees, officers, or other staff members, or to the organizations that support its research.

Foreword

Reasoned policymaking depends in part upon understanding among the branches of government of one another's problems and processes. There is no shortage of commentary suggesting the need for better communications between Congress and the executive branch. Yet the judicial branch, which has increasingly played a critical role in our system, has generally been neglected in discussions about interbranch relationships.

This book seeks to help redress this imbalance by focusing on the critical linkage between the federal judiciary and Congress. The consequences of the lack of understanding between the judiciary and Congress are becoming ever more acute. The legislature's inattention to the institutional well-being of the judiciary has made it increasingly difficult to attract able candidates to the federal bench and to retain those already on it. The gap has also made it harder for the courts to discern legislative meaning whenever they interpret statutes. Courts are thus often accused of distorting congressional will.

As this volume details, some of these long-standing problems can be mitigated by developing ground rules for communications between judges and legislators, ascertaining ways for Congress to better signal its legislative intent to the courts, and developing institutional mechanisms to improve relations between the branches.

This volume is part of a major project, begun at the invitation of the U.S. Judicial Conference Committee on the Judicial Branch, that seeks to determine how relations between the legislative and judicial branches can be improved. The papers in this volume are the product of a colloquium held at Brookings that brought together scholars from a variety of disciplines, members of the judiciary and Congress, and other interested persons. Robert A. Katzmann, editor of the volume and director of the project, has contributed a summary of the proceedings and an agenda for improvements between the branches.

The editor is grateful to the colloquium participants. For their critical and useful comments on the manuscript, he owes a special debt to Judge Frank M. Coffin, Judge Abner Mikva, Professor A. Leo Levin, Warren I. Cikins, Thomas E. Mann, and R. Shep Melnick. At the colloquium, Donna M. Dezenhall of the Brookings Center for Public Education and Maureen Weston were helpful. Brookings interns Daniel Hall, Kimberly Reed, and Jack Zorman aided the editor in various ways. William J. Brennan IV, then of the Federal Judicial Center, assisted in gathering data for one chapter.

The editor is very thankful to Nancy D. Davidson, who edited the manuscript with the help of Brenda B. Szittya. Richard Aboulafia verified its contents. The index was prepared by Margaret Lynch. Sandra Z. Riegler, Eloise Stinger, and Pamela Whelan provided administrative support, and Renuka D. Deonarain supplied secretarial skills as the manuscript was turned into a book. Louis Holliday and Michael Doleman provided assistance in preparing the manuscript and research materials. Laura Walker and the Brookings library staff also were most helpful.

The Brookings Institution is grateful to the Charles E. Culpeper Foundation, the Earhart Foundation, and an anonymous foundation for grants to support work on this volume.

The views ascribed to this book are those of the authors and should not be attributed to the trustees, officers, or other staff members of the Brookings Institution, or to the various funding sources.

Bruce K. MacLaury
PRESIDENT

JULY 1988
WASHINGTON, D.C.

Editor's Acknowledgments

I have many thanks to spread about, not only to those who helped produce this volume, but also to those who have lent their energies to this ongoing project. Foremost among these is Judge Frank M. Coffin, the chairman of the U.S. Judicial Conference Committee on the Judicial Branch, without whose vision this project would not have been undertaken. The wise counsel of Gilbert Y. Steiner, senior fellow in the Brookings Governmental Studies program, has been indispensable from the outset. I am grateful to the directors and officers of the Governance Institute, whose backing assured that this project could be pursued.

I appreciate the support at Brookings of President Bruce K. MacLaury; Thomas E. Mann, the director of the Brookings Governmental Studies program; and Warren I. Cikins, senior staff member of the Center for Public Policy Education and the organizer of the Brookings' Administration of Justice conferences, who introduced the panelists at the colloquium.

The members of the U.S. Judicial Conference Committee on the Judicial Branch provided valuable suggestions about the project. I benefited from the advice of the planning committee for the colloquium, consisting of Judge Coffin, Judge Abner J. Mikva, Judge Thomas J. Meskill, Judge J. Clifford Wallace, Professor A. Leo Levin, Dean Paul D. Carrington, Warren I. Cikins, Roger H. Davidson, Jeffrey W. Kampelman, William C. Kelly, Jr., and Gilbert Y. Steiner. In addition, discussions about various aspects of the project have been helpful with the following people: Judge Hugh H. Bownes, Judge John R. Brown, Judge James L. Buckley, Judge Warren Eginton, Judge Irving Hill, Judge Kenneth W. Starr, William R. Burchill, Jr., Benjamin L. Cardin, Robert Feidler, Kenneth Feinberg, Louis Fisher, Hillel Fradkin, Leonard Garment, Mark A. Goldberg, Stephen Hess, Mary Jane Hickey, Stephen Horn, Robert W. Kastenmeier, Herbert Kaufman, Leslie Lenkowsky, Paul C. Light, Thomas Main, Daniel P. Moynihan, William K. Muir, Jr., Gerald D. Rapp, Michael J. Remington, Steven R. Ross, Martin M. Shapiro, Thomas Thornburg, William Weller, and Russell R. Wheeler.

I am particularly grateful for the continuing support of Francis J. McNamara, Jr., and Helen D. Johnson, so necessary for the birth and continued life of this project.

A. Leo Levin and Charles P. Nihan, the former director and deputy director of the Federal Judiciary Center, respectively, provided a stimulating environment for my work over a period of several months.

I also extend thanks to the Judicial Conference of the District of Columbia Circuit for inviting me to participate at its meeting and to test various ideas about this project with the judges of the circuit. In that regard, I especially acknowledge the kindness of Chief Judge Patricia M. Wald, Judge James L. Buckley, and Judge Ruth Bader Ginsburg.

In addition to the aid provided by various foundations to the Brookings Institution, I appreciate the grants to the Governance Institute that contributed to the completion of this book from the M. D. Anderson Foundation, the Lynde and Harry Bradley Foundation, the Charles E. Culpeper Foundation, the Robert J. Kutak Foundation, the Henry Luce Foundation, the Mead Corporation Foundation, and an anonymous foundation.

Robert A. Katzmann
EDITOR

JULY 1988
WASHINGTON, D.C.

Contents

->>><<<-

Judges and Legislators

Introduction

Robert A. Katzmann

+>>X<<+

This study of judicial-congressional relations is rooted in the premise that the two branches lack appreciation of each other's processes and problems, with unfortunate consequences for both and for policymaking more generally. This colloquium volume can perhaps best be understood as an effort by the judiciary to bridge the distance with Congress, to ascertain the sources of tension, and to find pragmatic solutions to ameliorate them. It is the first immediate product of a long-term project examining the full range of relationships between the judiciary and Congress, begun under the auspices of the Brookings Institution and continuing in conjunction with the Governance Institute. The purpose of the inquiry is not to propose a radical restructuring of arrangements, but rather to determine if, how, and under what circumstances the judicial-congressional relationship might be improved. Such work may be especially timely as our Constitution enters into its next hundred years and we rededicate ourselves to the effort to realize its objectives.

Origins

A critical examination of judicial-congressional affairs, with the hope of improving relations between the branches, became part of the long-term agenda of the U.S. Judicial Conference Committee on the Judicial Branch in 1984. The U.S. Judicial Conference is the policymaking body of the federal judiciary, concerned with the administration of justice and charged by statute with making recommendations to Congress.[1] A key committee of the conference is the Committee on the Judicial Branch, responsible in part for advising and making recommendations to the Judicial Conference on matters

---

1. Created in 1922, with the vigorous support of Chief Justice William Howard Taft, the "Conference of Senior Circuit Judges," as it was then known, was to provide the federal judiciary with a centralized policymaking administrative and management capacity. It consists today of the chief justice of the United States, who serves as its chairman, the chief judge of each judicial circuit, the chief judge of the Court of International Trade, and a district judge from each judicial circuit. 28 U.S.C. sec. 331.

relating to the viability of the judicial office as a lifetime calling—salaries, benefits, and other perquisites. It is to disseminate such information and promote interest throughout the federal judiciary.

Chaired by Circuit Judge Frank M. Coffin, the fourteen-person committee is a diverse group, drawn from across the country and rich in experience. A distinctive dimension of the committee's profile is that many of its members have served in Congress.[2]

Upon assuming the chair of the committee, at the request of then Chief Justice Warren Burger, Judge Coffin proposed that its focus should include, in addition to its traditional concerns, a long-range program devoted to the increased understanding of and respect for the judiciary. At the core of such an agenda would be an examination of past, present, and future relations between Congress and the judiciary. As a former member of Congress and a federal circuit judge, Coffin had reached the view that the interaction of the two branches of government festered with enough misunderstandings and friction to impede the most effective functioning of both. The judiciary could not hope to strengthen its well-being without congressional support—and that depended upon a mutual appreciation of each branch's responsibilities, processes, and problems. With the backing of the chief justice and the approval of his committee, Judge Coffin moved to launch an inquiry, of which this colloquium volume is but a part.[3] Thus the idea for this project is directly traceable to Judge Coffin and the Committee on the Judicial Branch; their support has been a vital, sustaining force.

At the invitation of Judge Coffin, I began work with the Committee on the Judicial Branch to help create a process for considering important questions affecting relations between the courts and Congress. As presently envisioned, the project has three principal components: a book, which I will be writing throughout the duration of the enterprise, assessing relations

2. Since the project began, the roster from the House of Representatives has consisted at various times of Judge Coffin (elected from Maine), Judge Abner J. Mikva of the U.S. Court of Appeals for the District of Columbia Circuit (Illinois), Judge Thomas J. Meskill of the U.S. Court of Appeals for the Second Circuit (Connecticut), Senior District Judge James Harvey of the U.S. District Court for the Eastern District of Michigan (Michigan), Senior District Judge Oren Harris of the U.S. District Court for the Eastern District of Arkansas (Arkansas), and District Judge William L. Hungate of the U.S. District Court for the Eastern District of Missouri (Missouri). Former senators include Senior Judge Jack R. Miller of the U.S. Court of Appeals for the Federal Circuit (Iowa) and Judge Donald S. Russell of the U.S. Court of Appeals for the Fourth Circuit (South Carolina).

3. Indeed, the responsibility to "study and report to the Judicial Conference on past, present, and possible future relationships with Congress" became an explicit part of the committee's work in 1987. Executive Committee of the Judicial Conference, "Judicial Conference of the United States Report on Committee Jurisdiction," November 6, 1987.

between the judiciary and Congress; a preliminary colloquium identifying critical issues (the results of which are contained in this volume); and a series of workshops bringing together judges, legislators, scholars, members of the bar, and other interested citizens with the objective of achieving pragmatic solutions. From the outset, the project has benefited from the advice of a panel drawn from the Committee on the Judicial Branch. Apart from Judge Coffin, it has consisted of Judge Thomas J. Meskill of the U.S. Court of Appeals for the Second Circuit, Judge Abner J. Mikva of the U.S. Court of Appeals for the D.C. Circuit, and Judge J. Clifford Wallace of the U.S. Court of Appeals for the Ninth Circuit. In addition, a planning committee was created to provide counsel as to the project's early direction.[4]

From the beginning, our planning group recognized that the success of the enterprise would depend upon the continuing involvement of representatives of both branches. Thus we concluded that it would be desirable, as soon as practicable, to hold a preliminary colloquium, at which officials from each branch could present their views of the problems confronting them.

The Colloquium

Some forty-five people—including a Supreme Court justice, federal judges, a key member of Congress, legislative staffers, a state Supreme Court justice, representatives from the judicial branch, scholars, and members of the private bar—gathered in November 1986 for an all-day meeting at the Brookings Institution. The core of the session consisted of three panel discussions exploring (1) the constitutional and prudential reasons for the absence of communication between the branches; (2) the institutional arrangements through which each branch presents its views and assesses the problems of the other—including a preliminary examination of such topics as how the judiciary interprets legislative history and the way Congress addresses (or fails to address) the concerns of the federal courts; and (3) the kinds of practical steps that might be taken to improve judicial-legislative relations. This volume presents the papers prepared in conjunction with the colloquium,

---

4. The members of that planning group have included, in addition to the representatives of the Committee on the Judicial Branch, Professor A. Leo Levin, director of the Federal Judicial Center (who at times was represented by deputy director Charles Nihan); Roger H. Davidson of the Congressional Research Service; Johnny H. Killian of the Congressional Research Service; senior fellow Gilbert Y. Steiner of the Brookings Institution; senior staff member Warren I. Cikins of the Brookings Institution; William C. Kelly, Jr., of the law firm of Latham and Watkins; and Jeffrey W. Kampelman of the law firm of Shaw, Pittman, Potts and Trowbridge. Dean Paul D. Carrington of the Duke University School of Law also participated in one meeting of the planning group.

with a summary of the proceedings and a blueprint for the next phase of activity in the concluding chapters.

The keynote essay, written by Judge Coffin, poses the central issues that give rise to our work and identifies the fundamental questions for examination in the long term. Exploring changes in the institutional tapestry of the Republic over the last 200 years, Judge Coffin examines the areas of estrangement between the branches and calls for "all feasible reconciliation," specifying fruitful topics of inquiry.

The next contribution looks to history to provide a key to understanding the sources of friction. Conceivably, the seeds of the present circumstances might be found in the early American experience. In their study, covering the period from 1789 to 1800, historians Maeva Marcus and Emily Van Tassel show that in the absence of guidance from the Constitution, judges and legislators sought to find appropriate ways to communicate; indeed, the legislature encouraged the third branch to assume a role beyond adjudicating cases, to work more broadly with Congress and the executive to promote effective government. Thus events in the first years of the nation do not compel today's rigid separation and general lack of communication between the federal judiciary and Congress. This conclusion has important ramifications for our current effort to improve relations between the branches.

That historical inquiry provided a fitting ground for the first preliminary discussion of the colloquium, concerning the reasons for the lack of regular communication between the judiciary and Congress (the central points of which are distilled in a later chapter). Whatever the appropriate boundaries for interaction might be, it is necessary for each branch to understand the workings of the other. Each vitally affects the other, but without a clear recognition of the other's institutional processes and problems. The need to remedy such deficiencies in knowledge prompted the commissioning of two papers. One examines what legislators need to know about the judicial process; the second explores what judges should know about Congress. The authors of the former work, Representative Robert W. Kastenmeier, Democrat of Wisconsin, who has been for many years the chair of the Subcommittee on Courts, Civil Liberties, and the Administration of Justice of the House Committee on the Judiciary, and subcommittee counsel Michael Remington, provide a unique perspective from Capitol Hill. As they attempt to offer "a judicious legislator's lexicon" to the federal courts, Kastenmeier and Remington allude to the formidability of their task; they observe that "as participants in the legislative process, we are struck by the simple fact that few in Congress know much about or pay attention to the third branch of government."

In his essay, congressional scholar Roger H. Davidson seeks to provide judges with a basic understanding of Congress—a "critical tourist's survey of the legislative process." He starts from the premise that in order to understand today's congressional enactments, one must know something about law-makers—their objectives, working conditions, and procedures by which they process bills and regulations. The paper offers judges a look into the institutional milieu of a branch whose product they are often called upon to interpret, but with whose day-to-day environment they have virtually no contact. The work provides not only judicial understanding of the congres-sional experience, but also background for another facet of the project's mandate (discussed more fully in the last chapter): to explore ways to augment the judiciary's understanding of legislative history and determine how Congress might signal statutory intent more clearly to the courts. Too often discussions of statutory interpretation and legislative drafting take place in a vacuum. Knowledge of Congress is obviously useful in the search for, and assessment of, possible remedies to specific problems of statutory interpretation.

As will be described in the chapter summarizing the proceedings, consid-eration of problems of institutional capacity led to a lively exchange of views. But that examination was only a prelude to the colloquium participants' discussion of possible improvements. That preliminary search focused on the federal courts and the Congress (with some attention to the executive, too). As part of the investigation, an effort was made to ascertain what could be learned from other experiences.

In that regard, the contributions of Justice Hans A. Linde of the Oregon Supreme Court and Patrick S. Atiyah of Oxford University offer insights from the perspectives of the states and the British system, respectively. From the vantage point of a jurist and scholar, Linde notes that certain characteristics common to state courts and state legislatures distinguish their problems from those of the federal courts and Congress. At the same time, however, the pattern of institutional relations in the states casts doubt upon the shibboleths invoked to bar judicial involvement in legislative affairs at the national level. Indeed, for reasons that he explains, Linde observes that the "active partici-pation of state judges in the policy process is much more taken for granted and much less controversial than the involvement of federal judges in the national government."

Examining judicial-legislative relations in England, Atiyah shows how institutional differences between Britain and America influence the nature of the interaction between judges and lawmakers in the interpretation of statutes. He argues that the different role of the executive in the two countries is key to understanding the largely dissimilar character of relations between the judiciary and the legislature in the United States and England. If the English model suggests that little borrowing is possible, it also highlights, by contrast, the unique sources of tension between the legislative and judicial branches in the American system.

With these essays as background, colloquium participants engaged in three panel discussions, which are summarized. The volume concludes with an examination of the challenge ahead—an agenda that calls for research, workshops (focusing on ground rules for communication, understanding the legislative process, and mechanisms to improve judicial-congressional relations), and recommendations with the hope of facilitating practical results.

The Underlying Concerns

Robert A. Katzmann

※

Congress is largely oblivious of the well-being of the judiciary as an institution, and the judiciary often seems unaware of the critical nuances of the legislative process. But for occasional exceptions, each branch stands aloof from the other.[1] "The judiciary and Congress not only do not communicate on their most basic concerns; they do not know how they may properly do so," declared Judge Frank M. Coffin in his paper in this volume. "The condition," he continued, "is that of a chronic, debilitating fever."

It is the perception of many in the federal court system and on Capitol Hill that this state of affairs has had adverse effects not only on relations between the two branches, but also on public policy in general.[2] Consider the following examples.

—In the waning days of the 1986 legislative session, Congress tacked on to a childhood vaccine protection law a provision that could greatly increase the judicial work load, but did not provide federal courts with the necessary additional resources. Judges were charged with determining whether claimants are eligible for compensation due to illness or death resulting from vaccination.[3] One official of the court system estimated that the judiciary would have to hire and train 300 or 400 special masters to handle these cases. Courts would still have to decide the flood of expected appeals, running perhaps in the thousands. In spite of the obvious impact on the courts, Congress did not consult with the judiciary when it considered the legislation. A year of considerable uncertainty passed before the district courts secured relief from the legislature.[4]

1. The Senate's consideration of a controversial judicial nominee is such an exception. See Robert A. Katzmann, "Approaching the Bench: Judicial Confirmation in Perspective," *Brookings Review,* vol. 6 (Spring 1988), pp. 42–46.

2. See Robert A. Katzmann, "Needed: Congress-Judiciary Dialogue," *New York Times,* October 10, 1987, p. 31.

3. 100 Stat. 3743, 3755–3784.

4. Included in the mammoth continuing resolution that Congress enacted at the end of

—Even with respect to legislation directed principally at the administration of justice—for example, sweeping measures expediting trials, overhauling the bankruptcy system, and revising sentencing—Congress has acted without sustained communication with the very branch charged with implementing those changes.[5]

—Congress sought to deal with the deficit by mandating cuts throughout the federal government, including the courts. To comply, the judiciary had for a time to suspend civil jury trials, in violation of the Seventh Amendment to the U.S. Constitution.

—The courts' alleged difficulties in assessing legislative materials have sparked growing debate, even among judges themselves, about the role of the judiciary in statutory interpretation. At the colloquium, Justice Antonin Scalia differed with Judges Stephen Breyer and Abner Mikva as to the courts' usage of legislative history. Scalia claimed that courts, however unwittingly, have allowed themselves to be manipulated by cadres of congressional staffs, who distort legislative intent with an eye toward judicial consumption. Breyer and Mikva argued that, when properly applied, such materials can guide courts in the effort to discern legislative meaning.[6]

The Knowledge Gap and Its Consequences

To be sure, friction between the branches is in some measure inherent in the U.S. system. But these anecdotes illuminate a deeper-seated imperative—the

---

1987 is a provision placing much of the burden of these cases on the Court of Claims. *Congressional Record,* daily edition (December 21, 1987), pp. H12166–67, 12198. The Administrative Office of the U.S. Courts led the effort for this legislative change, undertaken without fanfare.

5. The measures referred to are the Speedy Trial Act of 1974, 88 Stat. 2076, and Speedy Trial Act Amendments of 1979, 93 Stat. 327; Bankruptcy Administration and Federal Judgeships Act of 1984, 98 Stat. 333; and Comprehensive Crime Control Act of 1984, 98 Stat. 1976.

6. As a circuit judge, Justice Scalia disputed judicial reliance on committee reports: "I think it time for courts to become concerned about the fact that routine deference to the detail of committee reports . . . [is] converting a system of judicial construction into a system of committee-staff prescription." *Hirschey* v. *Federal Energy Regulatory Commission,* 777 F. 2d 1 at 7-8 (D.C. Cir. 1985). More recently, Justice Scalia questioned the Supreme Court's use of legislative history. *INS* v. *Cardoza-Fonseca,* 475 U.S. 1009 (1987). For a summary of the discussion about the uses of legislative history at the colloquium among Justice Scalia, Judge Breyer, Judge Mikva, and Representative Kastenmeier, see "Summary of the Proceedings" below. More generally, see Robert A. Katzmann, *Institutional Disability: The Saga of Transportation Policy for the Disabled* (Brookings, 1986), pp. 15–78, 152–87; R. Shep Melnick, "The Politics of Partnership," *Public Administration Review,* vol. 45 (November 1985), pp. 653–60; "The Role of Legislative History in Judicial Interpretation: A Discussion between Judge Kenneth W. Starr and Judge Abner J. Mikva," 1987 *Duke Law Journal* 361; Martin M. Shapiro, *Who Guards the Guardians: Judicial Control of Administration* (University of Georgia Press, 1988); and Patricia M. Wald, "Some Observations on the Use of Legislative History in the 1981 Supreme Court Term," 68 *Iowa Law Review* 195 (1983).

need for the judiciary and Congress to better understand each other's problems and processes.

That this knowledge gap should exist is curious. After all, the system of checks and balances assumes that the branches will interact. Certainly, the Congress and the judiciary affect each other in important ways. That relationship extends beyond the Senate's traditional and familiar power to advise and consult with respect to judicial nominees. Congress directly affects the "administration of justice" by regulating the structure, function, and well-being of the courts. The legislature does this when it creates judgeships, determines court jurisdiction, sets judicial compensation, enacts criminal and civil laws, provides for attorneys' fees, or grapples with changes in the bankruptcy system.

For its part, the judiciary affects the course of legislation whenever it is called upon to interpret statutes—to discern legislative intent. Given the breadth of legislative activity, the courts' impact can be wide-ranging. In this age of statutes, judicial interpretation of statutes has become for courts an increasingly significant and time-consuming responsibility. It has become as important to the legislative process—for what the courts decide has obvious ramifications for Congress—as any single part of that process.[7]

If the impact of the judiciary on the legislature is great, the task for the judge is formidable, even daunting. Imagine the complicated nature of the inquiry for a court, whose interpretation shapes the meaning of statutes. Congress enacts a law; the statute becomes the object of litigation. The court must interpret the meaning of the words of the statute. Yet the language is often unclear. As the judiciary looks for guidance, it delves into the legislative history—the foundation on which judges seek to interpret statutory meaning. In so doing, the court must determine what constitutes legislative history and how to weigh its various parts, such as committee reports, conference committee reports, floor debates, and votes. It may have to penetrate layer upon layer of rules and procedures. At times the legislative history is ambiguous. In other situations, the problem results not from legislative imprecision but from silence: Congress has not addressed the issue. The court

7. I am grateful to Judge Abner Mikva for his observations on this point. Those statutory decisions can spark congressional efforts to overturn or modify them. See Beth Henschen, "Statutory Interpretations of the Supreme Court: Congressional Response," *American Politics Quarterly,* vol. 11 (January 1983), pp. 441–57; and Harry Stumpf, "Congressional Response to Supreme Court Rulings: The Interaction of Law and Politics," 14 *Journal of Public Law* 377 (1965). The interaction of the branches can involve not only statutes (the concern of this volume), but the Constitution as well. See Louis Fisher, *Constitutional Dialogues: Interpretation as Political Process* (Princeton University Press, 1988); and Walter F. Murphy, *Congress and the Court: A Case Study in the American Political Process* (University of Chicago Press, 1962).

is then asked to fill in the gaps, not only with respect to the meaning of statutory language, but also with regard to a whole host of commonly overlooked issues dealing with how and under what circumstances statutes are to be carried out.

When Congress, as a deliberative body, does not give explicit direction about its legislative meaning, it not only creates added burdens for the courts: it also increases the risk that the judiciary, in a good-faith effort to make sense of the problems before it, will interpret the statutes in ways that the legislature did not intend.

If Congress and the courts are to interact intelligently, each has to understand the other's activities. And that understanding must involve communication, direct or indirect, necessary for reasoned decisionmaking. If the executive and legislative branches were to cease regular communication, the breakdown of government would be considered likely. The absence of such communication between the judiciary and Congress should give equal cause for concern. Both branches are uncertain about how and under what circumstances they can interact.

In part, the courts are reluctant to maintain a greater presence because of the need to avoid prejudgment of issues that might come before them and because of the constitutional barriers against rendering advisory opinions. Even with regard to nonadjudicatory matters, some bearing directly on the administration of justice, there is concern that Congress might view such involvement as inappropriate.[8] In some measure, the perception that the judiciary is above the political fray enhances the third branch's legitimacy. But that posture is not without costs.

Current arrangements deprive Congress of the information needed to understand the capacity and limitations of the courts. Legislators might be more sensitive to the courts if they were more familiar with their problems. Moreover, without interaction, Congress cannot make use of judicial expertise when it revises laws. Courts that have had to wrestle with statutes may have something to contribute when the legislature considers changing them; indeed, they may be able to identify parts of legislation that need congressional attention. But the gulf between the branches has inhibited such input.

Perhaps even more fundamentally, distance has fostered among some on

8. For example, U.S. District Court Judge Walter T. McGovern of Seattle, who chairs the Judicial Conference's Committee on Judicial Resources, expressed misgivings about judges' contacting senators to fill judicial vacancies: "We don't think that it's appropriate for judges to simply on their own suddenly get on the telephone or personally visit the senator's office and say, 'We have this vacancy and we think it must be filled now.' " *Washington Post*, April 18, 1988.

Capitol Hill a basic hostility toward the judiciary. The view is that courts are usurpers of the electoral process. Judges, according to this perception, are unelected, imperial beings who twist legislation out of shape to impose their preferences on society. But this view ignores the irony: judicial action is often a consequence of legislative directives. Congress frequently passes the buck to the courts to avoid controversial choices and then blames judges for issuing decisions that it in fact required. Congress does not, of course, provide for a judicial role in only matters of great moment—as shown by the Standard (Apple) Barrel Act, the Horse Protection Act, and the Egg Products Inspection Act.[9] Indeed, exclusive of diversity cases, Congress has vested jurisdiction in federal courts in legislation covering over 300 subjects.[10] As the legislature adds to the judiciary's agenda, it might be more appropriate to focus on whether Congress provides the courts with resources necessary to fulfill their responsibilities, rather than to criticize judges for performing tasks that Congress has mandated they assume.

At the same time, the communications gap has made it difficult for the judiciary to keep abreast of major changes in the legislative process in the last several years. Fragmentation has increased as staffs have grown substantially and subcommittees have proliferated. Legislation is often not the product of reasoned deliberation, as the Founders envisioned, but of highly atomistic activity.[11] Courts are confronted with the difficult responsibility of making sense of vague and ambiguously worded statutes with often skimpy legislative

9. The Standard (Apple) Barrel Act sets forth the dimensions for a standard barrel of apples and provides for penalties of one dollar and costs for each barrel sold or offered for sale, recoverable in federal court (37 Stat. 250). The Horse Protection Act prohibits, in principal part, the transporting, moving, shipping, delivering, or receiving of any horse which is sore, "with reason to believe that such horse while it is sore may be shown, exhibited . . . sold, auctioned, or offered for sale in any horse show, horse exhibition, or horse sale or auction" with such exceptions as stated in law (84 Stat. 1404, sec. 5; 90 Stat. 915, sec. 6). The Egg Products Inspection Act seeks to ensure that eggs and egg products are "wholesome, otherwise not adulterated, and properly labeled and packaged" (84 Stat. 1620). In each of these cases, the courts are vested with jurisdiction to enforce the statute.

10. Attachments to letter from Chief Judge Charles Clark, U.S. Court of Appeals for the Fifth Circuit, to Senator Ernest F. Hollings, July 11, 1983.

11. Senator Daniel Patrick Moynihan of New York touched upon this last problem in connection with the Internal Revenue Service's effort to impose the "uniform capitalization rules" on authors. Noting that he was "considerably involved in writing them," Senator Moynihan argued that the rules, which were designed to provide a better matching of income and expenses of manufacturing property, did not apply to books. But a small footnote in a conference committee report that thereafter became law did seem to include books. Commented Senator Moynihan, "I was a member of the conference committee. I do not ever recall the subject's having been raised, nor does any senator or representative with whom I've talked. My best guess is that staff members wrote it into the report thinking it was *already* law. . . . It is not law, and must not be construed as law." *New York Times,* September 6, 1987, p. E14.

histories. The outcome is often a bewildering composition of ambiguous and even contradictory expressions of policy. It is often difficult to discern what constitutes legitimate legislative history. From the courts' perspective, distance has exacerbated difficulties as judges try to weigh statutory meaning. Without clear signals, the judiciary has understandable difficulty making sense of the legislative maze.

Such judicial interpretations have consequences for the distribution of power within Congress. The courts strengthen those forces—whether individual legislators, staffs, or committees—to the extent that judges give weight to the particular views expressed in the materials that are incorporated in the legislative record. Thus the various interests have some incentive to ensure that the record reflects their preferences.

How courts and Congress interact has ramifications beyond those branches; the character of that relationship affects the shape and development of policy. In that sense, the concern is not simply whether the courts have adequate resources or how to discern legislative intent, but how the judiciary and the legislature work together—or sometimes at cross-purposes—as they influence policymaking. The interplay of Congress and the courts has vital consequences for the administrative state itself. When the judiciary interprets a statute or mandates or restrains executive action, it perforce affects the administrative process. Just as the judiciary can bear upon the balance of forces within Congress, so its decisions can influence the relationships among agencies or competing factions within the bureaucracy, or the capacity of the president to control the executive branch. Indeed, a growing literature suggests that agency personnel often ally themselves with legislators and staffs to create legislative histories, knowing that one day that record may be grounds for a judicial decision. Policymaking can thus be thought of as dynamic and complex, as "a continuum of institutional processes [judicial, legislative, and administrative], sometimes acting independently, but often interacting in subtle and perhaps not always conscious ways to influence the behavior of other processes."[12]

---

12. See Katzmann, *Institutional Disability*, p. 9. More generally, see Steven Kelman, *Making Public Policy: A Hopeful View of American Government* (Basic Books, 1987); and Hans Linde and others, *Legislative and Administrative Processes*, 2d ed. (Foundation Press, 1981). Some studies with implications for law and policymaking have focused attention on such issues as the delegation of power from Congress to the administrative branch and agencies. See, for example, a recent symposium on "The Uneasy Constitutional Status of the Administrative Agencies," 36 *American University Law Review* 277 (1986). See also Peter Aranow, Ernest Gellhorn, and Glen Robinson, "A Theory of Legislative Delegation," 68 *Cornell Law Review* 1 (1983); Morris P. Fiorina, "Legislator Uncertainty, Legislative Control, and the Delegation of Legislative Power," 2 *Journal of Law, Economics, and Organization* 33 (1986); and Jerry L. Mashaw, "Prodelegation;

The fact that these patterns of relationships between the judiciary and Congress have important effects on governmental processes and policy suggests the perils of the present circumstance: in the absence of communication and mutual understanding, the quality of governance will inevitably suffer. It is, of course, too much to expect that institutions will act with perfect knowledge. Given the political and policy complexities surrounding particular issues, it is unrealistic to believe that those institutions can definitively address all the problems they face. Indeed, it would be naive to believe that all legislation can be stripped of ambiguity. Imprecise language can permit proposed legislation to secure needed support from diverse interests with differing and sometimes opposing views of various aspects of the bill's objectives. However, much ambiguity and lack of clarity are not deliberate; they come from the absence of forethought and the rush of fast-moving events, which are obstacles to consideration of every problem and issue. But at the very least, each institution can strive to overcome unnecessary tensions that prevent one from accurately assessing the processes and outcomes of the other.

Three Central Questions

If the foregoing analysis is correct, then three central questions must be addressed. First, what kinds of communications and patterns of relationships are appropriate between the judiciary and Congress? Second, how can courts better understand the legislative process and Congress more clearly signal its intent? Third, what kinds of mechanisms should be devised to promote informed interaction between the branches?

Determining What Is Appropriate

The Constitution provides no clear rules for determining the permissible limits of communications between the legislature and the judiciary. Indeed, it says little about the nature of the interaction between them. Some guidance does come from the article III "cases or controversies" requirement barring courts from deciding abstract, hypothetical, or contingent questions. Because

---

Why Administrators Should Make Political Decisions," 1 *Journal of Law, Economics, and Organization* 81 (1985). On executive control, see, for instance, Peter L. Strauss, "The Place of Agencies in Government: Separation of Powers and the Fourth Branch," 84 *Columbia Law Review* 573 (1984); and Thomas O. McGarity, "Presidential Control of Regulatory Agency Decisionmaking," 36 *American University Law Review* 443 (1986). On judicial deference to agency decisions, see Colin Diver, "Statutory Interpretation in the Administrative State," 133 *University of Pennsylvania Law Review* 549 (1985); and Leslie E. Gerwin, "The Deference Dilemma: Judicial Responses to the Great Legislative Power Giveaway," 14 *Hastings Constitutional Law Quarterly* 289 (1987). On courts and policymaking, see Donald L. Horowitz, *Courts and Social Policy* (Brookings, 1977); and R. Shep Melnick, *Regulation and the Courts: The Case of the Clean Air Act* (Brookings, 1983).

of it, the judiciary has from the beginning felt constrained from issuing advisory opinions to the legislative and executive branches. But, as discussed in a later chapter, judges in the early days of the Republic performed congressionally assigned tasks that did not require the decision of cases or subordinate them, as jurists, to a nonjudicial administrative hierarchy.[13] This participation came despite the Constitutional Convention's rejection of judicial involvement in a council of revision—suggesting perhaps that Congress and the presidency, once they began operating, determined that a judicial presence, in at least some nonadjudicatory matters, was on balance beneficial.

These early cases involving judicial refusal to render advisory opinions were grounded mostly on the separation-of-powers doctrine. Although that doctrine might mean that one branch cannot encroach upon the functions unique to another or be made to assume tasks that diminish it within the constitutional scheme, it does not follow that complete separation is required. The Constitution, after all, created "separated institutions sharing powers," not separate institutions.[14]

If the separation-of-powers doctrine does not by itself compel such distance, are there any statutes that effectively lead to the gulf between the branches? A statute does exist that precludes federal officers and employees from using federal funds for lobbying activities. Its relevant section states:

No part of the money appropriated by any enactment of Congress, shall, in the absence of express authorization by Congress be used directly or indirectly to pay for any personal service, advertisement, telegram, telephone, letter, printed or written matter, or other device, intended to influence in any manner a Member of Congress, to favor or oppose, by vote or otherwise, any legislation or appropriation by Congress . . . ; *but this shall not prevent officers or employees of the United States or of its departments or agencies from communicating to Members of Congress, through the proper official channels, requests for legislation or appropriations which they deem necessary for the efficient conduct of the public business.*[15]

The Department of Justice has interpreted the "official channels" exception

13. Also see Russell Wheeler, "Extrajudicial Activities of the Early Supreme Court," *Supreme Court Review* (1973), pp. 123–58.

14. The phrase is Richard E. Neustadt's. See his *Presidential Power: The Politics of Leadership* (Wiley, 1960), p. 33.

15. 18 U.S.C. 1913 (emphasis added). For a brief description of the legislative history, see Louis Fisher, *The Politics of Shared Power: Congress and the Executive,* 2d ed. (Congressional Quarterly Press, 1987), pp. 55–56.

as allowing judges to expend appropriated funds for the purpose of contacting members and congressional committees to express their views on legislation. Because federal judges do not have direct superiors, the attorney general concluded that it was inappropriate to engage in legalistic arguments as to whether federal judges speak through "proper official channels" whenever they take a position with respect to matters of judicial concern.[16] For its part, the U.S. Judicial Conference has tried to avoid any appearance of improperly using appropriated funds to influence Congress.

If the separation-of-powers doctrine does not by itself preclude all communications between the legislature and the judiciary, and if statutes do not require such distance, then what are the circumstances in which judges and legislators should interact? The task, as will be discussed in this volume, is to devise guidelines for communication that are prudent and that give direction as to such matters as the manner, form, and timing of interaction.

Making Sense of the Legislative Process

Difficulties in understanding the legislative process and thus discerning congressional intent can only hinder relations between the judiciary and Congress. In the effort to enhance the courts' knowledge of Congress, it would be useful to begin by examining the inadequacies of traditional modes of statutory construction and to present some of the alternative conceptions of judicial interpretation of statutes, specifically their assumptions about the way Congress works.

The traditional modes by which courts interpret statutes rely on the "canons of statutory construction."[17] These canons include the following precepts: the starting point is the language of the statute; if the language is plain, construction is unnecessary; penal statutes are to be construed narrowly, but remedial statutes broadly; statutes in derogation of the common law are to be strictly construed; the expression of one thing is the exclusion of another; repeals by implication are disfavored; and every word of a statute must be given significance. As Karl Llewellyn long ago observed, these maxims are hardly useful guides to construction.[18] For almost every canon, one might call upon an equal and opposite canon; a canon seemingly exists to support every possible outcome. There is no canon for ranking or choosing between canons. As Judge Richard Posner has written: "If a judge wants to interpret

16. The memorandum opinion for the Attorney General, "Applicability of Antilobbying Statute (18 U.S.C. sec. 1913)—Federal Judges," 2 *Opinions of Office of Legal Counsel* 30, 31 (1978).

17. See, for example, J. G. Sutherland and C. Dallas Sands, *Statutes and Statutory Construction,* 4th ed. (Wilmette, Ill.: Callaghan, 1972).

18. Karl N. Llewellyn, *The Common Law Tradition: Deciding Appeals* (Little, Brown, 1960).

a statute broadly, he does not mention the plain-meaning rule; he intones the rule that remedial statutes are to be construed broadly, or some other canon that leans toward the broad rather than the narrow. If he wants to interpret the statute narrowly, he will invoke some other canon."[19]

If the canons are of limited utility, other approaches have been advanced as guides to statutory construction. Each rests on assumptions about the workings of the legislative process and about how to determine legislative intent.[20] One influential view—a "public interest" construction, advanced by, among others, Hart and Sacks—maintains that "every statute and every doctrine of unwritten law developed by the decisional process has some kind of purpose or objective." Thus unclear wording can be made comprehensible by identifying the purpose and policy it embraces and then deducing the outcome most consistent with that purpose or policy. This perspective conceives of the legislative process as deliberative, informed, and efficient, with decisions made only after legislators have gathered all the relevant data and given such information due consideration.[21]

A variety of other positions reject this vision of the way Congress works, but differ among themselves as to the implications for the way courts should interpret legislation. What might be loosely labeled as the "law and economics" or "public choice" school makes use of the principles of market economics to account for decisionmaking. Its adherents paint the legislative process as driven by rational, egoistic, utility-maximizing legislators whose primary motivation is to be reelected. According to this view, "Legislation is a commodity demanded and supplied much as are other commodities, so that legislative protection flows to those groups that derive the greatest value from it regardless of overall social welfare, whether the latter is defined as wealth, utility, or some other vision of equity or justice."[22] The laws that are passed tend to benefit the cohesive special interest groups that lobby the legislature. Members of Congress will enact laws that transfer wealth to those special interests and reduce efficiency at the expense of society. At the same time,

19. Richard A. Posner, *The Federal Courts: Crisis and Reform* (Harvard University Press, 1985), p. 276.

20. For an early classic discussion, see Max Radin, "Statutory Interpretation," 43 *Harvard Law Review* 863 (1930); and James Landis, "A Note on Statutory Interpretation," 43 *Harvard Law Review* 886 (1930).

21. Henry M. Hart, Jr., and Albert Sacks, "The Legal Process: Basic Problems in the Making and Application of Law" (Harvard Law School, 1958), pp. 166–67. For an instructive overview of this and other approaches, see William N. Eskridge, Jr., and Philip P. Frickey, "Legislation Scholarship and Pedagogy in the Post-Legal Process Era," 48 *University of Pittsburgh Law Review* 691 (1987); and Eskridge and Frickey, *Cases and Materials on Legislation: Statutes and the Creation of Public Policy* (West, 1988).

22. Posner, *The Federal Courts*, p. 263.

laws that benefit the public will be few because of the "collective action" problem. That is, "rational self-interested individuals will not act to achieve their common or group interests" because the benefits being sought are collective to the groups as a whole; hence the rational individual has an incentive to be a free rider.[23] It is thus by no means automatic that interest groups will arise to press legislators to enact legislation benefiting the public interest.

This vision of the legislature, in contrast to the "public interest" conception, is bleak. Legislators, eager to be returned to office, avoid choices on critical issues that could antagonize energized groups. They do not work to develop coherent policy, but seek to accommodate the preferences of interest groups through ad hoc bargaining. Evading their responsibility, legislators adopt vague statutes vesting policymaking duties in administrators who must stumble through a mine field of unresolved problems.

Against this background, various approaches to guide judicial interpretation have been offered. Judge Posner, a leading proponent of the law and economics school, supports the method of "imaginative reconstruction." First, "the judge should try to put himself in the shoes of enacting legislators and figure out how they would have wanted the statute applied to the case before them." If that fails, "as occasionally it will, either because the necessary information is lacking or because the legislators had failed to agree on essential premises, then the judge must decide what attribution of meaning to the statute will yield the most reasonable result in the case at hand—always bearing in mind that what seems reasonable to the judge may not have seemed reasonable to the legislators, and that it is their conception of reasonableness, to the extent known, rather than the judge's, that should guide decision."[24]

Judge Frank Easterbrook argues that it is the court's task to determine whether a particular law is general-interest legislation or special-interest legislation. If statutes are designed to overcome "failures" in markets, then it makes sense, he argues, to use the remedial approach to the construction of statutes, at least most of them. If "on the other hand, statutes are designed to serve private interests, to transfer the profits . . . of productive activity to a privileged few, to replace the outcomes of private transactions with monopolistic ones, then the judge should take the beady-eyed contractual approach." In distinguishing between general- and special-interest legislation, the judge should determine whether the statute is specific or general, look

---

23. Mancur Olson, Jr., *The Logic of Collective Action: Public Goods and the Theory of Groups* (Harvard University Press, 1965), p. 2.

24. Posner, *The Federal Courts,* pp. 286–87. As Judge Posner notes, "There is nothing new in this suggestion."

for the indications of profit-seeking legislation, and delve into the legislative process ("who lobbied for the legislation? . . . what deals were struck in the cloakroom?").[25] For his part, because of what he perceives as the inclination of legislators to enact profit-seeking laws, Richard Epstein supports as an antidote a broad role for the courts in reviewing economic legislation.[26]

Students of what Robert Weisberg terms the "new legal process" assert that although the legislative process may fail to achieve procedural and substantive justice, it can be reformed.[27] Lawmaking, according to this perspective, involves value creation, not simply bargaining among exogenously defined interests. Further, courts and agencies should actively seek to realize "public" or "common" values, and the branches of government should encourage conversation and dialogue to achieve justice and rationality in the law.[28]

Still another conception of the legislative process, seen through the lens of participant-observers, accepts legislation as legitimate but regards legislative history as susceptible to distortion and manipulation. Courts, in this view, should restrict themselves to the "plain meaning" of the statute. Many laws, of course, are not clear on their face. If Congress does not approve of the court's interpretation, then it can modify the judiciary's ruling or from the start enact legislation that is unambiguous on its face.[29] Another strand of thought, hermeneutics, questions whether statutes of a previous generation, even if seemingly clearly worded, can be interpreted true to their original

25. Frank H. Easterbrook, "The Supreme Court 1983 Term—Foreword: The Court and the Economic System," 98 *Harvard Law Review* 4 (1984). Compare with Jonathan Macey, "Promoting Public-Regarding Legislation through Statutory Interpretation: An Interest Group Model," 86 *Columbia Law Review* 223 (1986).

26. Richard Epstein, *Takings: Private Property and the Constitution* (Harvard University Press, 1985).

27. See Robert Weisberg, "The Calabresian Judicial Artist: Statutes and the New Legal Process," 35 *Stanford Law Review* 213 (1983).

28. See, for example, Frank Michelman, "The Supreme Court 1985 Term—Foreword: Traces of Self-Government," 100 *Harvard Law Review* 4 (1986); Cass Sunstein, "Legal Interference with Private Preferences," 53 *University of Chicago Law Review* 1129 (1986); E. Donald Elliott, Bruce A. Ackerman, and John C. Millian, "Toward a Theory of Statutory Evolution: The Federalization of Environmental Law," 1 *Journal of Law, Economics, and Organization* 313 (1985); Guido Calabresi, *A Common Law for the Age of Statutes* (Harvard University Press, 1982); Owen Fiss, "Foreword: The Forms of Justice," 93 *Harvard Law Review* 1 (1979); Abram Chayes, "The Role of the Judge in Public Law Litigation," 89 *Harvard Law Review* 1281 (1979); and Michael A. Fitts, "The Vices of Virtue," *University of Pennsylvania Law Review* (forthcoming).

29. Among those who believe that greater deference be given to the plain meaning rule are Justice Scalia and Judge Kenneth Starr of the U. S. Court of Appeals for the D.C. Circuit. See the chapter below summarizing the colloquium discussion; also see Judge Starr's remarks in "Judicial Review of Administrative Action in a Conservative Era," 39 *Administrative Law Review* 353, 363 (1987).

meaning; according to this view, the current generation cannot understand the past in its own terms, free from modern prejudices and preconceptions. As a linguistic matter, moreover, words change their meaning.[30] For others, legislative history is an indispensable aid to understanding congressional meaning. What is needed is the development of procedures to identify the weight to be given to various parts of the legislative history, to signal that which is legitimate.[31]

The role of the judiciary in reviewing legislation is in no small measure dependent upon subjective perspectives about the proper allocation of responsibilities among courts, Congress, and various parts of the administrative branch. I leave for another time an analysis of those particular conceptions.[32] For present purposes, it is important to note that despite their differences, most of these approaches share a concern with the process by which Congress operates, indeed, with the ways in which the branches of government interact. Their perspectives are based upon assumptions about how Congress functions, the factors affecting legislative outcomes, and the ability of the judiciary to make sense of congressional intent. Thus they should to one degree or another share an objective of this enterprise: that is, through an empirical examination of the way Congress works, to ascertain how courts can better interpret statutory meaning and to determine whether and how Congress can clarify legislative history. Theories about how courts should interpret legislative history can be advanced with greater confidence to the extent that they are informed by an appreciation of the complex reality of the legislative process.

Most of these approaches concentrate on how courts should interpret statutes; they are less concerned with the extent to which relationships between Congress and the judiciary can be routinized so that the two branches can interact more fully to their mutual benefit. This project involves consideration of whether and how the courts might play a helpful role in identifying problems with statutes they have interpreted, perhaps alerting Congress to such difficulties and providing some input as the legislature revises those laws.

---

30. See Hans-Georg Godamer, *Truth and Method* (New York: Crossroad Publishing, 1982); Eric D. Hirsch, Jr., *Validity in Interpretation* (Yale University Press, 1973); and Paul Brest, "The Misconceived Quest for the Original Understanding," 60 *Boston University Law Review* 204, 221–224 (1980).

31. See the chapter by Judge Frank Coffin and remarks of Judge Mikva and Representative Kastenmeier in the chapter summarizing the colloquium discussion; and Abner J. Mikva, "Reading and Writing Statutes," 48 *University of Pittsburgh Law Review* 627 (1987).

32. The foregoing survey was not meant to be exhaustive. The focus was on those approaches concerned directly with legislation. Thus I have not discussed the work of "critical legal scholars," who have not as yet turned their attention to statutes.

Creating Mechanisms

For those engaged in governance—the practitioners in the judicial and legislative branches—the matter of devising practical measures to reduce tensions, improve relations, and facilitate informed decisionmaking is of special importance. It is necessary to blend both theory and practice. The problem has at least two dimensions: the creation of a process in which representatives of both branches, uncertain about the very propriety of meeting, can examine critical questions; and the identification of discrete issues, susceptible of resolution. As discussed in detail in the final chapter, what is required is a concrete agenda focused on how institutional arrangements can be structured so that the judiciary and Congress can function with heightened awareness of each other's processes. Among the subjects to be examined are how to improve legislative drafting, clarify legislative intent and history, and transmit judicial opinions dealing with statutes to relevant congressional bodies. Meriting consideration as well are changes within the judiciary and Congress, the feasibility of a role for the executive branch, and the lessons from other approaches (for instance, law revision commissions in the states and devices to promote cooperation such as those found in the federal-state arena). Through this effort, intended to produce pragmatic recommendations, the hope is to further institutional comity between the courts and Congress.

The *Federalist* Number 86:
On Relations between the Judiciary and Congress

Frank M. Coffin

->>X<<-

Lest this essay be deemed a fraud and a hoax, let me assure the reader that it is not an actual communication recently received from Messrs. Madison, Jay, and Hamilton. It is, rather, what I am quite sure they would say if I but had a better ability to hear them.

Almost 200 years ago, when the youngest of our trio was thirty and the oldest forty-two, we seized the opportunity to respond to doubters of the Constitution with a series of eighty-five essays called *The Federalist,* which we wrote under the name of Publius. Although some historians claim that the luminous presences of our elders, Washington and Franklin, had more to do with ratification, we have always felt that the *Federalist* did its part.

Now by some eccentric dispensation, as the nation ends its second century, we are given the privilege of adding one more essay—only one. This of course makes us feel like Tantalus: when we stoop to drink, the water recedes, as does the fruit above when we reach for it. We have reached a decision not to recommend any change in the old charter. This was never our mission. And, remembering the tribulations the fifty-five of us had during our four torrid months in Philadelphia when the country had fewer than 4 million inhabitants, we are loath to see the nation become Tantalus today.

Our focus therefore is not on changing the Constitution but on finding ways to improve its workings between the two branches of government that make and interpret the laws and possess the greatest continuity—or inertia— in the conduct of their business. The institution of the presidency has been richly studied and written about. But the interrelation of Congress and the

This essay first appeared in *The Brookings Review*, vol. 4 (Winter–Spring 1986), pp. 27–31.

judiciary remains as unexplored today as the western territories were in our time. We wrote in number 47 of the separation of the branches and in number 48 of the connection that should exist among them. But neither Montesquieu nor the British or colonial experience gave us more than the foundation.

The lack of any superstructure has produced the following state of affairs. The judiciary and Congress not only do not communicate with each other on their most basic concerns; they do not know how they may properly do so. Legislators enact laws without considering either their burden on courts or how they might be interpreted. The paradox is that when the judiciary exercises the powers Congress has thrust upon it, it is reviled as power hungry. Legislators, required to stand periodically for reelection, are suspicious of, antagonistic to, and ever ready to restrain and humble their secure, life-tenured colleagues.

The judges, for their part, facing increasing responsibilities along with criticism for exercising them, and sensitive to ever-accreting restrictions and diminishing standards affecting their life and work, are in danger of losing the respect, serenity, and independence that the Constitution sought to vouchsafe. The condition we describe, if not an acute crisis, is that of a chronic, debilitating fever. We therefore dedicate this eighty-sixth Federalist paper to both branches and their happier coexistence.

Our Earlier Pronouncements

In number 48 we made so bold as to criticize some of our colonial forerunners for being wary only of the danger to liberty of a grasping hereditary magistrate. We warned of the equal danger from legislative usurpation, pointing out that "the legislative department alone has access to the pockets of the people," thus creating a dependence on the part of the other branches.

In contrast, in number 78, we supposed that "the Judiciary . . . will always be the least dangerous to the political rights of the Constitution; because it will be the least in a capacity to annoy or injure them . . . [having] no influence over either the sword or the purse. . . ." We explained that lifetime tenure was necessary both to attract the most able judges and to assure "uniform adherence to the rights of the Constitution, and of individuals." And in number 79 we wrote that the parallel guarantee, the Constitution's provision barring any diminution in judges' compensation, "put it out of the power of [the legislative branch] to change the condition of the individual for the worse."

We now see that we were imperfect prophets. We would not change what we said about the power of the legislative department. But we did not accurately foretell the nature of the judiciary. We underestimated the impact on society of judicial decisions applying the Constitution and statutes. In the eyes of many, this influence has made the judiciary a source of danger. Others view it as the last bastion of liberty. We recognize the existence of this deeply felt division of opinion. We should, therefore, have called the judiciary not "the least dangerous," but the most vulnerable branch. Unlike the persons in the executive and legislative branches, judges are appointed for life to their position and are wholly dependent upon the legislative branch for the maintenance of satisfactory working conditions and emoluments.

What Has Changed

In viewing the progress of our Republic over these two centuries, we have seen with both humility and pride how well the Constitution has served and still serves its people. What we see is not a cause for basic constitutional change, but rather a need to address nonconstitutional means of improving the institutional relations between Congress and the judiciary.

That the national interest calls for the very best in judges and legislators has always been true but never more so than in these, your times. The two kinds of officials have grown, under our Constitution, into quite different species. Both share, however, the dubious honor of being the butt of criticism, satire, and caricature. It is equally true that in moments of the gravest stress, as in the squalid Watergate affair, both Congress and the judiciary were justly perceived as saving strengths for the nation. Yet the corona of approbation is all too short-lived among our unruly and restless populace. This fact takes on new significance in a time when the reservoirs of the ablest candidates for both the bench and the legislature are being drained.

Nearly 200 years ago we wrote of the limited number of persons endowed with the mind and character to perform complex judicial labors "with utility and dignity." We now realize more than we ever could have imagined how the development of the country and of civilized life has placed the judiciary in the vortex of conflicting individual and societal values: a sixtyfold increase in the population; the tensions among sectors of the economy; the encroachments on the liberty of the individual necessitated by the interest of all in regulating space, commerce, labor, consumption, the environment; all the complications introduced not only by the industrial revolution but by the postindustrial age; the change in mores of the people and their varying attitudes—as deeply held and vehemently expressed as ever—on desegregation, abortion, religion, pornography, capital punishment. All of these forces of change have at some point forced the federal judiciary to resolve bitter disputes, interpret our old Constitution, and in the process advantage or disadvantage either the majority or minorities and individuals.

As the work of the judiciary has changed, so has its life style. Gone are the days when a Justice Story could also be a bank director. We see that today judges are held to canons of ethics, disciplinary procedures, financial reporting, and standards of disengagement in social, business, and political matters that not even the most monastic of us could have foreseen. Coupled with these developments, an erosion in judges' standard of living for nearly two decades has resulted in more and more judges' resigning their office and likely candidates' refusing appointment.

If the judiciary has been affected by two centuries of change, the lineaments of its traditional work are still prominently in place: the highly trained and experienced lawyer-judge, respecting time-honored professional disciplines, deciding actual cases on the basis of his own research and thinking, aided only by a small staff. True, the modern federal judiciary now has its own bureaucracy, the Administrative Office of the United States Courts. But this office is still a small support staff in a world of giants, handicapped by limited resources and, more particularly, by the absence of clear boundaries of its permissible range of operations.

How different are the work, the pace, and pressures of the senator and representative! Here, too, we have seen a similar shallowing of the reservoir of the ablest political leaders. The demands of campaigning effectively, representing the electorate conscientiously, and legislating responsibly are such as to be exhausting; they discourage some politicians from continuing in office more than a few short years. The catalogue of pressures is both depressing and cataclysmic: the volume, complexity, and variety of new legislation; the proliferation of committees; the growth and escalation in importance of the staffs of members and of committees; the lack of time to read and reflect; the power of special interests and single-issue groups; the costs of attaining and retaining office; the distorting demands of television; the increasing rate of turnover and resignations among the members; the near disappearance of the revered veteran statesman; and, most alarming, the erosion of respect for the legislature itself.

These conditions, keenly felt no doubt by all members, have insidious effects on the relationship between the judiciary and Congress. Harried members can all too easily be goaded to anger by those whose ox a judge has gored. They feel vulnerable to the demagogic criticism of those who would lead an all too willing but unthinking electorate to castigate any effort to improve congressional compensation. Any such considerations can only be strengthened by a factor we may not have fully anticipated in providing for permanency of judicial tenure—the human tendency of an elected official whose lease on office must be painfully renewed periodically on the hustings to consider a tenured judge so highly favored as to need or deserve no further consideration.

The tensions of the times, it seems clear to us, have thus created an estrangement between the two branches. This has been brought to pass even though most federal judges have been at one time intimately associated with representatives and at least one senator whose sponsorship was a key to his or her appointment to the bench; a number of judges have served in Congress; and various committees of the judiciary and Congress perform discrete functions together harmoniously. The separation, therefore, is an institutional one, and its speedy amelioration is in the best interests of this Republic.

Areas of Estrangement

It is not difficult for the interested observer to discern the signs of unnecessary distance between the two branches. We stress "unnecessary," for we realize that the underpinning of our doctrine of separation of powers is a recognition of man's inherent self-aggrandizing nature and the necessity of invoking the different interests of the three branches to check and restrain each other—a condition of permanent tension. But just as tensions and disagreements in a workable and enduring marriage do not normally foreshadow estrangement, so need they not in our constitutional structure.

Here, then, are some of the points of abrasion we have noted. In torrential floods of new legislation, laws are passed without regard to their impact on judicial resources. Sometimes laws directed solely to changing a part of the judicial establishment are enacted without consulting the affected judges. When deliberations over complex legislation affecting the judiciary extend over several years, the contribution of thinking from the judiciary may be solicited in only the earliest stages.

In pointing to the lack of preenactment opportunity for the judiciary to give its views, we do not for a moment exhume the idea of a council of revision contained in Resolve 8 of the Virginia Plan, which one of us helped to formulate. This would have required judges to join with the executive in passing on a law's validity before its enactment. Short of so pronouncing, however, we sense a considerable uncertainty as to how far the judiciary may properly go in giving its views on the policy of a proposed law, as distinguished from its sheer workability. Issues of policy and issues of workability tend to merge.

At the other end of the spectrum, there would seem to be room for a more systematic and effective way for the legislature to obtain the postenactment views of the judiciary, the better to remove obscurity, redundancy, and inconsistencies through amendment. Often these views are contained as holdings or dicta in judicial opinions. But as yet these nuggets, if such they are, are nowhere systematically collected and analyzed. Moreover, there may be other ways in which the experience of the judges who have dealt with legislation may be made available to Congress.

On occasion legislative efforts are launched to "restrain" or otherwise monitor judges. We do not write of the plethora of efforts to limit the jurisdiction of courts; such attempts have always been made and no doubt will continue so long as there exist differences of views as to what courts should do. What we refer to are efforts to specify in detail how judges should conduct their deliberations, when they should be disqualified from hearing a case, and how they should be disciplined (short of impeachment) for malconduct. There seems to us to be a fine line between the kind of oversight that is proper for Congress to exercise and the kind that encroaches on the ability of judges to practice their calling with independence. Even if saner heads prevail, the very mounting of such efforts seems an unnecessary and corrosive harassment.

Another area, shrouded by the fog of uncertainty, is that of the kind and manner of communications that should be encouraged between Congress and the judiciary. Just as we wrote in number 48 that the principle of separation of powers "does not require that the legislative, executive, and judiciary departments should be wholly unconnected with each other," so also we would say that the departments should, consistent with their own mission, seek ways to communicate effectively with each other.

This advice was unneeded when the Constitution was drafted. The entire national government was a small community. In 1789 the Senate membership consisted of twenty-six, the House of sixty-five, the judiciary of nineteen; in 1790, the Department of State had nine employed. Often the limited lodging arrangements in our new capital meant that officials of all three branches ate from the same table. With time and growth and increased specialization, communication, except in the most formal sense, has become a greater problem for the judiciary and Congress than it has for the executive, whose platoons of liaison representatives regularly walk their beat on Capitol Hill.

The essence of the problem can be summed up by saying that the overarching and simplistic commandment, "thou shalt not lobby," does not begin to recognize the multiple levels and purposes of desirable communication in both directions between the two great branches. Worse, the negative nature of the commandment and its criminal sanction chill any effort to explore ways of meeting perceived needs.

The anomalous result is that in an age when Congress is inundated by information and opinion from every group, entity, and individual with an interest in getting a law passed, it hears from the judiciary chiefly on two occasions: (1) when a legislative committee has formally asked the Judicial Conference of the United States—the policymaking body of the federal judiciary—for its views on a specific piece of legislation, and (2) when a legislative committee has asked a judicial committee or a judge to testify before it.

Limiting permissible communication to these two channels disserves the judiciary, Congress, and the citizenry. What if one or many judges have views on legislation contrary to those expressed by the Judicial Conference? Should they be permitted to send those views to the congressional committee or to ask to testify before it? If so, what restraints, if any, should be observed? Should the Judicial Conference itself be permitted to communicate its views even though no request has come from a legislative committee? Should a judge or the Judicial Conference be permitted to send views critical of existing legislation? If so, what are the limits of propriety?

May judges prevail on a third party to formally present their views on, for example, the adequacy of their emoluments and other benefits? May judges consult and cooperate with groups of citizens who themselves are committed to working for a judiciary of quality and independence? If so, what ought to be the ground rules of permissible association and representation?

Turning the coin to its other side, should a legislator ever be permitted to express a concern or opinion in a litigated case of public importance on trial or on appeal? If so, under what conditions and restraints? How should a senator or a representative communicate complaints of possible misconduct by a judge? Should a legislator and a judge be permitted to communicate directly with each other on legislation, new or old? On the repair or construction of court facilities? On candidates for judicial office? Should legislators and judges within a state or region be encouraged to meet formally and informally? If so, how can the boundaries of propriety best be defined and preserved?

Finally, in the critical forum of judicial confirmation hearings, is it possible to arrive at a consensus on the kinds of questions from legislators and answers from judges that properly serve the legitimate interests of the interrogators without entrenching upon the dignity, impartiality, and independence of the judicial nominee? By consensus we do not mean a catalogue of proper and improper questions, but rather an atmosphere of inquiry flowing from a basic shared value that asking for prejudgments on specific issues endangers the quality and independence of judges so catechized.

A Call for All Feasible Reconciliation

Having had some 200 years to reflect on our earlier writings, we realize that we may have made too much of our mentor, Baron de Montesquieu. We blush a bit in recalling what we said in number 47: "The British Constitution was to Montesquieu what Homer has been to the didactic writers on epic poetry"—particularly since we quoted him as characterizing the British king, rather than the prime minister, as the "sole executive magistrate." Nevertheless, we realize that we, though acknowledging him as our "oracle," were creating a system of government quite different from that in our erstwhile mother country.

The separation of powers set out in our Constitution is, we can justly proclaim, our own invention. With two centuries of experience to survey, including wars foreign and domestic, depressions, and scandals, we feel humbly proud of the proven worth of the concept. But we also sense that the time has come to attempt to soften the edges where the judiciary and Congress rub. Not, we are quick to say, through constitutional changes. We are in entire accord with the homely philosophy, "If it isn't broken, why fix it?" On the other hand, if something, although not broken, shows the sign of strain, we deem it only prudent to try to ease that tension. So we commend to your good judgment the finer tuning that can be brought about by a new consensus and some new practices and procedures.

The key to such a limited effort is process. As we look back on our experiences in Philadelphia, the process really began with reading not only Montesquieu's *L'Esprit des lois,* other books, and the constitutions of the various states, but reflecting on our experience under the Articles of Confederation. It continued, as you know, with a bountiful measure of written proposals. And both our reading and our writing were hammered into shape on the anvil of months of discussion and debate. Of course, we were discussing momentous propositions. But although Michelangelo's towering David represents a prodigious investment of time, talent, and energy, so also does Bellini's loaf-sized Salt Cellar of Francis I.

The starting point for a constructive process is asking the right questions. This suits us well, for at this juncture we have only questions on improving relations between the judiciary and Congress; indeed, if we had answers, there would be no need for the process we have described. We would begin by a look backward. What was the nature of communication and relationships between the makers and the adjudicators of law at the birth of our nation? What can be discerned about our intent? What changes have taken place during these two centuries?

Then we would be most interested in a look at the present: what perceptions, assumptions, and biases does each branch harbor about the other; what ones are both false and harmful; how can they best be changed?

Such an examination would clear the building site of underbrush and accumulated debris. We would then think it desirable to undertake three major lines of inquiry. The first would delve into the principle of separation of powers and the multitude of situations in which it is invoked. The objective would be to identify the kinds of issues, functions, hazards, and benefits that dictate the most absolute or "pure" separation; those that merit a less than complete separation; and those where the advantages of collaboration and ease of communication far outweigh those of separation. Out of such an inquiry might happily emerge certain standards or criteria that could guide future relationships between these two branches.

A second inquiry, more detailed than the first, would survey the existing ways in which courts participate in the legislative process and the ways in which Congress directly and indirectly affects the judicial process; such a survey would attempt to devise meaningful categories, such as general legislation, justice-oriented legislation, court and judge-oriented legislation; the areas of frustration felt by each as the result of actions of the other; the present levels and modes of communication; and the organizational structure and procedures of each that help or hinder effective communication.

The third inquiry, built upon the first two, would be a search for improved ways of communicating and acting, honoring separation where separation is called for, but encouraging communication and even collaboration where such are permissible. This study would draw upon the experience of the states and even other countries; it would seek ways to strengthen and broaden the structural capacity of the courts to initiate communications with and respond to communications from Congress, utilizing various levels, modes, and procedures. It would seek ways in which Congress could take advantage of judicial experience in interpreting various statutes, minimize risks of judicial misinterpretation of legislative history, and avoid the fortuitous imposition of unintended burdens on courts. This pragmatic search for improved methods of conducting the law-creating business of the nation would, in our view, also embrace ways to stimulate a greater community of interest and shared respect. We can still learn from Britain—no longer from its institutions but from the camaraderie of social intercourse that occasionally envelops cabinet ministers, members of Parliament, and even judges. Is there a need for facilities and provisions for occasional meetings and social and educational programs? If so, what kind?

As we view this task of tuning the organs of our government, we hark back to the words of the philosopher Hume with which we closed our last appeal to the public in number 85. Observing that attaining the right balance in any large society is beyond the reach of the reflection and reason even of genius, Hume then wrote: "The judgments of many must unite in the work; experience must guide their labor; time must bring it to perfection, and the feeling of inconveniences must correct the mistakes which they inevitably fall into, in their first trials and experiments." After 200 years it is not too early to let "the feeling of inconveniences" help correct mistakes. We wish you well.

—Publius

Judges and Legislators in the New Federal System, 1789–1800

Maeva Marcus and Emily Field Van Tassel

-»»X«-

The current lack of communication between the federal judiciary and Congress is widely assumed to have its roots in the Constitution and early historical experience. According to this view, it should come as no surprise that Congress and the courts do not communicate well today—for they have never done so. To be sure, the Constitution provides few particulars about the relationship between the courts and the legislature, and in the early days of the Republic, views differed about what that relationship should be. In the absence of clear guidelines, judges sought to be responsive both to those who believed that the judiciary should promote effective government and to those who believed that the separation of powers constrained such a role. From the beginning federal judges hit upon a distinction, based on the judicial structure created by Congress, that preserved an independent stance for the judiciary at the same time that it allowed justices to maintain political relationships with both the executive and legislative branches of government. The distinction could be instructive to those who seek to improve relations between the branches today.

The government emerging from the turmoil of the Revolution and the shaping of the Constitution naturally reflected its origins. As Ralph Lerner has noted, the first Supreme Court justices "were not narrow professional lawyers, but revolutionary patriots and statesmen whose involvement in the founding and ratification controversies made it natural for them to think

The authors would like to thank James Buchanan, Charles Geyh, Dan Marcus, and Stanley Katz for their comments on earlier versions of this article, and they would particularly like to thank the staff of the Documentary History Project at the Supreme Court—James Buchanan, Christine Jordan, James R. Perry, and Stephen Tull—for collecting, transcribing, and annotating many of the documents cited here. Many of these documents will appear in *The Documentary History of the Supreme Court of the United States, 1789–1800*, vols. 2, 3 (Columbia University Press, forthcoming).

politically and to feel some proprietary relationship to the new order."[1] Not only had they been involved in the creation of the new government, but of the twelve men who sat on the Supreme Court in its first decade, six had served in the Continental Congress, four in the Confederation Congress, and two in the federal Congress. Only five of the justices had not served in any national congress before their appointment to the court; all five, however, had participated in their states' ratification conventions. Samuel Chase was the only justice who had not been a delegate to either the Constitutional Convention or his state's ratification convention.[2]

When Congress, in the Judiciary Act of 1789, imposed on the Supreme Court justices the duty to ride circuit as lower federal court judges, it gave the justices both a semipolitical assignment and a vehicle for their continued politicization. These "republican schoolmasters," as Ralph Lerner describes them, were the only federal officials with regular ongoing contact with virtually all regions of the country and thus were representatives of the federal government to the citizenry in ways that individual elected officials could not be.[3] Instructed to explicate the laws and structure of the new government to the country at large, an essentially political task, the justices could hardly avoid thinking of themselves in political terms.[4] The charge that the judges gave to grand juries at the opening of each circuit court, in which they explained what constituted violations of law that the juries were to investigate, along with any embellishments that the judge chose to add, became the vehicle for this explication. The grand jury charge took them outside the limits of a case or controversy and allowed them a forum for political discourse that they frequently used to full effect. The jurors to whom the justices spoke were often the already converted, and their frequent requests that the justices allow their charges to be printed in local newspapers, where they would be picked up and reprinted by politically sympathetic newspapers up and down the country, ensured a broad dissemination of the justices' federalist interpretations.[5]

1. Ralph Lerner, "The Supreme Court as Republican Schoolmaster," *Supreme Court Review* (1967), p. 131.
2. For background on the justices, see their individual biographical headnotes in Maeva Marcus and James R. Perry, eds., *The Documentary History of the Supreme Court of the United States, 1789–1800,* 1 vol. to date (Columbia University Press, 1985).
3. Lerner, "The Supreme Court as Republican Schoolmaster," p. 127.
4. See, for example, Thomas Jefferson to Edmund Randolph, May 8, 1793, Thomas Jefferson Papers, Library of Congress.
5. Ibid. In an item in the *Augusta Chronicle,* November 26, 1791, criticizing James Iredell's charge to the Georgia grand jury in fall 1791, "Philanthropos" commented that "we see his Honor labouring to reconcile the Grand Jury (*and through them the bulk of the people*)" to the Excise Act of 1791. (Emphasis added).

Circuit riding also ensured that the early Supreme Court justices would maintain and reinforce their ties with other members of the founding generation, many of whom served in Congress. Although James Sterling Young avers that informal relations between Court and Congress were virtually nonexistent after the government took up residence in the new federal city of Washington, District of Columbia,[6] justices and congressmen met each other before the move on both social and political grounds on circuit, at home, and in the capital.

Formal Separation versus Informal Cooperation

The arms'-length relationship that has developed over the years between the judiciary and Congress simply was not contemplated by many during the early years of the Republic. The rigid formal institutional separation that exists today between the two branches was largely of the judges' own making. Many in the first Congress believed that cooperation between the branches could coexist with the separation-of-powers doctrine. James Madison, for instance, despaired of congressional ability to create a judicial system that was not "defective both in its general structure, and many of its particular regulations." He recognized that Congress was limited in what it could effectively accomplish and was resigned to passing the Judiciary Act, in spite of manifold deficiencies, in the hope that "the system may speedily undergo a reconsideration under the auspices of the Judges who alone will be able perhaps to set it to rights."[7] Madison had already made clear in his remarks on separation of powers—prepared in support of the Constitution in the form of *Federalist* number 47—that an absolute and inviolable division between branches would be impracticable. There he spoke only to the criticism of executive appointment of judicial officers; in the instance of the Judiciary Act, it is evident that his vision of the actual operation of the separation doctrine took him even further from a strict division between branches.

Madison was not alone. The duties imposed by Congress on the judiciary,

6. James Sterling Young, *The Washington Community, 1800–1828* (Columbia University Press, 1966), pp. 77–79. But see Russell Wheeler, "Extrajudicial Activities of United States Supreme Court Justices: The Constitutional Period, 1790–1809" (Ph.D. dissertation, University of Chicago, 1970), p. 203.

7. James Madison to Edmund Pendleton, September 14, 1789, printed in Robert Rutland and Charles Hobson, eds., *The Papers of James Madison* (University of Virginia Press, 1979), vol. 12, p. 402. Attorney General Edmund Randolph shared Madison's confidence in the judges' ability to "set it to rights." Upon Congress's request for a report on judicial reform in 1790, Randolph wrote to Associate Justice James Wilson asking for his aid in the undertaking. Edmund Randolph to James Wilson, August 5, 1790, Society Miscellaneous Collection, Pennsylvania Historical Society.

the requests for judicial assistance by both the legislative and executive branches, and the myriad formal and informal interbranch communications respecting the functions of the new government and particular desires for fine-tuning and even major overhauls suggest that the designers and architects of the new system had no precise or uniform view of how the branches should relate in practice.

Separation of powers was a new and relatively untried political concept when the U.S. government began its operations in 1789.[8] Court, Congress, and executive were uncertain of its practical effects or limits, particularly in relation to the developing American theory of balanced government. For although the separation-of-powers theory had gained ascendancy during the Revolution, at the cessation of hostilities the less radical among the revolutionary leaders turned back to traditional political thought and grafted parts of the old ideas of balanced government onto separation of powers "to provide a new, and uniquely American, combination of the separation of powers and checks and balances."[9] By creating this American hybrid, the federalist constitutional architects effectively cut off recourse to experience or previous theory for solutions to the problems that were bound to arise under the new system.[10]

The Constitutional Convention dealt with the separation-of-powers doctrine most directly in its application to executive-legislative branch relationships, flirting with a quasi-parliamentary system in which the executive would have been a creature of the legislature. In the early years of the Republic, separation between these two branches was not rigid: in drafting legislation congressional select committees frequently consulted closely with executive department heads most concerned with the proposed legislation, and Congress seriously

8. Although Virginia had laid out the doctrine completely and succinctly in its 1776 Constitution, Vile notes, "It is true . . . that the division of functions between the branches of the governments of the States was not always consistently followed through, and that in their practical operation the early State governments deviated considerably from the spirit of the doctrine." M. J. C. Vile, *Constitutionalism and the Separation of Powers* (Oxford: Clarendon Press, 1967), p. 119. See also Gordon S. Wood, *The Creation of the American Republic, 1776–1787* (University of North Carolina Press, 1969), pp. 448–63. The Georgia Constitution of 1777 "boldly proclaimed Montesquieu's celebrated doctrine of the separation of powers in the first paragraph—only to utterly disregard the doctrine in the articles that followed. . . ." Albert Saye, *A Constitutional History of Georgia, 1732–1945* (University of Georgia Press, 1948), p. 100.

9. Wood, *Creation of the American Republic*, pp. 453, 548–53, 560–62; Vile, *Constitutionalism*, p. 122.

10. The hybridization occurred in areas such as Senate approval of executive appointments and treaties, the presidential veto, and the doctrine of judicial review. See, for example, William Loughton Smith to Edward Rutledge, May 24, 1790, Letters of William Loughton Smith to Edward Rutledge, South Carolina Historical Society.

considered, though finally rejected, giving department heads the right to join in floor debate over legislation.[11]

Applied to judicial relations with the other two branches, the theory of separation of powers seemed even more ambiguous. The Virginia Plan for the new Constitution had proposed a council of revision composed of the executive and some complement of the federal judiciary. The plan envisioned a council charged with the oversight of legislative acts and vested with a limited veto, presumably over those acts not consonant with the Constitution.[12] The notion of a council of revision was not new: New York had such a body, and other proposals were made using the form in the 1780s.[13] And in 1790 the head of the new judicial branch, Chief Justice John Jay, apparently speaking of New York's system, explained to Justice Edward Rutledge that "[a] Council of Revision . . . still appear to me to be useful. The Executive and the Constitution cannot otherwise be well guarded against the weight of power of an unchecked Legislature. . . ."[14] Separation of powers, then, while fiercely championed by some as an article of faith not susceptible to compromise, was a mutable doctrine to others, unclear in its extent and subject, within strict limits, to practical concerns.[15]

Because of the ambiguity created in the Constitution by the coexistence of the separation-of-powers doctrine with a system of checks and balances, and because Congress often required the judges to act in ways not wholly consistent with a strictly independent judiciary performing only judicial tasks, federal judges from the first days of the Republic had to wrestle with questions of proper behavior. Judges appointed by President Washington may not have known the specific points of the debate in the Constitutional Convention over the judges' possible participation in a council of revision, but they were too deeply involved in the ongoing political debate not to be aware of the

11. Alfred H. Kelly and Winfred A. Harbison, *The American Constitution: Its Origins and Development,* 4th ed. (W. W. Norton, 1970), pp. 132–36, 169–70.

12. The Virginia Resolutions Presented to the Constitutional Convention on May 29, 1787, printed in Michael Kammen, ed., *The Origins of the American Constitution: A Documentary History* (Penguin, 1986), p. 24.

13. See Hamilton's discussion in *Federalist* number 73 in Jacob E. Cooke, ed., *The Federalist* (Wesleyan University Press, 1961), pp. 492–99; and Wood, *Creation of the American Republic,* pp. 435–36, 455–56.

14. Draft of letter from John Jay to Edward Rutledge, November 14, 1790. Excerpt from an advertisement by autograph dealer Kenneth W. Rendell, Newton, Mass. Since an excerpt is all we have of this letter, it is impossible to tell precisely to what Jay was referring or why he was discussing a council of revision.

15. Examples of absolutist views on the separation-of-powers doctrine can be found in the thought of Nathaniel Chipman and later Thomas Jefferson. Vile, *Constitutionalism,* pp. 162–66.

broad arguments: the need for an independent judiciary, as against the desire to make use of the talents of eminent men. Putting those arguments together with the actual text of the Constitution, the judges could begin to formulate, as circumstances arose, the policy that would inform their actions. Certainly they believed that the Framers of the Constitution had intended federal judges to be independent, for they had given them tenure of office during good behavior and salaries that could not be diminished during their incumbencies (article III, sec. 1). Moreover, the Constitution contained a specific prohibition against serving in the U.S. Congress while holding any other federal office (article I, sec. 6). Otherwise the Constitution was silent about the activities of federal judges. It seemed to leave the judges free to decide for themselves whether to get involved in the political life of the nation. No constitutional bar existed to judges' holding positions in the executive branch or running for political office. Nor did any provision keep them from giving advice, formally or informally, to an official of the executive branch or to a member of Congress. Thus, as the first decade in the life of the federal judiciary unfolded, the judges could be seen behaving in ways that reflected the ambivalent nature of their constitutional charge.

Because the justices of the Supreme Court met at the national capital (New York in 1790, Philadelphia for the remainder of the decade), it naturally fell to them to fashion a policy that the other federal judges could follow. In response to a series of events in the early 1790s, the justices articulated a distinction between the Court as an institution and its members as individuals. As an institution the Supreme Court would adhere scrupulously to the separation-of-powers doctrine to ensure that nothing would interfere with its constitutional duty to be the final impartial arbiter in cases and controversies properly presented to it. But as individuals the justices freely participated in a range of activities that might have compromised their independence as an institution.

Institution versus Individuals

The justices first made the distinction publicly in response to duties assigned to them under the Invalid Pensions Act of 1792.[16] Under the act, a disabled

16. 1 Stat. 243. John Jay had actually expressed his belief in the distinction as early as 1789 in a letter to William Cushing discussing administrative matters to be worked out in the new court system. He notes: "It is to be regretted that the Circuit Court cannot proceed for want of a Seal—but as the Statute enables the *sup. Court*, and not the Judges of it to provide one, I am inclined to think that no order on the Subject by the Judges *out* of Court, would be regular. [I]f so, the Delay is unavoidable, and must continue until the Sitting of the Court in February." John Jay to William Cushing, December 7, 1789, in Marcus and Perry, eds., *Documentary History of the Supreme Court,* vol. 1, p. 682.

revolutionary war veteran could apply for a pension by appearing before the circuit court of the United States for the district in which he lived and proving that he had been wounded during the war in the service of the United States, that his disability kept him from pursuing his usual employment, and that he had not deserted. The circuit court, after verifying the invalid's claims, had to inquire into the nature and degree of the disability and then recommend to the secretary of war whether the applicant should receive a pension and in what amount. If the secretary suspected no "mistake or imposition," he was to add the invalid's name to the pension list of the United States. But if he had any such suspicions, the secretary could withhold the applicant's name from the list and report his action to Congress.[17]

At the first terms of the circuit courts following passage of the Invalid Pensions Act, the judges refused to carry out the duties assigned by the act. Their objection was that it was unconstitutional for the court as an institution to perform those duties. As explained by the judges of the Circuit Court for the District of New York:

> That, by the constitution of the United States, the Government thereof is divided into *three* distinct and independent branches; and that it is the duty of each to abstain from and to oppose encroachments on either.
>
> That neither the *legislative* nor the *executive* branch can constitutionally assign to the *judicial* any duties but such as are properly judicial, and to be performed in a judicial manner.
>
> That the duties assigned to the circuit courts by this act are not of that description, and that the act itself does not appear to contemplate them as such, inasmuch as it subjects the decisions of these courts made pursuant to those duties, first to the consideration and suspension of the Secretary of War, and then to the revision of the Legislature; whereas, by the constitution, neither the Secretary of War, nor any other executive officer, nor even the Legislature, are authorized to sit as a court of errors on the judicial acts or opinions of this court.[18]

All the justices of the Supreme Court agreed. When an invalid veteran appeared before the Circuit Court for the District of Pennsylvania, Justices

17. 1 Stat. 244, secs. 2, 4.

18. Extract of the minutes of the Circuit Court for the District of New York, April 5, 1792, contained in a letter from John Jay, William Cushing, and James Duane to George Washington, April 10, 1792, printed in *American State Papers, Miscellaneous* (Washington, D.C.: Gales and Seaton, 1834), vol. 1, pp. 49, 50.

James Wilson and John Blair, along with Judge Richard Peters, refused to proceed:[19]

1. Because the business directed by this act is not of a judicial nature. It forms no part of the power vested by the constitution in the courts of the United States. The circuit court must, consequently, have proceeded *without* constitutional authority.

2. Because, if upon that business the court had proceeded, its *judgments* (for its *opinions* are its *judgments*) might, under the same act, have been revised and controlled by the Legislature and by an officer in the executive department. Such revision and control we deemed radically inconsistent with the independence of that judicial power which is vested in the courts, and, consequently, with that important principle which is so strictly observed by the constitution of the United States.[20]

The judges at the Circuit Court for the District of North Carolina, Justice James Iredell and Judge John Sitgreaves, added their sentiments to those of their brethren in the other circuits. "No decision of any court of the United States," they asserted, "can, under any circumstances, in our opinion, agreeable to the constitution, be liable to a reversion, or even suspension, by the Legislature itself, in whom no judicial power of any kind appears to be vested but the important one relative to impeachments."[21] All the justices came to the same conclusion: the Constitution forbade the circuit courts, as institutions, to carry out the duties assigned to them by the Invalid Pensions Act.

Conscious of the humanitarian purposes of the act and wishing to find a way to perform the duties stipulated by it, some justices agreed that they would, as individuals, act as commissioners and hear the claims of the disabled veterans. As the judges of the Circuit Court for the District of New York stated:

19. The court refused to consider the petition of William Hayburn to be placed on the pension list of the United States. Copy of the opinion of the Circuit Court for the Pennsylvania District in the case of William Hayburn, an Invalid on his petition to be put on the list of pensioners of the United States (Record Group 267, National Archives); and *Hayburn's Case,* 2 U.S. (2 Dall.) 409 (1792).

20. James Wilson, John Blair, and Richard Peters to George Washington, April 18, 1792, printed in *American State Papers, Miscellaneous,* vol. 1, p. 51. Emphasis in original. In revealing their opinion to the president, these judges noted that "to be obliged to act contrary either to the obvious directions of Congress, or to a constitutional principle, in our judgment equally obvious, excited feelings in us which we hope never to experience again." Ibid.

21. James Iredell and John Sitgreaves to George Washington, June 8, 1792, printed in ibid., p. 53.

As, therefore, the business assigned to this court by the act is not judicial, nor directed to be performed judicially, the act can only be considered as appointing commissioners for the purposes mentioned in it by *official* instead of *personal* descriptions.

That the judges of this court regard themselves as being the commissioners designated by this act, and therefore as being at liberty to accept or to decline that office.[22]

Although they could not execute the invalid pension duties as a court, the judges thought it perfectly legitimate to conduct the business as commissioners out of court, but in the same courtroom.

Some of the judges questioned their authority to sit as commissioners, however, and one, James Wilson, refused to hear any claims in any capacity. Their doubts, however, focused on whether they could interpret the Invalid Pensions Act of 1792 as allowing them to act as commissioners, not on whether it was proper for judges to assume such extrajudicial tasks. As stated by Judges Iredell and Sitgreaves:

[Could we] be justified in acting under this act personally in the character of commissioners during the sessions of a court; and could we be satisfied that we had authority to do so, we would cheerfully devote such part of our time as might be necessary for the performance of the service. But we confess we have great doubts on this head. The power appears to be given to the court only, and not to the judges of it.[23]

Nevertheless, the judges told President Washington that they would think more about the question, because they wished to carry out the benevolent purposes of the act.

After a great deal of soul-searching, Justice Iredell eventually decided that he could act as a commissioner. In a written precis of his views, Iredell related that he had struggled with the construction that could be given to the Invalid Pensions Act, especially because "authorities" for whom he had the "highest respect" had differed with him.[24] Nonetheless, Iredell believed

22. Extract of the minutes of the Circuit Court for the District of New York, April 5, 1792, printed in ibid., p. 50. Emphasis in original.

23. Ibid., p. 53.

24. Iredell was thinking of Justice James Wilson, who refused to act as a commissioner. As Iredell wrote to his wife, "We have had a great deal of business to do here, particularly as I have reconciled myself to the propriety of doing the Invalid-business out of Court. *Judge Wilson altogether declines it.*" James Iredell to Hannah Iredell, September 30, 1792, printed in Griffith McRee, *Life and Correspondence of James Iredell* (New York: Peter Smith, 1949), vol. 2, p. 361. Emphasis in original.

that he could interpret the act to warrant the judges, as individuals, acting as commissioners. Iredell explained that

> Congress may probably have meant, in using the expression "Circuit Court", rather a designation of the Persons in whom they chose to repose such confidence, than a description to be strictly confined to its legal import, . . . there are expressions in the act which in my opinion lead to a very probable supposition that Congress may have contemplated it as a personal rather than a judicial exercise of power.[25]

In concluding that he could undertake the duty to hear the invalid pension claims, Iredell appended one caveat:

> This not being any part of my duty as a Judge (for so I consider it), but a Trust which I may or may not execute, I ought not to do it if it will be in any manner inconsistent with my Judicial Duty. If therefore it appeared to me that this question could by any possibility [?] come before me as a Judge, either in the Circuit or the Supreme Court, I ought not to exercise the authority. But I do not think it can. Therefore, having no reason of a public nature to decline the execution of the Trust, I readily accept it.[26]

25. Reasons for acting as a Commissioner on the Invalid Act [October 1792], Charles E. Johnson Collection, North Carolina State Department of Archives and History.

26. Ibid. In fact, in the February 1794 term, two cases came before the Supreme Court involving the rights of invalid pensioners, *Ex parte Chandler* and *United States* v. *Yale Todd,* but Justice Iredell did not attend court for the entire term because of illness. Neither case is reported by Dallas in the *U.S. Reports,* but they are recorded in the minutes and docket of the Supreme Court. Marcus and Perry, eds., *Documentary History of the Supreme Court,* vol. 1, pp. 222, 223, 226, 228, 494. Congress apparently began to doubt the propriety and wisdom of assigning the invalid pension duties to the circuit courts and in February 1793 changed the law. The new act replaced the circuit court judges with district judges or any three persons commissioned by those judges and reduced their role merely to collecting the evidence and transmitting it to the secretary of war. 1 Stat. 324–25. Congress also seemed to have doubts about the judges' interpretation of the 1792 act to allow them to hear invalid pension claims as commissioners, for in the new act Congress ordered the secretary of war and the attorney general to seek an adjudication of the Supreme Court "on the validity of any such rights claimed under the act aforesaid [the 1792 act], by the determination of certain persons styling themselves commissioners." Ibid., p. 325, sec. 3. In the case of *U.S.* v. *Yale Todd* the Supreme Court decided that the determinations of the commissioners were not valid. Marcus and Perry, eds., *Documentary History of the Supreme Court,* vol. 1, p. 228. The Court gave no rationale for its decision. The finding of no legal rights for the invalids could mean that the justices found the 1792 act unconstitutional or that, as a matter of statutory construction, the judges were not authorized by Congress to sit as commissioners.

The justices of the Supreme Court further developed their distinction between what the Court could do as an institution and what they as individuals might undertake when, in the summer of 1793, President Washington asked Secretary of State Thomas Jefferson to seek a formal opinion from the Supreme Court on questions involving the interpretation of treaties and the proper behavior of the United States in relation to the belligerent nations of Europe.[27] The matter of advisory opinions had been taken up during the debates in the Constitutional Convention. Charles Pinckney, an opponent of the plan for a council of revision, had proposed that the justices of the Supreme Court be required to render advisory opinions "upon important questions of law, and upon solemn occasions" when requested by the president or Congress.[28] Pinckney submitted his proposal to the Committee on Detail, where it disappeared. The convention did not reject the proposal, and Russell Wheeler speculates that it failed to emerge from the Committee on Detail because it was deemed redundant rather than repugnant.[29] The committee may well have assumed, Wheeler believes, that the president and Congress could and would request advisory opinions without the need of a constitutional directive. And, in fact, the executive and Congress did come to the Court for advisory opinions, only to be rebuffed by a separatist Court.

In accordance with Washington's request for a formal opinion from the Supreme Court, Jefferson wrote a letter to the judges, making it clear that the executive branch made no assumptions as to the propriety of the Court issuing advisory opinions.[30] What the president apparently had in mind was not only receiving specific answers to problems the government had encountered, but also getting authoritative judgments from the Court that would give more weight to his public pronouncements on the subject.[31] Introducing

27. Jefferson to Chief Justice Jay and associate justices, July 18, 1793, John Jay Papers, Columbia University. The questions are enclosed in this letter.

28. Max Farrand, *The Records of the Federal Convention* (Yale University Press, 1937), vol. 2, p. 341.

29. Russell Wheeler, "Extrajudicial Activities of the Early Supreme Court," *Supreme Court Review* (1973), p. 129.

30. This type of request must be distinguished from simply asking advice from the justices, on a personal basis, on a great variety of matters of state. President Washington, for example, availed himself of the knowledge and good judgment of Chief Justice John Jay on many occasions. That this occasion was different in kind was obvious to all involved.

31. "The President," Jefferson noted, "would therefore be much relieved if he found himself free to refer questions of this description to the opinions of the Judges of the supreme court of the US. whose knowledge of the subject would secure us against errors dangerous to the peace of the US. and their authority ensure the respect of all parties." Jefferson to Chief Justice John Jay and associate justices, July 18, 1793, John Jay Papers, Columbia University.

his request, the secretary of state described the difficulties that the United States had been encountering with the powers of Europe and the necessity of answering a number of questions that concerned the peace of the nation. "*These questions,*" wrote Jefferson, "depend for their solution on the construction of our treaties, on the laws of nature & nations, & on the laws of the land; and are often presented under circumstances *which do not give a cognisance of them to the tribunals of the country.*" But before receiving the answers to these questions, the president wanted to know first whether, in the justices' opinion, "the public may, with propriety, be availed of their *advice on these questions?*"[32] That the Court might not comply with the president's request already had been intimated privately to Washington by Chief Justice Jay.[33]

In the justices' reply to Jefferson's letter, they distinguished the judicial branch from the other branches of government as a separate and independent institution. The judges' highest priority seemed to be their ability to perform their judicial tasks impartially. Their letter to President Washington indicated that they had considered "the Lines of Separation drawn by the Constitution between the three Departments of Government" and had noted their being "in certain Respects checks on each other—and our being Judges of a Court in the last Resort." Thus they had decided that these considerations afforded "strong arguments against the Propriety of our extra-judicially deciding the questions alluded to; especially as the Power given by the Constitution to the President of calling on the Heads of Departments for opinions, seems to have been purposely as well as expressly limited to the *executive* Departments."[34]

The justices may have been even more reluctant to assay an opinion on the questions put to them because they knew that cases already before the lower federal courts involved these issues.[35] And they did not want the executive branch to think that it was a part of their official duty to advise the president when asked, for in the justices' minds that could be an interference with their primary constitutional duty to be impartial judges "in the last resort." The judges did not say that they personally could never give the president their opinions, but indicated that as an independent institution the Court could not be officially called upon to render that service.

32. Ibid. Emphasis in original.
33. Wheeler, "Extrajudicial Activities," p. 150. For an excellent discussion of the whole advisory opinion question, see pp. 144–58.
34. Letter from John Jay, James Wilson, John Blair, James Iredell, and William Paterson to George Washington, August 8, 1793, Record Group 59, National Archives. Emphasis in original.
35. See, for example, *United States* v. *Henfield* (U.S. Circuit Court for the District of Pennsylvania, 1793), printed in Francis Wharton, *State Trials of the United States during the Administrations of Washington and Adams* (Philadelphia: Carey and Hart, 1849), pp. 49–89.

Judicial-Congressional Relations

Individually, judges continued to give advice to both president and Congress, despite the possibility that the subjects involved could later come before the courts.[36] For the remainder of the 1790s the judges certainly did advise Congress, when asked, on matters of legislation, but always in their individual capacities, never as a court.[37] When, toward the end of the decade, Congress attempted to amend the Judiciary Act of 1789, the justices openly worked with a congressional committee that was to bring forth a new bill. Justices William Paterson and Bushrod Washington actually offered a bill of their own to the House committee dealing with the judiciary. According to Samuel Sewall, the chair of that committee, "Judge Paterson and Judge Washington were with the Committee according to appointment and favoured us with the details of a bill calculated upon the plan which had been suggested, and which in the principal points will be adopted by the Committee."[38] After the committee had formulated and reported its bill, Representative Robert Goodloe Harper wrote to Justice Paterson at the request of "some gentlemen in Congress," asking the judge to communicate his views on the bill. Harper closed his letter with a suggestion that the other justices ought to look at the bill too:

> Being of opinion that the Judiciary establishment cannot be rendered complete, without an uniform system of Practice and pleadings for the Courts of the United States, I beg leave, by the desire of the same gentlemen, to suggest that no persons can be so competent to that task as the judges, and to request that they will be pleased to give it their attention.[39]

The judges thus continued to adhere to the distinction they had set up early

---

36. Justice Iredell's protestations to the contrary when he decided to act as a commissioner in order to hear the claims of invalid veterans do not strike us as good evidence of the reluctance of judges individually to advise on subjects that might later come before them in court. In our view Iredell made as strong a statement as he could to justify his acting as a commissioner, because he wanted to act as one so as not to defy Congress's benevolent purpose. He must have known that there was a possibility that the claims that he adjudicated as a commissioner could eventually end up in federal court, as in fact at least two of them did.

37. In the contemporary age, the judiciary has distinguished between commenting on legislation that directly affects operation of the judicial system and other kinds of legislation. As to the former, the Judicial Conference of the United States responds to congressional inquiries.

38. Sewall to William Cushing, February 25, 1800, William Cushing Papers, Massachusetts Historical Society.

39. Harper to William Paterson, May 10, 1800, William Paterson Papers, Rutgers University.

in the decade: they involved themselves individually in political matters that they would not consider as a court.[40]

Congress itself seemed to recognize this dichotomy when in formal statutes it assigned particular duties to the chief justice of the United States. Legislation passed on August 12, 1790, to provide for a reduction of the public debt, for example, made the chief justice one of the Sinking Fund commissioners, along with the president of the Senate, the secretary of state, the secretary of the treasury, and the attorney general.[41] Because the tasks given to these commissioners required them to exercise administrative discretion, Congress apparently wanted individuals who were worthy of the public trust to serve on the commission, and the chief justice seemed an ideal choice. During the discussion of the creation of the Sinking Fund no opposition developed against using a member of the judiciary in this manner.[42]

The institutional-individual distinction was a logical response to the problem of maintaining a check on the encroachments of the other branches on the judiciary while allowing the government to take advantage of the judges' skills and talents. The judges also found the dichotomy persuasive when they, in turn, had requests to make of Congress. As was the case in the justices' manner of responding to Congress and the executive, their manner of approaching Congress evolved incident by incident as they faced the ambiguities of the American separation-of-powers doctrine.

On occasion individual justices and district court judges made specific requests to Congress to modify existing legislation or pass new legislation. When individuals wished to make a formal presentation to Congress as a body, they did it through the president. When, for example, hardship and injustice to hapless litigants threatened to result from a Supreme Court interpretation of a procedural rule, James Iredell undertook, through the president, to let Congress know of the problem, noting that the justices "were persuaded that if the mischief had been foreseen by Congress as resulting from the law in question, it would never have existed." Referring to a request

40. See, for example, letters of John Jay to Alexander Hamilton, November 28, 1790, printed in Henry P. Johnston, *Correspondence and Public Papers of John Jay* (New York: Burt Franklin, 1970), vol. 3, pp. 409–11; to Egbert Benson, March 31, 1792, printed in ibid., p. 417; and to Rufus King, December 22, 1793, printed in Charles King, *Life and Correspondence of Rufus King* (New York: DeCapo Press, 1971), vol. 1, pp. 509–10.

41. 1 Stat. 186.

42. For a discussion of the appointment of the chief justice as a Sinking Fund commissioner, see Wheeler, "Extrajudicial Activities," pp. 140–44, and citations therein. The chief justice also was appointed one of the inspectors of the coins produced by the U.S. Mint, another job that needed a trustworthy person to fulfill the duties in order to maintain public confidence. 1 Stat. 246.

President Washington had made to the entire court two years earlier, Iredell expressed his presumption that

> it is not only proper for a single judge, but his express duty when he deems it of importance to the public service, to state any particular circumstances that occur to him in the course of his personal experience which occasion unexpected difficulties or inconveniences in the execution of a system so new and in many respects unaided by any former examples.[43]

As if not completely convinced by the propriety of acting alone, however, Iredell added, "I therefore, sir, take the liberty to state some circumstances of great moment that occurred in the last Southern Circuit, which was attended by no other Judge of the Supreme Court but myself."[44] The president and Congress saw nothing amiss in Iredell's request: the suggestion was communicated, and Congress changed the offending provision.[45]

Later in the decade an indignant Judge Peters, of the U.S. District Court for the District of Pennsylvania, complained to President John Adams about his duties under the Debtors' Relief Act of 1796, fuming, "I can hardly suppose Congress meant to commit any part of the judiciary authority of the United States into a situation so inefficient and degrading." The act required the district judge to go to the jail to hold the proceedings and to certify the same to the jailer.[46] Among Peters's complaints were that the judge had no authority to order the prisoner brought to a "more fit and convenient place," nor any authority to enforce orders or punish contempts. "If it be," Peters speculated, "as it appears, an extra-judicial transaction, it is doubtful whether persons, other than the debtor, taking false oaths, before either the Judge or Commissioners, can be punished for perjury." Clearly Peters was unhappy about the duties imposed by the debtors' law: he concluded somewhat threateningly, "I choose to forget all questions about constitutional authority to compel a Judge to perform extra-judicial duty."[47]

43. James Iredell to George Washington, February 23, 1792, printed in Harold Syrett, ed., *The Papers of Alexander Hamilton,* 26 vols. (Columbia University Press, 1961–79), vol. 11, p. 46.

44. Ibid.

45. The president communicated the suggestion through the attorney general. See Tobias Lear to the Attorney General of the United States, February 24, 1792, Record Group 59 M179, National Archives. For the enacted legislation, see 1 Stat. 275, sec. 9.

46. 1 Stat. 482.

47. *Message from the President of the United States, Accompanying A Representation from the Judge of the District of Pennsylvania, and A Report of the Attorney-General,* January 18, 1798 (Philadelphia: Joseph Gales, 1798), pp. 4–5.

When judges wished to lobby Congress individually for legislative changes, however, they approached the congressmen directly, on an informal basis, apparently without raising any separation-of-powers concerns. The most sustained informal congressional-judicial relationships of which we have evidence are those between Justice James Iredell and his brother-in-law Senator Samuel Johnston, and between Rhode Island District Court Judge Henry Marchant and various members of Congress. Scattered correspondence between other justices and congressmen, such as that between Chief Justice John Jay and Senator Rufus King, suggests that the practice of informal lobbying or conferring between the two branches was, if not commonplace, then certainly not unusual during the formative decade of the U.S. constitutional system.[48]

James Iredell counted on his brother-in-law to remedy that most egregious defect of the judicial arrangement, Supreme Court circuit riding, which in Iredell's mind affected him more severely than any of the other justices; his personal crusade soon transformed the issue into one of institutional concern. And Judge Marchant tirelessly badgered Congress, through his friends, to raise his salary. In an era when fathers cautioned their sons to be circumspect in what they committed to paper and thence to the mails, when political allies routinely communicated in cipher, and when correspondents admonished each other to use seals, destroy letters, or return sensitive material, the fact that neither Iredell nor Marchant showed any compunction about sending their petitions through the mail, or even at times publicizing them, indicates that their informal use of friends in Congress did not strike them as improper.

The justices detested circuit riding. It was onerous, hard on their health, and required them to be away from their families for as long as six months out of the year.[49] The justices' dislike of circuit duties was itself a cause of

48. See, for example, Samuel Johnston to James Iredell, November 13, 1791, Charles E. Johnson Collection, North Carolina State Department of Archives and History; Samuel Johnston to James Iredell, November 26, 1794, McRee, ed., *Life and Correspondence of James Iredell*, vol. 2, pp. 430–31; Henry Marchant to Theodore Foster, November 12, 1791, Theodore Foster Papers, Rhode Island Historical Society; Henry Marchant to Benjamin Bourne, December 24, 1791, Benjamin Bourne Papers, Rhode Island Historical Society; and John Jay to Rufus King, December 22, 1793, Rufus King Papers, New York Historical Society. In addition, Thomas Johnson noted to James Iredell in 1792 that "Some time ago I took the Liberty of communicating to a Gent in Congress my wish" that the judiciary system might be amended in a particular way. "But from his Answer," Johnson ruefully admitted, "I do not think that or either of *several other Hints* will gain Attention." Thomas Johnson to James Iredell, March 31, 1792, Charles E. Johnson Collection, North Carolina State Department of Archives and History. Emphasis added.

49. See Thomas Johnson to George Washington, January 16, 1793, Marcus and Perry, eds., *Documentary History of the Supreme Court*, vol. 1, p. 80.

ongoing judicial-congressional relations at first informally, through personal contacts, and then formally, through the president.

It was also a source of some rancor among the justices. In February 1791 James Iredell wrote an angry letter to Justices Jay, Cushing, and Wilson, decrying the system they had devised whereby each justice would receive a permanent circuit assignment. Iredell, who, with Rutledge, would have been permanently assigned to the most burdensome of the circuits, the Southern Circuit, remonstrated strongly against the unfairness of the justices' decision to reject a rotation of circuits:

> I must take the liberty to add, that if contrary to my wishes and expectations you should still continue to be of opinion that as the law stands at present it must receive the construction you gave it at New York, and therefore that decision is to remain unaltered, I shall be under the painful necessity of trying in some manner whether an alteration of the law in that particular cannot be obtained. . . .[50]

John Jay replied to Iredell the next day, acquiescing in a reexamination of the question of rotation. "If the Decision on it at New York should on further Consideration appear to have been erroneous," conceded Jay, "it ought to be relinquished." But contrary to Julius Goebel's suggestion that Iredell's threat must have shocked a Court that "had thus far steered clear of anything resembling political self-help," Jay indicated his willingness for Iredell to do what he might. After noting his sympathy for the "great and unequal" inconveniences of the Southern Circuit, Jay concluded: "and yet Sir! an adequate Remedy can in my opinion be afforded only by legislative Provisions."[51]

As the problem of permanent assignments heated up in the ensuing year, relations among the justices evidenced notable strain.[52] Jay reiterated his view

50. James Iredell to Justices Jay, Cushing, and Wilson, February 11, 1791, James Iredell Sr. and Jr. Papers, Duke University.

51. John Jay to James Iredell, February 12, 1791, Charles E. Johnson Collection, North Carolina Archives; and Julius Goebel, *History of the Supreme Court of the United States,* vol. 1: *Antecedents and Beginnings to 1801* (Macmillan, 1971), p. 557. On Iredell's part, he had engaged in "political self-help" as early as August 1790 when he drafted a bill to change the times of various southern circuit courts to make the order of holding those courts more convenient for whoever rode the southern circuit. The bill, in Iredell's handwriting, passed on August 11, 1790. 1 Stat. 184.

52. See James Iredell to John Jay, January 17, 1792, James Iredell Sr. and Jr. Papers, Duke University; and James Iredell to Thomas Johnson, March 15, 1792, C. Burr Artz Public Library, Frederick, Maryland.

that congressional action was the only possible remedy, specifying that he meant by that a complete abolition of the circuit system, rather than a statutory rotation.[53] Meanwhile, Iredell had "applied to several Members of Congress that the law may be amended so as to compel a rotation."[54]

The judges seemed to believe there was a chance of getting Congress to relieve them of the circuits. Relief apparently hinged on a plan described in a letter from Thomas Johnson to James Iredell: "Mr. Blair mentioned to me also and indeed it was the principal purpose of his Letter that he Mr. Wilson & yourself were willing to give up 500 Dollars each to put the Circuit Business in a different Train, but that Mr. Jay and Mr. Cushings Inclination was not known to you." Johnson indicated his complete assent to go along with the plan, but urged Iredell not to allow "the Measure to be delayed if you have not their Answer; there's hardly Time left now," he continued with a rising sense of urgency, "and if this Opportunity is lost we shall not have another soon so good."[55] Iredell replied to Johnson on March 15: "I am very glad you approve of our offer—but I apprehend unless it is unanimous it cannot be proposed."[56]

Jay harbored serious misgivings about the propriety of the action suggested. The proposal to Congress was apparently to be made informally, according to Jay, but it was also to be made by the justices acting in concert and thus at least to all appearances as a court. Jay seems to have believed that the boundaries between informal, individual supplications and institutional actions were being blurred and warned that "the Sentiments of *Congress* on this point should be pretty well ascertained before the Proposal is made."[57]

While Jay did not explicitly invoke the separation-of-powers doctrine as a bar to Iredell's proposal, his doubts clearly focused on the reaction Congress might have to such quasi-congressional activity on the part of the Court. "To me it appears doubtful whether it would be recd. [by Congress] with pleasure—If they should regard it as conveying an Implication not flattering to their Ideas of their own Dignity, it would produce disagreable Strictures." He belittled its chances of acceptance on a final point: "As a mear Matter of

53. John Jay to James Iredell, March 3, 1792, James Iredell Sr. and Jr. Papers, Duke University. "The objections heretofore stated to a Rotation strike me as insuperable; . . . I had flattered myself that the system would have been revised during the present Session." Ibid.

54. James Iredell to Thomas Johnson, March 15, 1792.

55. Thomas Johnson to James Iredell, March 9, 1792, Charles E. Johnson Collection, North Carolina State Department of Archives and History.

56. James Iredell to Thomas Johnson, March 15, 1792.

57. John Jay to James Iredell, March 19, 1792, enclosed in John Jay to William Cushing, March 19, 1792, Robert Treat Paine Papers, Massachusetts Historical Society. Emphasis in original.

Bargain, I should think it an excellent one on our parts, but not a very handsome one on theirs."[58]

By March 31, for whatever reason, Iredell's plan apparently had been abandoned.[59] But his personal, informal activities may well have born fruit in the form of the rotation bill that was passed on April 14, which provided that no judge would be required to ride the same circuit until every other justice had attended it, unless he should consent to do so.[60]

In August 1792 the justices made a formal appeal to Congress, placing it before Congress through the agency of the executive. As they explained in a letter to President Washington,

> Your official connection with the Legislature and the consideration that applications from us to them, cannot be made in any manner so respectful to Government as through the President, induce us to request your attention to the enclosed representation and that you will be pleased to lay it before the Congress.[61]

Far from making mention of how the system could be changed, through salary reduction or otherwise, the judges forbore making any suggestion at all, admitting that "it would not become them to suggest what alterations or system ought in their opinion to be formed and adopted."[62] The only relief provided by Congress was to reduce the number of justices required on a given circuit from two to one.[63]

In an early instance of informal interbranch cooperation, Secretary of the Treasury Alexander Hamilton, Senator Rufus King, and Chief Justice John Jay consulted about the best way for the federal government to deal with the resistance to the whiskey excise.[64] Hamilton, writing with some vehemence

58. Ibid. If the plan was to contribute $500 apiece for the purpose of funding a separate circuit court, the bargain would indeed be a bad one for Congress, as the lowest paid district court judge received compensation of $800 a year—the amount went up to $1,800 for the District of South Carolina. 1 Stat. 72.

59. On that date Thomas Johnson wrote to James Iredell expressing regret that "you did not make the proposition for giving up a part of the salary." Referring to the plan as "the Act," Johnson opined that "we were better circumstanced to get a Change than we shall soon be again." March 31, 1792, Charles E. Johnson Collection, North Carolina State Department of Archives and History.

60. 1 Stat. 252–53.

61. Justices of the Supreme Court to George Washington, August 9, 1792, Record Group 46, National Archives.

62. Ibid.

63. 1 Stat. 333–34.

64. For a recent history of the rebellion, see Thomas P. Slaughter, *The Whiskey Rebellion: Frontier Epilogue to the American Revolution* (Oxford University Press, 1986).

to Jay, decried the lack of respect for the government shown by the whiskey rebels: "There is really My Dear Sir a crisis in the affairs of the Country which demands the most mature consideration of its best & wisest friends." After suggesting to Jay that "one point for consideration will be the expediency of the next Circuit Court's noticing the state of things in that quarter," Hamilton adds "perhaps it will not be amiss for you to converse with Mr. King."[65]

No sense of impropriety or violation of separation of powers informs Jay's reply to Hamilton. Jay and King conferred on the problem and jointly concluded that "neither a Proclamation nor a *particular* charge by the court to the G.Jury would be adviseable at present." Probably Jay believed that a particular charge would either be ignored, embarrassing the federal court, or tend further to inflame the passions of the westerners. "If matters can pass on *Sub Silentio* untill the meeting of Congress," Jay suggested, "I think all will be well."[66] Although questions might have been raised if the executive had formally requested a particular charge to the grand jury or if Congress had appointed a committee to confer with the chief justice, informal consultations such as described above seem not to have been perceived as improper.

Congressional failure to realize and act upon the immediate needs of the "least dangerous" and often most impotent governmental branch was a problem from the beginning. Although it was understandable that the body of men entrusted with setting the new government in motion might be unable to see to every detail at once, it is clear that at least one justice had little patience with congressional logjams. William Cushing found himself confronting a possible piracy prosecution on his first circuit, with no law to act under. He was aware of a bill respecting federal crimes and punishments, which, as he explained to John Lowell, had been "sleeping sometime" because of other matters before Congress. "I am urging the completion of it," he continued, "without which I do not know in what predicament our Courts will be in as to carrying into Execution punishments for pyracies & felonies on the h. Seas & some other matters."[67]

In a more dramatic interplay of court and Congress arising from congressional administration of the courts, Congress responded to a judicial "emergency" request with a speed hard to imagine in the twentieth century. Although it had provided for the adjournment of courts from day to day until a quorum could be made, Congress had failed to provide for the

65. Alexander Hamilton to John Jay, September 3, 1792, printed in Syrett, *Papers of Alexander Hamilton*, vol. 12, pp. 316–17.

66. John Jay to Alexander Hamilton, September 8, 1792, printed in ibid., pp. 334–35.

67. William Cushing to John Lowell, April 4, 1790, Hampton L. Carson Collection, Free Library of Philadelphia.

eventuality that a quorum could not be made at all.[68] Ordinarily judges simply assumed the power to adjourn to the next session. On November 30, 1792, for example, the U.S. District Judge for North Carolina, John Sitgreaves, opened court and then adjourned from day to day until December 11. When Justice Thomas Johnson still failed to appear, Sitgreaves adjourned the court to the next term.[69] But in Connecticut, in 1794, the failure of a Supreme Court justice to appear caused great upheaval. The U.S. district judge, the marshal, and attorneys, parties, and witnesses from all over the state appeared for the opening of court on April 25 and attended for nearly a week with no word as to why a Supreme Court justice had not arrived.[70] The clerk of the court, Simeon Baldwin, wrote to Congressman Uriah Tracy explaining that "serious difficulties were apprehended by the Counsel from a discontinuance & some doubts were entertained of the legal opperation of a revival of the causes by a Legislative Act." Baldwin continues:

It was therefore thought adviseable to continue the Court by daily adjournments untill a Judge should arrive who has power to continue the Causes—or untill Congress should empower the marshall or some other person to adjourn the Court & continue the causes to the next stated term—all parties are now dispersed with that expectation, the District Judge left town last fryday having advised the Marshall to keep alive the Court untill a Judge should arrive or Congress direct.[71]

Judge Richard Law had written the week before to Senator Oliver Ellsworth, Justice Wilson, and Justice Paterson about the problem. By May 12 Ellsworth had introduced an adjournment bill, which became law on May 19. Having appeared to adjourn the court "from day to day" every day for a month, the marshal was finally rewarded on May 30 when he read in court "An Act further to authorize the adjournment of Circuit Courts," allowing him to adjourn to the next term.[72]

The Connecticut adjournment crisis is more than simply another episode in the long history of problematic judicial-congressional interplay. It shows

68. 1 Stat. 73, sec. 6.

69. Minutes of the Circuit Court for the District of North Carolina, Record Group 21, U.S. Federal Archives and Records Center, East Point, Georgia.

70. U.S. District Judge Richard Law attended only for the first three days. Docket Book, Circuit Court for the District of Connecticut, Record Group 21, U.S. Federal Archives and Records Center, Waltham, Massachusetts.

71. Simeon Baldwin to Uriah Tracy, May 5, 1794, Baldwin Family Papers, Yale University.

72. Senate Legislative Journal, vol. 2, p. 78; and 1 Stat. 369. For a new twist on the problem, see Richard Peters to Edmund Randolph, January 7, 1795, Record Group 46, National Archives.

yet another way in which the two branches were not rigidly separated. The Judiciary Act of 1789 had granted the courts of the United States the power "to make and establish all necessary rules for the orderly conducting business in the said courts, provided such rules are not repugnant to the laws of the United States."[73] In the Connecticut case, the circuit court's rulemaking power came into conflict with the specific congressional stipulation as to adjournments. The judicial system could probably have operated more efficiently had the authority to make administrative decisions been not only lodged with the courts, but effectively left with them rather than being selectively removed through congressional acts. A pure separation of powers would have dictated this result.

Insights from History

Because of the novel implementation of the separation-of-powers doctrine in the United States and the different understandings of what the doctrine entailed, no clear precedents existed to guide the justices' behavior in their relationships with other branches of government. The ambiguous nature of that doctrine led the justices to evolve a way to maintain their institutional independence while still functioning as integral and effective officers of the new government. Congress, by statutorily creating, through the establishment of the circuit court system, an apparent distinction between the Supreme Court as an institution and the judges who composed it, suggested a paradigm for judicial-congressional relations that the judges chose to follow. While adhering to it at least in their relationship with other branches, the justices nevertheless deplored its application to their primary judicial task as a court of last resort. As the justices informed Congress:

> The distinction made between the Supreme Court and its Judges, and appointing the same men finally to correct in one capacity, the errors which they themselves may have committed in another, is a distinction unfriendly to impartial justice, and to that confidence in the Supreme Court, which it is so essential to the public Interest should be reposed in it.[74]

Although Congress finally responded to this complaint and relieved the justices, a mere century later, of their circuit duty, the doctrine of separation

73. 1 Stat. 73, sec. 17.
74. Justices of the Supreme Court to Congress, August 9, 1792, Record Group 46, National Archives.

of powers continues to complicate efforts to define the proper relationship between judges and legislators.[75]

The methods worked out by the first federal judges to deal with the quandary of interbranch relations cannot provide a blueprint for solutions to contemporary problems: the vast differences between the tiny federal judiciary of the eighteenth century and the comparatively vast judicial bureaucracy of today make the folly of such a proposal self-evident. What history can offer is insight into the practical understanding of the people who set in motion the American experiment about the range and limits of proper behavior when the theory of separation of powers and the need for effective government were apparently at odds.

What history shows is that the experience of the first decade under the Constitution did not establish the pattern for the current relationship between the federal judiciary and Congress. Quite the contrary. And that finding might serve as a lesson for—indeed, hearten—those who seek to improve communications between the branches.

75. The act was passed March 3, 1891. Felix Frankfurter and James M. Landis, *The Business of the Supreme Court* (Macmillan, 1927), pp. 97–101.

A Judicious Legislator's Lexicon to the Federal Judiciary

Robert W. Kastenmeier and Michael J. Remington

->>X<<-

The failure of communication between the two branches of government is an issue that has implications not just for judges and legislators but also for lawyers, public servants, administrators, lobbyists, academicians, legislative staff, and ordinary citizens. As participants in the legislative process, we are struck by the simple fact that few in Congress know much about or pay attention to the third branch of government. This lexicon describes those elements of the federal judiciary that should interest the conscientious legislator (as well as the serious staff member). Our principal purpose is to increase the legislature's understanding of the judicial branch. Our paper is eclectic in approach and based in large part on personal experience.

The Federal Judiciary

The federal judiciary can be compared with an integrated circuit or "chip," which is a complex of switches that control the flow of electric current. The city blocks of a chip are transistors, which are interconnected to perform electronic functions. The federal court system is a complex of decision points that control the flow of justice. The key components of the system are judges who resolve cases and controversies affecting aggrieved parties and administrative personnel who control the decisional currents.

We depict the federal judiciary in the same fashion as a circuit engineer would analyze a chip, by creating a schematic representation on paper in order to describe the total design. We begin with the first layer, the constitutional core. Next we discuss the overlay of statutorily created inferior courts and administrative structure. Then we assess the interface between the judicial branch and the legislative branch. The second major part of our paper is a shorter but more analytical examination of specific problems in the relationship between the two branches and of ideas for improvement.

54

The paper concludes on an optimistic note about the future of interbranch relations.

Our goal is to encourage the members of each branch to see interbranch problems from the perspective of the other branch. We would hope that differences and similarities in perspective may merge and a common language leading to increased communications and better understanding may be developed.

Constitutional Underpinnings

In January of every odd-numbered year, all newly elected members of Congress stand in their respective chambers before family and friends and take an oath to "support and defend the Constitution of the United States against all enemies foreign and domestic."[1] The importance of the oath is underscored by an understanding that a term of office does not begin until an investiture ceremony has occurred. Just what the oath means, and whether members of Congress actually read the Constitution before the ceremony, is not clear even to the trained eye. Given the level of debate about constitutional questions, it is fair to conclude that members' commitment to the Constitution is uneven.[2]

The most important part of the Constitution concerning the federal courts—article III—may be the most ignored. Questions about tenure in office, diminution of salary, inferior courts, the status of the Supreme Court, impeachment of federal judges, can all be answered by resorting to the constitutional roadmap provided by the Framers.

The opening sentence of the first section of article III states that "the judicial power of the United States, shall be vested in one Supreme Court, and in such inferior courts as the Congress may from time to time ordain and establish." The second sentence states that "the judges, both of the Supreme and inferior courts, shall hold their offices during good behavior, and shall, at stated times, receive for their services, a compensation, which shall not be diminished during their continuance in office." The life tenure of federal judges and the bar against diminution of salary while in office are created not for the benefit of the judges, but for the benefit of the judged.

Other than ordaining the creation of the Supreme Court, the Constitution is almost completely silent on the issue of federal court organization. The Constitution specifically confers authority on the policymaking branch (Con-

---

1. The form of the oath is set forth in 5 U.S.C. sec. 3331 (1976). The oath is constitutionally required of all members of both the House and Senate (art. VI, clause 3).

2. Abner Mikva, "How Well Does Congress Support and Defend the Constitution?" 61 *North Carolina Law Review* 587 (1983).

gress) to decide the size and composition of the Supreme Court, as well as the structure and organization of the inferior courts. In short, from the birth of our nation the issue of court reform has been a public policy question, not one reserved to judges and lawyers.

Congressional power to punish individual members of the judiciary is narrow. Federal judges hold their offices for life, can be removed only by impeachment, and cannot have their salaries reduced while in office. However, the recent impeachment of Harry E. Claiborne (a district judge from the District of Nevada) reaffirms that all federal judges are "civil officers of the United States" within the meaning of article II, section 4, of the Constitution and can be removed from office for the commission of "high crimes and misdemeanors" in the constitutional sense.[3] Commission of, and conviction for, a criminal offense are not preconditions for impeachment.

Section 2 of article III sets forth the nine classes of cases and controversies to which the judicial power of the United States extends—for example, cases arising under the Constitution and federal laws, and controversies between citizens of different states.

The Framers anticipated judicial review and the ability to invalidate federal and state legislative enactments, although they did not mention them specifically in the Constitution. Hamilton wrote the classic explanation:

> The interpretation of the laws is the proper and peculiar province of the courts. A constitution is, in fact, and must be regarded by the judges as a fundamental law. It therefore belongs to them to ascertain its meaning, as well as the meaning of any particular act proceeding from the legislative body.[4]

The statement in article VI that "the Constitution . . . shall be the supreme law of the land" coupled with the provision in article III extending the judicial power of the United States ". . . to all cases arising under this Constitution" makes abundantly clear that constitutional questions were indeed intended to be justiciable.

"Congress has an independent and affirmative obligation continually to determine the constitutionality of legislation," according to several legislative reports of the House Committee on the Judiciary.[5] When article III of the

3. The Claiborne impeachment is discussed in greater detail below.

4. *The Federalist,* no. 78.

5. *Magistrate Act of 1978,* H. Rept. 95-1364, 95 Cong. 2 sess. (Government Printing Office, 1978); *Judicial Councils Reform and Judicial Conduct and Disability Act of 1980,* H. Rept. 96-1313, 96 Cong. 2 sess. (GPO, 1980); and *Court of Appeals for the Federal Circuit Act of 1981,* H. Rept. 97-312, 97 Cong. 1 sess. (GPO, 1981).

Constitution is implicated, Congress's responsibility should be taken seriously. There are modest signs that this is happening, albeit in an ad hoc fashion. During recent Congresses, the House Judiciary Committee has filed legislative reports on such subjects as the Federal Magistrate Act of 1979, the Judicial Conduct and Disability Act of 1980, and the Court of Appeals for the Federal Circuit Act of 1981, all containing detailed constitutional analyses.[6]

While conscientious consideration of constitutional questions by Congress does not decide the ultimate issue of whether a public law passes constitutional muster, a reviewing court certainly can benefit from the congressional debate. Sitting en banc, the Ninth Circuit recently considered the constitutionality of consent trials by U.S. magistrates pursuant to the Federal Magistrate Act of 1979. Finding that the statute satisfied constitutional dictates, the court stated that considerable weight should be given to constitutional determinations by Congress: "The House Committee gave explicit consideration to the issue of constitutionality, and concluded that consent of the parties suffices to overcome objections based on constitutional grounds."[7] At the very least, this statement is a clear signal that Congress need not be timid about its duty to defend the Constitution. The more vigilant Congress becomes in asking and answering constitutional questions, the more weight will be accorded those answers by reviewing courts.

The Constitution establishes a federal government assigned certain enumerated powers and also state governments that exercise all the powers not delegated to the Union. Courts in the United States therefore occupy two distinctly different realms: state and federal. Suits filed each year in the state courts of general jurisdiction outnumber those filed in federal courts by some fifty times. Final decisions of the highest courts of the states are reviewable by the Supreme Court. The supremacy clause of the Constitution (article VI, clause 2) renders the Constitution, laws, and treaties of the United States as much a part of the law of every state as its own constitution and local laws.

The power to appoint federal judges is divided between the president and the Senate, which gives advice and consent (article II, section 2). Political factors have always been a salient feature of the appointing process, and there are only two ways to change this: through self-restraint on the part of the president and the Senate (unlikely), or through reduction of judicial independence and power of federal judges (unwise) so that less politically motivated individuals would seek the job.

Article I of the Constitution—the legislative branch's beacon—specifies

6. Ibid.
7. *Pacemaker Diagnostic Clinic of America* v. *Instromedix,* 725 F.2d 537, 542 (9th Cir. 1984).

that "Congress shall have the power . . . to constitute tribunals inferior to the Supreme Court" (section 8). Beginning with the creation of the Court of Claims immediately before the Civil War, Congress has exercised its article I authority to create specialized courts whose judges do not hold office for life. By limiting terms of office, the legislative branch maintains the flexibility to modify or abolish the tribunal at any time in response to changing societal, legal, or political conditions. Today, article I courts are located in the executive branch of government (the Tax Court, the Court of Military Appeals, and the territorial courts) and in the judicial branch (the U.S. Claims Court and the bankruptcy courts). Congress has created thousands of article I (without lifetime tenure) judicial officers, counting both U.S. magistrates and administrative law judges.

The constitutional grants of authority in articles I and III have provided Congress with the significant responsibility of overseeing the functioning of the federal court system. The creative genius of the Founding Fathers is that they counterbalanced the broad legislative power by granting independence and autonomy to an antimajoritarian branch of government—the judiciary. In effect, the Framers made it extremely difficult to change the basic judicial system. The result is a constructive tension that has contributed to the resiliency of the judiciary and has equipped it to prevent trespass by its coordinate branches of government.

Adjudicatory and Administrative Structure: An Institutional Analysis

A legislator who wants to legislate, a counsel who must give advice, and a legislative case worker who is asked to resolve a constituent's problem can more effectively and responsibly satisfy their respective duties when equipped with a working knowledge of the institutional framework of the federal judiciary.

ADJUDICATORY STRUCTURE. The statutory distribution of the judicial, or adjudicative, power of the United States has been a political problem since the heady days of drafting and implementing the Constitution. The constitutional grant of authority to the Congress to create inferior courts was exercised almost immediately after ratification of the Constitution by enactment of the Judiciary Act of September 24, 1789.[8] This great statute, owing its origins to Senate Bill No. 1 in the first session of the First Congress, was signed into law the day before the final vote on the Bill of Rights, thus establishing a hierarchial system of federal courts, not of judges. The new

8. 1 Stat. 73.

system was composed of three tiers: district courts of first instance; intermediate appellate tribunals (circuit courts); and the constitutionally created Supreme Court of final review. The three tiers were, however, occupied by two types of judges (district judges and Supreme Court justices).

Similar to every other court reform proposal that has been enacted in American history, the Judiciary Act of 1789 was a political compromise. The act established an organizational framework for the federal court system that lasted virtually unchanged for nearly one hundred years.

Over time, the major failing of the act was felt at the intermediate court level. In an increasingly robust country of growing boundaries and population and new legal relationships, litigation increased and cries for court reform were heard. Finally, in 1891 the Evarts Act was enacted, creating nine regional courts of appeals, with judges to sit full time on these courts.[9] The Evarts Act provided for the first time in federal law that the Supreme Court would have control over its docket to the extent that it was granted discretion as to whether to hear certain types of cases designated by statute and appealed from the newly created circuit courts of appeals. Despite this ameliorative action, the Supreme Court's work load remained too heavy. In the Judges' Act of 1925, the Court's obligatory review jurisdiction was largely eliminated and the role of certiorari or discretionary jurisdiction was expanded.[10] There remains a narrow category of cases that Congress has identified as meriting the immediate and mandatory attention of the Supreme Court.

Since 1789 the organizational principle of the federal judiciary has been regional, with a substantial dose of localism. The Judiciary Act of 1789 organized each state (thirteen at the time) as a single federal district. Now many states are divided into several districts, and California and New York each have four districts. There are ninety-one districts in all. An entire chapter of title 28 of the U.S. Code is devoted to the organizational structure of the federal judiciary. Chapter 5 delineates the framework of the ninety-one district courts on a state-by-state basis, the divisions per district (if any), and the places of holding court for each division or district. Congress constantly is being asked to create new districts (most recently another district in California), establish divisions, and create new places of holding court.

There are now thirteen circuits: twelve of these are regional and the thirteenth is the Court of Appeals for the Federal Circuit. Created by statute

9. 26 Stat. 826. As a political gesture to sentiment, Congress elected to keep the circuit courts but abolished their appellate jurisdiction. The anachronism of two courts of roughly equal weight—the district and circuit courts—was statutorily ended on January 1, 1912 (36 Stat. 1087).

10. 43 Stat. 936.

in 1982, the Court of Appeals for the Federal Circuit—which is housed in Washington, D.C.—has nationwide jurisdiction over certain types of cases, including patent, merit systems protection, and government contracts.[11] The newest geographic circuit is the Eleventh Circuit, which was split from the former Fifth Circuit on October 1, 1981.

The judicial branch of government, through the Judicial Conference of the United States, takes the position that changes in the geographic configuration and organization of the existing judicial districts and circuits should be enacted only after a congressional showing of strong and compelling need.

Congress has responded to the inexorably spiraling work load of the federal courts by constantly augmenting the number of judges and by increasing the number of units into which the system is divided. Presently, there are 575 district judges; 168 circuit judges; and, of course, 9 Supreme Court justices. It is customary to describe the structure of the federal judiciary as pyramidal, with the bulk of the judges at the base, fewer on the slopes, and very few at the apex. The addition of more district than circuit judges, coupled with increasing responsibilities being granted to U.S. magistrates (280) and U.S. bankruptcy judges (284), makes the judicial structure today resemble an eroded mountain range more than a majestic pyramid.

Since the localism of the federal judiciary corresponds closely to the localism of political districts for election to Congress, a representative or senator often takes more interest in a question of local judicial organization than an issue of nationwide import. A quick glance at the table of contents to congressional hearings on judicial branch issues confirms this proposition. In hearings on district court organization before the House Judiciary Subcommittee on Courts during the Ninety-fifth Congress, nineteen members of Congress presented oral and written statements on court organization bills.[12] During House hearings on proposals to create a Court of Appeals for the Federal Circuit, not a single member addressed views to the Courts Subcommittee.[13] Similarly, hearings on the pressing issue of the Supreme Court's work load crisis did not stimulate a sole member statement.[14]

11. 96 Stat. 25.

12. *Federal District Court Organization Act of 1978,* Hearings before the Subcommittee on Courts, Civil Liberties, and the Administration of Justice of the House Committee on the Judiciary, 95 Cong. 2 sess. (GPO, 1978).

13. *Court of Appeals for the Federal Circuit—1981,* Hearings before the Subcommittee on Courts, Civil Liberties, and the Administration of Justice of the House Committee on the Judiciary, 97 Cong. 1 sess. (GPO, 1981).

14. *Supreme Court Workload,* Hearings before the Subcommittee on Courts, Civil Liberties, and the Administration of Justice of the House Committee on the Judiciary, 98 Cong. 1 sess. (GPO, 1983).

The House Committee on the Judiciary has found that the federal judiciary cannot be expanded indeterminably without impairing its high quality, agreeing with Justice Frankfurter that "a powerful judiciary implies a relatively small number of judges."[15] Whether one concurs with the political palliative of creating judgeships, it can hardly be questioned that judges are like better roads: they solve short-term problems, but over the long run they cause more congestion. From a numerical and organizational perspective, the federal judiciary is becoming more bureaucratic and much more complicated. As judge and staff resources have increased over time, there has been an equal—if not greater—growth in the administrative work imposed on the courts. And, ominously, the pending backlogs of criminal and civil cases and appeals have actually increased.[16]

ADMINISTRATIVE STRUCTURE. During the first one hundred years of the federal judiciary, there was not much concern about judicial administration. The work load was relatively low, and the numbers of judges and subordinates were well within manageable limits. In the latter part of the nineteenth century, with the development of the modern industrial state, however, new and largely unforeseen pressures were thrust on the courts and the legal profession. Social, technological, and economic changes placed tremendous burdens on the legal system, whose job it was to direct and organize those changes. However, the need to improve the administration of justice was not immediately recognized.

Progressive pressures for change were put in focus in 1906, when Roscoe Pound gave a classic address to the American Bar Association on the popular dissatisfaction with the administration of justice. The Pound speech planted a seed for reform, which sprouted and matured sixteen years later. Under the tutelege of Chief Justice (former President) William Howard Taft, legislation was enacted in 1922 that achieved two objectives.[17] First, the chief justice was given the authority to take specific actions to meet the changing needs of the federal courts. Second, and more important, the 1922 act established the Conference of Senior Circuit Judges (today known as the Judicial Conference of the United States). The conference was allocated general responsibility to make a comprehensive survey of the business in the federal courts, prepare plans for the transfer and temporary assignment of judges to

15. *Abolition of Diversity of Citizenship Jurisdiction*, H. Rept. 95-893, 95 Cong. 2 sess. (GPO, 1978); see Felix N. Frankfurter, "Distribution of Judicial Power Between United States and State Courts," 13 *Cornell Law Quarterly* 499, 515 (1928).

16. *Annual Report of the Director of the Administrative Office of the U.S. Courts, 1986* (GPO, 1987), pp. 2 (table 1), 8 (table 4), 15 (table 6).

17. 42 Stat. 837.

meet varying docket demands, and submit to Congress suggestions concerning uniformity and the expedition of the federal courts' business. The judicial branch, through the conception of the conference, acquired a policymaking body—a corporate board of directors—vested with fact-finding capabilities and authority to recommend legislative changes to Congress. Considered together, these changes comprised the first congressional effort in this nation's history to treat the federal judicial system as a single entity for administrative purposes. The yeoman efforts of Pound and Taft were part of a broader trend toward the adoption of efficient and rational methods of government in an increasingly industrial and urban setting, but this fact should not diminish the consequence of their contributions.

Although the 1922 reform was a significant political step forward, it exposed a need for further legislative action. The Judicial Conference, meeting only once a year and lacking an administrative staff, was unable to discharge its responsibilities effectively. Furthermore, without a comprehensive, reliable system of gathering and recording statistics, court reformers—including members of Congress—were hard-pressed to identify and formulate solutions to judicial branch problems.

Seventeen years later, in response to these needs, Congress acted again, passing the Administrative Office Act of 1939.[18] The House report underlined the significance of this bill by stating that it ". . . is the most important ever presented to Congress for the improvement of Federal judicature."[19] By enacting the Administrative Office Act, Congress achieved at least three major objectives. First, an entirely new institution—the Administrative Office of the U.S. Courts—was created to assume the responsibility of administering the federal courts, including preparation of the judiciary's budget, which previously had been prepared by the Department of Justice. One of the principal congressional purposes in enacting the 1939 act was the elimination of the Department of Justice as the controlling fiduciary for a constitutionally coordinate and independent branch of government. The Administrative Office was also given responsibility for gathering statistics about the federal courts' work load and reporting these statistics annually to both Congress and the Judicial Conference. In addition, the conference's own power was augmented by giving it supervisory authority over the Administrative Office, which was created to serve the conference by implementing and executing conference orders and policies. As candidly described by Judge Elmo Hunter, the

18. 53 Stat. 1223.
19. *Administration of U.S. Courts,* H. Rept. 702, 76 Cong. 1 sess. (GPO, 1939), p. 4.

Administrative Office ". . . was not intended to play a policy formulation role of its own."[20]

Second, through decentralization, Congress forged another new institution: the judicial councils of the circuits, which were to work for the effective and expeditious transaction of the business of the courts. The act specified that the councils had general order-making authority, a power that has never been granted to the Judicial Conference.

Third, the legislation provided for a judicial conference in each circuit, to be composed of all the circuit's district and circuit judges, together with designated members of the bar. The conferences were authorized to review their circuit's business and to study how the administration of justice in the circuit might be improved. These conferences have stimulated communications between bench and bar and are an untapped resource for improving understanding between judges and Congress.

After enactment of the Administrative Office Act of 1939, nearly three decades went by before passage of the next major administrative reform. In 1967 the Federal Judicial Center was established within the judicial branch and given responsibilities over research, judicial education, and systems development.[21] The authorizing legislation also provided that the center would be the source of recommendations to Congress, the Judicial Conference, and the legal community in general. In order to meld the center into the federal judiciary, Congress created a governing board chaired by the chief justice and composed of the director of the Administrative Office and five judges elected by the Judicial Conference.

In 1971 Congress created the office of Circuit Executive, a court administrator assigned to the courts of appeals with various responsibilities such as improving internal management and organization, serving the chief judge of the circuit, and staffing the circuit council.[22]

In 1976 Chief Justice Warren E. Burger established a Legislative Affairs Office, breaking precedent with the past. Placed in the Administrative Office, the office was charged with diverse liaison responsibilities, including the formulation of the Judicial Conference's legislative program and the presentation and promotion of the program to Congress. Today, it is hard to imagine the federal judiciary functioning without a legislative affairs officer.

---

20. *Federal Judicial Branch,* Hearings before the Subcommittee on Courts, Civil Liberties, and the Administration of Justice of the House Committee on the Judiciary, 97 Cong. 1 sess. (GPO, 1981), pp. 7, 12.

21. 81 Stat. 664.

22. 84 Stat. 1907.

Federal Judicial Administration

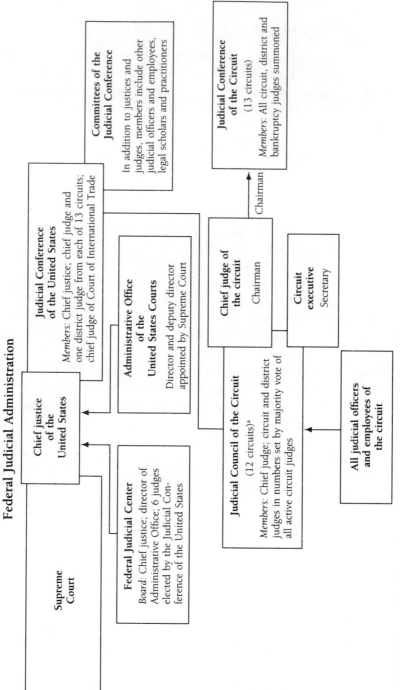

Source: Administrative Office of the United States Courts, Office of the General Counsel, November 1985.
a. The Federal Circuit is not within the statute establishing judicial councils (28 U.S.C. Sec. 332).

In 1980 Congress, building on the preexisting judicial structure, enacted the Judicial Councils Reform and Judicial Conduct and Disability Act.[23] This legislation increased the circuit councils' power and authority, democratized their membership, and specifically assigned to them the responsibility of deciding matters of judicial misconduct and disability. Moreover, the Judicial Conference was empowered to enact rules governing judicial discipline and given order-making authority in this limited arena.

The State Justice Institute was authorized in 1984 and asked by Congress to work cooperatively with the federal judiciary in order to improve the justice rendered by state courts.[24] As described by Senator Howell T. Heflin, its chief sponsor in the Senate, it is a nonprofit national institute that provides technical and financial assistance to State courts, which ". . . share with the Federal courts the awesome responsibility of enforcing the rights and duties of the Constitution and laws of the United States."[25]

Under the leadership and encouragement of former Chief Justice Burger, a number of institutions have been created during the past two decades: the National Center for State Courts (a research organization that studies state judicial matters); the National Judicial College (an educational center for the training and continuing judicial education of state judges); and the Institute for Court Management (a training institution for professional court administrators). These organizations, not statutorily created and therefore not governmental entities, can nonetheless be quite helpful to congressional offices in the constant quest to get information about problems of the justice system, to obtain statistical data, and to discuss issues with experts in the field of court administration.

The first century of this nation's history witnessed the constitutional and statutory creation of a court structure. During the second century, the most salient feature of legislation affecting the federal judiciary has been the establishment of administrative entities linked to, but not really part of, the federal courts. (See the figure on page 64 for an overall view of the federal judicial administrative structure.) No one knows what the third century holds in store.

The Legislative-Judicial Nexus

In order to know anything about government, one must see it in action, and the best way to experience the frontier between branches of government is to sit in the office of a subcommittee of the House Judiciary Committee,

23. 94 Stat. 2035.
24. 98 Stat. 335, sec. 201.
25. *Congressional Record* (February 24, 1981), p. 2831.

telephone in hand, fielding questions about senior judges and social security, judicial discipline, and magistrates' retirement benefits. Alternatively, one should be in a senior member's office during Judicial Conference week, when large numbers of influential federal judges descend on Washington, D.C., and seek meetings.

Institutional relations between the two branches of government occur along the entire spectrum of oversight, appropriations and the budget, investigations, program legislation, rules of procedure, the confirmation process, pay and perquisites, and impeachment, judicial discipline, and ethics. While the judiciary does not have a separate authorization process, specific programs are reviewed periodically. Personal relations also exist throughout the two branches. Indeed, there was a period in U.S. history when a very high percentage of federal judges had previously served in Congress (see the paper by Maeva Marcus and Emily Van Tassel in this volume). These individuals normally did not reject their political relationships built over time, nor should federal judges today who have had the honor of serving in Congress. In any event, an iron curtain does not exist between the two branches of government; a more apt analogy would be a low-lying fence shared by good neighbors. We now analyze the gates in the fence through which institutional and sometimes personal communications flow.

OVERSIGHT. Congressional oversight of most government endeavors is highly diffused, exercised by numerous standing committees and subcommittees with much overlapping and duplication of responsibility.[26] Oversight of the federal judiciary, however, is not so spread. The House and Senate Committees on the Judiciary oversee the federal courts (with the exception of the Supreme Court), and it is rare for another committee to encroach upon this turf.

Admittedly, oversight is most effective when Congress is able to exercise control over a recalcitrant agency or reverse an unacceptable action, either by amending an authorization, using the confirmation process to educate a nominee, or attaching a rider to an appropriations measure. Because such tools are not readily available to bring pressure to bear on the federal judiciary, oversight arguably has not been as successful as it could have been in remedying the flaws of the judicial branch.

Although Judge Abner Mikva has commented that "there is no traditional

26. As contemplated by the Legislative Reorganization Act of 1970, oversight is the "review and study, on a continuing basis, of the application, administration, and execution" of the law, agencies, and subject matter within a committee's or subcommittee's jurisdiction. 84 Stat. 1140, sec. 118.

oversight of the courts,"[27] Judge Elmo Hunter—testifying for the Judicial Conference at a hearing before the Senate Judiciary Subcommittee on Courts—stated to the contrary:

> In the past three Congresses, the House Subcommittee on Courts, Civil Liberties and the Administration of Justice has routinely conducted oversight hearings and published a record of those proceedings. . . . Let me note for the record that the Judicial Conference has thoroughly cooperated in that oversight—and in fact has repeatedly sought and is now seeking more of it.[28]

The Judicial Conference is not the only arm of the federal judicial branch that has been subjected to congressional oversight; the Federal Judicial Center and the Administrative Office both have been periodically scrutinized. Further, as part of its oversight function, Congress receives annual reports of the directors of the Administrative Office and the Federal Judicial Center.

Last, the implementation and effectiveness of recent statutory changes affecting the judiciary have been examined by congressional subcommittees. Oversight hearings reviewing the execution of legislative enactments have been held on such subjects as the Magistrate Act of 1979, the Judicial Discipline Act of 1981, the Pretrial Services Act, and the Court of Appeals for the Federal Circuit. On occasion, defects in language in the original law have been identified and corrective legislation has ensued. As a general proposition, the judicial branch has a good track record of implementing congressional edicts. And congressional oversight, on the whole, has generally been of a cooperative, rather than hostile, nature.

THE AUTHORIZATION PROCESS.   The judicial branch institutionally endorses oversight of its statutory structure and administration, while at the same time it vigorously opposes all efforts to enact into law an annual authorization process, such as that which exists for nearly all executive branch agencies. When an annual or multiyear authorization is required by law, appropriations must be expressly authorized. In short, two "look-sees" are required: one by the legislative (authorizing) committee and the second by the money (appropriations) committee. Each committee has a different objective: the legislative committee gives permission for the activity and sets a maximum allowance;

27. Abner J. Mikva and Patti B. Saris, *The American Congress: The First Branch* (New York: Franklin Watts, 1983), p. 313.

28. *Federal Judicial Salary Control Act of 1981,* Hearings before the Subcommittee on Courts of the Senate Committee on the Judiciary, 97 Cong. 2 sess. (GPO, 1982), pp. 37–38.

the appropriations committee establishes and fills the bank account with taxpayer funds that actually can be spent in any given year.

Proponents for an annual authorization posit that the federal judiciary does not receive the normal oversight that has proven beneficial to other endeavors of government, and that greater illumination of court programs would assist public understanding. Senator Jesse Helms has argued:

> I feel that the courts, as much as any other part of government, should be required to operate in the sunshine with all the facts regarding their programs and activities fully before the public and the peoples' representatives. The appropriations process alone is insufficient to achieve that goal.[29]

However, opponents have argued that the inevitable result of an authorization requirement would be congressional meddling in judicial policy and decisionmaking. They claim the authorization would become an easy target for legislative efforts to circumscribe "judicial activism" in such emotional areas as busing, school prayer, and abortion. Any restriction on the independence and autonomy of the judiciary, such as authorization riders, would violate the basic constitutional text. From a more practical perspective, such a two-step process—authorization and appropriation—could ultimately lead to less oversight because of the overriding need to keep the courts functioning. Robert Bork has observed, "You may have to rush the process and actually get less oversight than you now have."[30]

For the time being, the judiciary has avoided being subjected to a statutorily mandated authorization; however, it has continuously operated under the constitutional stricture that "no money shall be drawn from the treasury, but in consequence of appropriations made by law" (article I, section 9).

APPROPRIATIONS AND THE BUDGET. As stated above, the judiciary's appropriation is a permanent authorization; consequently, the budget receives annual review only by the House and Senate Appropriations committees, and more specifically, by the two respective subcommittees with jurisdiction over the judicial branch's appropriation.

The appropriations process for the federal judiciary, similar to that of the executive branch, operates in two steps. First, the budget document is prepared by the Administrative Office in a form approved by the House and Senate Appropriations committees. The document is provided to the Office

29. Ibid., p. 4.
30. Ibid., p. 11.

of Management and Budget (OMB) and incorporated into the president's budget. By statute, the OMB is precluded from changing the judiciary's request, but comments and criticism may be provided to the appropriate committees.

Second, the budget request is formally presented to Congress. Hearings are held early in the year, with judicial branch witnesses appearing to justify and answer questions about the request. Normally, these witnesses consist of the chairman of the Judicial Conference's Budget Committee, the directors of the Administrative Office and Federal Judicial Center, the chief judges of the Court of Appeals for the Federal Circuit and the Court of International Trade, and two associate justices of the Supreme Court.

The judiciary's share of the federal budget has never exceeded one-tenth of 1 percent in any given year. Most of the judiciary's expenditures are "uncontrollable" expenses, since the courts are primarily service oriented and highly labor intensive and reactive.

The working relationship between the Appropriations committees—especially the House committee, which plays a more active role—and the judiciary is clearly an amicable one, based on mutual respect. There is much interaction between committee staff and Administrative Office personnel; the hearing process is short, swift, and to the point; and the judiciary's budget request is generally granted.

INVESTIGATIONS.   The General Accounting Office (GAO) serves Congress as auditor of the federal checkbooks and as investigator of fraud, abuse, and inefficiency. With regard to the federal judiciary, the GAO periodically audits the Judicial Survivors' Annuities Fund and the Federal Judges' Retirement Fund. Either upon requests from congressional committees or on its own initiative, the GAO has conducted studies on such diverse issues as reduction of the civil case backlog, places of holding court, jury utilization, automation, court reporters, probation and parole, public defenders, the Speedy Trial Act, sentencing reform, and protection and security of grand jury information.

A member of Congress who wants to identify waste in public expenditures or improve the delivery of government services is well advised to consider requesting a GAO audit or investigation. The final report may take several years, but the result is usually worth the wait. GAO investigations of judicial branch activities have proved to be helpful to the courts and have been met with commitments of cooperation rather than expressions of hostility. GAO recommendations for change and suggested improvements have generally been well received and are usually implemented by the Judicial Conference.

Sometimes the recommendations assume statutory form, ultimately being considered by Congress.

PROGRAM LEGISLATION. When Congress enacted the first Judiciary Act almost two hundred years ago, program authorization for the federal judiciary began. It has continued unabated to this day. The entire judicial pyramid, with the exception of the apex (the Supreme Court), is the result of program-by-program legislation.

Judges appear routinely as witnesses before the House and Senate Judiciary committees to testify on pending bills having to do with judicial administration. Testimony on behalf of the Judicial Conference has been proffered on legislative proposals relating to the creation of judgeships, diversity of citizenship jurisdiction, magistrates reform, the rules enabling process, pretrial services, judicial survivors' annuities, and the creation of new courts.

In fact, the chief justice, acting according to statutory requirement, submits a report to Congress on the biannual proceedings of the Judicial Conference and its recommendations for legislation.[31] The conference proceedings, which are published as a part of the annual report of the director of the Administrative Office of the U.S. Courts, are a useful guide to the conference's past and present policy positions.

FEDERAL RULES OF PROCEDURE. Congressional authority to regulate practice and procedure in the federal courts has been acknowledged by the Supreme Court since the earliest days of the Republic. Congress may exercise that power by delegating to the Supreme Court or to other federal courts authority to make rules that are not inconsistent with the statutes or Constitution of the United States. By enacting the various rules enabling acts, Congress has delegated the power to prescibe rules regulating civil and criminal procedures, appellate proceedings, bankruptcy, and evidence.[32] In exchange for that delegation, Congress has retained the power to override rules that have been promulgated pursuant to these acts.

One noted jurist and commentator on the subject, Judge Jack Weinstein, has noted that "the history of rule-making at the federal level . . . shows a practical accommodation between the legislature and the courts."[33] Despite the feeling that the rule-making process has been successful, there are several identifiable flaws. In 1973 Congress did not accept the Federal Rules of

31. 28 U.S.C. sec. 331.
32. See 28 U.S.C. secs. 2071, 2072, 2075, 2076; 18 U.S.C. sec. 3771.
33. Jack B. Weinstein, *Reform of Court Rulemaking Procedures* (Ohio State University Press, 1977), p. 77.

Evidence, primarily because of doubt about whether the rules were within the rule-making authority delegated by Congress. William Hungate (then a representative and now a judge) observed at the time during floor debate:

> The fundamental rights and human relationships which will be affected by the rules, both in and out of the courts, require that the rules be permitted to become effective only if, when, and to the extent they are affirmatively approved by the Congress.[34]

To overcome any problem, Congress considered the rules of evidence as a legislative proposal with the usual requirements—affirmative approval by each chamber and presentment to the president for signature.

For two Congresses in a row, the House of Representatives has passed legislation to reform the entire rule-making process.[35] That legislation is premised on the recognition of three major problems in the current process: (1) there is a lack of openness; (2) the rules should not supersede statutes; and (3) there are too many local rules, often of an overlapping and inconsistent nature.

The Judicial Conference has cooperated with congressional efforts to improve the process. Under the firm leadership of Judge Edward T. Gignoux (former chairman of the Standing Committee on Practice and Procedure), administrative improvements have been implemented and the legislative reform efforts supported. The U.S. Senate, however, has not acted on Rules Enabling Act reform.

THE CONFIRMATION PROCESS.   The Constitution provides another link between the Congress and the judicial branch: the power of the Senate to "advise and consent" to the confirmation of all lifetime-tenured federal judges and many fixed-term judicial officers. Much has been written about the relationship of the Senate and the president in this regard, but there is scant analysis of the appointment process as a communication channel between Congress and the courts.[36]

Lifetime tenure is a suit of armor shielding against politicization of the federal judiciary. Nonetheless, as Judge Mikva has realistically observed, "Congressional unhappiness with the role of courts is reflected, in the long

---

34. *Congressional Record* (March 14, 1973), p. 7646.

35. For further information about the House bills, see *Rules Enabling Act,* H. Rept. 99-422, 99 Cong. 1 sess. (GPO, 1985).

36. See, for example, Joseph P. Harris, *The Advice and Consent of the Senate: A Study of the Confirmation of Appointments by the United States Senate* (Westport, Conn.: Greenwood Press, 1968); and Congressional Quarterly, *Powers of Congress,* 2d ed. (Washington, D.C.: CQ, 1982).

run, in the philosophies of the judges placed on the bench."[37] Judges do read the election results, and new appointees normally agree with the final outcome.

The confirmation process serves as something more than an inquiry into the capabilities, background, and philosophy of prospective federal judges. It becomes a forum for senators, especially those who are members of the majority party, to instruct and lecture nominees on their views about the federal judiciary. This communications channel, occurring in a Senate hearing room open to the public, can be a sobering experience for lower court judges who are being elevated to higher judicial office. Expressions of support or criticism and questions directed at these individuals are heard far beyond the walls of the hearing room, long after the nominee is confirmed.

Appointments to the district courts are made after consultation by the president with individual senators of the same political party who represent the state where the appointment is being made. Senatorial courtesy allows a senator of the same party as the president to thwart a nomination. The chief executive has greater power when making appointments to circuit court judgeships, and greater still for nominations to the Supreme Court. Surprisingly, before 1950, Supreme Court nominees were not even invited to appear before the Senate Judiciary Committee. Justice Abe Fortas was the first nominee for chief justice ever to testify before the committee. During Chief Justice Rehnquist's recent confirmation hearings, senators solicited his views on everything from structural reform to administrative matters affecting the federal courts. At times, a neutral observer might mistakenly have thought that an oversight hearing was in progress.

In the final analysis, the nomination and confirmation process is one that not only stimulates communications between the legislature (particularly the Senate) and the judiciary, but also brings the executive into the relationship.

PAY AND PERQUISITES.   No discussion about the relationship between Congress and the courts can be complete without an examination of pay and perquisites. This subject is arcane and confusing, even to the most experienced members and staffers; it also is an issue that is readily politicized.

Clearly, Congress can react negatively to the judicial branch through swift punitive actions. Congressional punishment of the Supreme Court is nothing new: in 1816 Congress refused to appropriate money for a court reporter because of displeasure with a Supreme Court decision.[38]

Legislative retaliation often involves judges' salaries. In 1964 Congress augmented the salaries of all federal judges, with the exception of Supreme

37. Mikva and Saris, *The American Congress,* p. 314.
38. *Martin* v. *Hunter's Lessee,* 14 U.S. (1 Wheat.) 304 (1816).

Court justices, by $7,000; the justices were given $4,500. The legislative history provides evidence that the lesser pay hike was related to a controversial Supreme Court decision.[39]

Section 140 of Public Law 97-92, sponsored by Senator Robert Dole, is a recently enacted statutory provision that bars pay increases for federal judges except as specifically authorized by Congress.[40] When he offered section 140 as an amendment during Senate floor consideration of the pending joint resolution to continue appropriations, Senator Dole observed:

> What the amendment does is to put an end to the automatic, backdoor pay raises for Federal judges. We had an example of that here about 2 months ago, the so-called midnight pay raise for Federal judges.[41]

Clearly, Senator Dole was referring to the decision of the Supreme Court in *United States* v. *Will*, holding that annual cost-of-living adjustments in pay, pursuant to law, became permanent for judges at midnight on October 1, the start of the fiscal year in question.[42] The Court further held that congressional action thereafter to vitiate the increases came too late, violating the constitutional prohibition (in article III) against reducing judicial salaries.

Senator Dole later clarified the intent of his amendment, explaining that it had been offered for another senator as an accommodation: "My staff and I were under the strong impression that the language was intended solely to apply to the single fiscal year that the overall legislation affected."[43] Nonetheless, the comptroller general has steadfastly construed section 140 as permanent legislation, finding that the statutory language and nature of the provision show that permanency was the intent of Congress.

The major problem with salary freezes (not diminution, which would be unconstitutional) due to disenchantment with judicial decisionmaking is that this tactic does not work. As aptly observed by Robert Bork during congressional testimony:

> The Supreme Court of the United States is not going to overrule *Roe*

---

39. *Reynolds* v. *Sims,* 377 U.S. 533 (1964); 78 Stat. 400; see *Congressional Record* (July 2, 1964), pp. 15843–46. Senator John G. Tower observed: "It should be further noted that since the Supreme Court seems to reason it should legislate and amend the Constitution, perhaps members of the Supreme Court should receive a salary no higher than that received by the legislators." *Congressional Record* (July 2, 1964), p. 15844.

40. 95 Stat. 1183.

41. *Congressional Record* (November 19, 1981), p. 28439.

42. 449 U.S. 200 (1980).

43. Letter of March 18, 1985, from Senator Robert Dole to Charles A. Bowsher (Comptroller General of the United States).

v. *Wade* in order to get a salary increase. That decision may be overruled but not for that reason. Penalizing the entire judiciary by continuing to allow their compensation to be reduced by inflation because of dissatisfaction with particular decisions would not only be mean-spirited but would be wholly ineffective. Indeed, its only result would be to deter more and more good lawyers from accepting judgeships.[44]

In short, judges cannot be bought for the price of a salary increase.

There is of course no hard and fast rule that all federal employees are entitled to annual cost-of-living increases in order to keep pace with inflation. In fact, during fiscal year 1986 no federal employees received across-the-board adjustments. But it is arguable that singling out judges for a separate category to be punished flies directly in the face of article III, which promotes judicial branch autonomy and independence from fear of public or congressional reprisals. Ultimately, questions rising to a constitutional magnitude may be raised.

There are signs of clearing on an otherwise stormy horizon, showing that improvements and better relations are in store. Just before adjournment *sine die* of the Ninety-ninth Congress, Senator Dole authored legislation to repeal the Dole amendment. The repealer passed the Senate as an amendment to an unrelated court reform measure, but died in the House as time expired.

Pursuant to a recent reform—tacked to the continuing appropriations resolution for fiscal year 1986—the Commission on Executive, Legislative, and Judicial Salaries (the Quadrennial Commission) now operates under more efficient procedures in making recommendations about pay rates for top federal executives, members of Congress, and federal judges.[45] The commission is required to report its recommendations to the president by December 15 every four years and the president will accept, modify, or reject them. In turn, the president's recommendations will become effective unless disapproved by a joint resolution agreed to by Congress not later than thirty days after the recommendations are transmitted.[46]

---

44. *Federal Judicial Salary Control Act of 1981*, Hearings, p. 77.

45. 99 Stat. 1185, 1322–23.

46. In December 1986 the Quadrennial Commission recognized the erosion in a federal judge's pay over the past eighteen years (in real terms, of almost 40 percent) and recommended significant pay raises. President Reagan exercised his authority to modify the proposal, drastically reducing the proposed pay levels. The president suggested in his budget that the salaries of district judges be modestly increased to $89,000 and those of circuit judges to $95,000. The commission's recommendations for other judicial officers were reduced even more sharply. Congress attempted to roll back any pay raises, but the thirty days for congressional review passed and the new salaries went into effect.

The refrains "You can live on it, but you can't die on it," or "Federal judges should not have to stay in the YMCA when they travel" could be muted with improvements to judicial perquisites. Slowly but surely this is being done. The Ninety-ninth Congress substantially improved the Judicial Survivors' Annuities System, authorized actual travel expenses for federal judges, and created a new system of recall for magistrates, bankruptcy judges, and Claims Court judges. Retirement reform for magistrates and bankruptcy judges is under way.

Judicial survivors' annuities, leave policy, retirement, travel expenses, official duty stations, and pay are not only complicated issues standing alone, but from a parliamentary perspective they create confusion because they often cross committee jurisdictional lines. For example, a bill to provide a retirement system for U.S. magistrates equal to that for bankruptcy judges was, in the opinion of the House parliamentarian, recently misreferred to only the House Judiciary Committee; he deemed it was also within the province of the Post Office and Civil Service Committee.[47] Judicial survivors' annuities legislation was, just before House floor consideration, referred to the Appropriations Committee because an entitlement was created.[48]

Confoundment about the substance and parliamentary thickets can be avoided, as has been shown on numerous occasions, by conscientious legislative work and good communications between representatives of Congress and the judiciary.

IMPEACHMENT, JUDICIAL DISCIPLINE, AND ETHICS.   Until recently, the impeachment process would not have been mentioned as a communications channel between the two branches. The removal from office of Harry E. Claiborne, however, serves notice on all lifetime-tenured federal judges that they could be impeached for the commission of "high crimes and misdemeanors" in the constitutional sense. A factual showing that a felony offense has been committed could suffice, and mere reliance on a conviction may not be enough. During parts of the Claiborne impeachment, the Senate galleries were filled with federal judges who, by happenstance, were in town for a meeting of the Federal Judges Association. A preponderance of their interest and comments centered on the fourth article of impeachment, which charged that Judge Claiborne should be removed from office for committing a "misdemeanor" because he had "betrayed the trust of the people of the

47. See H.R. 5454, 99 Cong. 2 sess. (1986).

48. See Judicial Improvements Act of 1985, H.R. 3570, 99 Cong. 1 sess.; and *Congressional Record,* daily edition (December 16, 1985), pp. H11998, 12000.

United States and reduced confidence in the integrity and impartiality of the Judiciary."[49]

Imploring the Senate to convict on this article, the chairman of the House managers (Peter W. Rodino, Jr.) put the question in eloquent, but nonetheless harsh, terms:

> The judges of our Federal courts occupy a unique position of trust and responsibility in our system of government: They are the only members of any branch who hold their office for life; they are purposely insulated from the immediate pressures and shifting currents of the body politic. But with this special prerogative of judicial independence comes the most exacting standard of public and private conduct.[50]

The Senate voted to convict Judge Claiborne of violating article IV by a vote of 89 to 8.[51]

This message, however, in no way reduces judicial independence. One highly respected federal judge (Frank M. Johnson, Jr.) had previously registered agreement: "Judicial independence must incorporate some notion of accountability."[52]

Recognizing that judicial independence and public accountability are not mutually exclusive, several years ago Congress—with the close cooperation of the Judicial Conference and the Chief Justice of the United States—enacted the Judicial Conduct and Disability Act of 1980.[53] The act establishes procedures and a mechanism within the judicial branch to consider and respond to complaints against judges. Most complaints are handled initially by the chief judges of the circuits and then by the judicial councils of the circuits, but when impeachable offenses are identified, the councils and the Judicial Conference are empowered to refer the matter directly to Congress.

Federal judges must satisfy exacting ethical standards regarding personal finances. The Ethics in Government Act of 1978 requires all judges to file personal financial reports containing a full statement of assets, income, and liabilities as well as those of spouses and dependent children.[54] The act also

---

49. See Markup of H.R. 461, Impeachment of Judge Harry E. Claiborne, in *Conduct of Harry E. Claiborne, U.S. District Judge, District of Nevada,* Hearing before the House Committee on the Judiciary, 99 Cong. 2 sess. (GPO, 1986), p. 81.

50. *Congressional Record,* daily edition (October 7, 1986), p. S15496.

51. Ibid. (October 9, 1986), p. S15762.

52. Frank M. Johnson, Jr., "Judicial Independence Once More an Issue," 65 *American Bar Association Journal* 342 (1979).

53. 94 Stat. 2035.

54. 92 Stat. 1851–61.

mandates that the Judicial Conference establish a Judicial Ethics Committee responsible for administering the act. With the approval of the conference, the committee can submit recommendations for legislative change directly to Congress. The Judicial Ethics Committee is the only conference entity to be statutorily required.

Legislative and Judicial Branch Relations: Problems and Opportunities

There are not many guideposts for resolving problems and identifying opportunities for improving relations between the branches. The *Congressional Record*, the Congressional Research Service, and voluminous records and reports of national conferences on the administration of justice yield only sparse information. A case in point is the otherwise excellent report of the Council on the Role of Courts, which inexplicably neglects even to mention the congressional role.[55] Commenting on the communications gap, Judge Frank Coffin—speaking for Madison, Jay, and Hamilton—writes elsewhere in this volume that "the interrelationship of Congress and the judiciary remains as unexplored today as the western territories were in our time." So, without maps in an unfamiliar land, we will make five brief points about the geography that exists between the legislative and judicial branches of government. The five points differ somewhat in depth of field: the first three are wide-angle thoughts and the latter two are focused on specific problems. The unwavering bearing is straight toward the need to improve understanding and communications between the two branches.

Changing Institutions in a Changing Society

Just as the Industrial Revolution dramatically changed American society in the late eighteenth and early nineteenth centuries and had a direct impact on this nation's justice system, so too is the present information revolution being felt by our institutions, including both Congress and the courts.

Today, technology is accelerating the pace of change far beyond anyone's expectations. The role of law in our society is, and has always been, to

55. Jethro K. Lieberman, ed., *The Role of Courts in American Society* (St. Paul: West, 1984). In a similar vein, the attorney general of the State of Washington, Slade Gorton, indicated to the Pound Conference that a point of view had been "totally ignored during the course of the conference." Speaking as an elected official, he explained his discomfort: "I appear to be the only substantive speaker at this conference who was elected by the people of a state to an office which the voters perceived to be a policy-making position." A. Leo Levin and Russell R. Wheeler, eds., *The Pound Conference: Perspectives on Justice in the Future* (St. Paul: West, 1977), pp. 224–25.

organize, redirect, and legitimize changes that started outside the law. Legislators rely on courts and judges to deal with the ceaseless flux in as rational and consistent a way as possible.

Societal and technological changes ripple throughout the court system. According to a report by the Office of Technology Assessment, "The resulting surge of scientific and technological disputes into the judicial arena is likely to put substantial strain on the institutional resources of the judiciary."[56] For confirmation one only need look to explosive increases in the numbers of intellectual property cases filed in federal court, examine the changing nature of the criminal law (including the creation of new crimes), and assess recent legislative enactments that create new causes of action (for example, the Electronic Communications Privacy Act, the Semiconductor Protection Act of 1984, and the Anti-Drug Abuse Act of 1986).

The contemporary Congress is no longer the part-time and deliberative institution it was during the days of Henry Clay and Daniel Webster. Instead, it is a large, bustling enterprise that tries—sometimes successfully and sometimes unsuccessfully—to keep pace with a constantly changing society and a demanding clientele. The role of the political representative has become infinitely more difficult and more exacting.

Similarly, today's federal judges have vastly different jobs and pressures than their predecessors. Far busier, having less time to reflect, present-day judges preside over large numbers of complex proceedings that are characterized by complicated discovery, numbers of pretrial motions, and long trials.

An advanced degree in statistics is not necessary to assess the significance and relevancy of growth of personnel in both branches. First, over a thirty-year period, the judiciary has shown a much faster growth rate than Congress, both in staff and overall budget. Second, in several years, the appropriation for the judicial branch will pass that of the legislative branch.[57]

The budget numbers and employee data for both the legislative and judicial branches show them to be dramatically different institutions from what they

56. U.S. Office of Technology Assessment, *Intellectual Property Rights in an Age of Electronics and Information* (GPO, 1986), p. 286.

57. In fiscal year 1961 the appropriation for the legislative branch was approximately $140,930,800; the appropriation for fiscal year 1986 was $1,783,255,000, roughly an elevenfold augmentation. Norman J. Ornstein, Thomas E. Mann, and Michael J. Malbin, *Vital Statistics on Congress, 1987–1988* (Washington, D.C.: Congressional Quarterly, 1987), p. 150. In fiscal year 1961 the total budget for the federal judiciary, excluding the Supreme Court, was $50,686,900; the total for fiscal year 1986 was $1,044,000 (the judiciary's first "billion dollar budget"), a twentyfold increase. *Annual Report of the Director of the Administrative Office of the U.S. Courts, 1961* (GPO, 1962), p. 189; *1986* (GPO, 1987), p. 77.

were several decades ago. Whether they have become bureaucratized (in the negative sense of the word) is a subject of open debate. What cannot be contested is the explosive rate of growth within both branches. Given the attendant difficulties of management and delegation of authority, judges and congressmen find themselves in the same boat. Judge Alvin Rubin's well-known statement about the task of judging today ("too much work, too little time to do it, the necessity of delegation, inefficient management, the dilution of responsibility for decision-making") could just as appropriately be directed at Congress.[58]

There is a growing trend among some judges and certain law professors to criticize the role played by professional staff on Capitol Hill. For example, Justice Scalia, while sitting on the Circuit Court for the District of Columbia, complained about the staff drafting of committee reports.[59] His thesis, that legislative history is entitled to less judicial deference when drafted by staff, is unsettling—certainly to those who work on Capitol Hill. Not only does it ignore the fact that most reports are distributed to members in advance of consideration of specific legislation, but it also denies one of the most salient characteristics of the modern-day Congress. Admittedly, many reports are drafted by staff. But so are judicial opinions and judges' bench memos.

Judicial distrust of staff work raises more questions about modern American government and delegation of authority than it answers. A canon of construction that legislative history is entitled to little or no judicial deference could have serious ramifications not only for the legislature but for the judiciary as well. At the very least, daunting questions are raised. Should elected representatives give less respect to judicial opinions written in large part by law clerks? Are dispositive motions or cases resolved by U.S. magistrates entitled to any less deference than judgments entered by district judges? Should one ignore the existence of staff attorneys for the circuits, who accomplish a great deal of substantive work? If full deference is to be given for the work product of constitutional officers (members of Congress and presidentially appointed judges) and less respect is to be awarded for the ruminations of staff, will this not ultimately reduce overall respect for the rule of law (both as formulated by the peoples' representatives and as interpreted by the courts)?

Quite frankly, it would be much better to focus on the reason for the enormous growth in staff for the two branches of government. Certainly, it is not that judges and congressmen work less or are less conscientious. The

58. Alvin B. Rubin, "Bureaucratization of the Federal Courts: The Tension Between Justice and Efficiency," 55 *Notre Dame Lawyer* 648, 654 (1980).

59. See *Hirschey* v. *Federal Energy Regulatory Commission*, 777 F.2d 1, 6–8 (D.C. Cir. 1985).

cause, to paraphrase Justice Powell, ". . . is the escalating extent to which citizens turn to the courts and [to the Congress] for the resolution of claims and controversies of all kinds."[60]

Obviously, it is outside the scope of this discourse to examine and explain the enormous increases in case filings for federal judges or constituent work for members of Congress. A major reason both branches have larger support staffs is because citizens ask government to do more and more, and not because of a mere desire to build empires.

Why are societal changes and the resultant modifications to government institutions of relevance to interbranch relations? The plain answer is that the more tensions within an institution, the more likely tempers will flare and frustrations will fester. The more voices that speak in either branch, the more difficult the role of formulating policy, interpreting messages, and understanding the substance. Simply put, the task of communicating among the coordinate branches becomes infinitely harder. Bureaucratic growth and work load have created an estrangement when what is needed is a rapprochement.

Leadership

High-level public servants must march ahead, but not too far ahead, for if they move too fast, there will be no followers. The political process depends on the leadership of these individuals and their ability to ask the right questions, seize ideas, and mold consensus and compromise around solutions to problems.

There is no large political constituency for court reform. Members of the legal profession do form an articulate, intelligent, and vocal political community, sometimes individually and sometimes in associations. In the long run, however, lawyers have a great tendency (perhaps derived from their legal education) to approach issues in a highly individualistic manner, and bar associations tend to look after the interests of their members. Leadership of the bench and bar thus becomes an arduous and time-consuming endeavor. The political task of shepherding court reform proposals through Congress is a great responsibility, certainly "no sport for the short-winded."[61]

Building upon the dedication to court reform of former Chief Justices Taft and Hughes, Chief Justice Warren E. Burger pledged during his confirmation hearings that in order to "see the judicial system functions more efficiently,"

60. Lewis F. Powell, "Are the Federal Courts Becoming Bureaucracies?" 68 *American Bar Association Journal* 1370, 1371 (1982).

61. Arthur T. Vanderbilt, ed., *Minimum Standards of Judicial Administration* (National Conference of Judicial Councils, 1949), p. xix.

he would "devote every energy and every moment of the rest of [his] life to that end."[62] During his seventeen years as chief justice, Burger made true on his promise to devote himself to making the system work better. He worked behind the scenes on many issues of public policy import. Sometimes he received credit and sometimes he was criticized for meddling in legislative affairs, but there is no question that he contributed in countless ways to improving this nation's justice system.

Without leadership, a branch of government is rudderless and without bearings. Without leadership, a branch cannot communicate candidly and openly with a coordinate branch.

With leadership, a branch need not fear the future and will not be paralyzed by the present. With it, interbranch communications—speaking with a confident and clear voice—can transpire on a broad range of issues.

Chief Justice Burger's leadership of the judicial branch has been met by equally strong and effective leadership in the legislative branch from chairmen and ranking minority members of the relevant congressional committees and from leaders of both houses.

The tools of leadership—intellectual power, personal courage, and communications skills—have also been wielded by the chairmen of Judicial Conference committees and the chief judges of the circuit courts of appeals.

Ideas

Ideas are the critical mass of communications and the fuel of politics. An idea is an incitement for belief, and if believed it is acted upon, unless, in Justice Holmes's words, "some other belief outweighs it or some failure of energy stifles the movement at its birth."[63]

The legislative and the judicial branches have systemic difficulties with communications. Yet ideas are the daily currency of judges and elected officials. Every time a judge renders an opinion, thoughts are set forth. Each proposal for legislation is derived from an idea about how to solve a problem. Why is it then that judges and legislators personally find it so difficult to share ideas with each other?

Many followers of Congress question whether an individual, having planted the kernel of a notion, can see its germination and maturation into a public law. The argument is made that the modern Congress is obliged to place inordinate emphasis on the "big picture" and seemingly intractable issues of budget deficits, national defense, trade, crime, and the environment. Modern

---

62. *Nomination of Warren E. Burger,* Hearing before the Senate Committee on the Judiciary, 91 Cong. 1 sess. (GPO, 1969), p. 5.

63. *Gitlow* v. *New York,* 268 U.S. 652, 673 (1925).

lobbying techniques require representatives, senators and their respective staffs to spend their finite time listening to employees of government agencies and well-heeled lobbyists. Any spare time must be spent serving constituents and, of course, fund-raising or campaigning for reelection. At first blush, the conclusion is inescapable: a single individual, even though armed with a good idea, does not stand a chance of effectuating a policy change.

This conclusion is erroneous. A person can set forth a thought, see it translated into a legislative proposal, and ultimately witness the enactment of a public law.

There are several examples in the arena of court reform. In January 1977 Judge Harold Leventhal took advantage of a concurring opinion to express an idea. He exhorted Congress to enact "a general statute permitting transfer between [federal courts] in the interest of justice, including specifically but not exclusively those instances when complaints are filed in what later proves to be the 'wrong' court."[64] On April 2, 1982, President Reagan signed the Federal Courts Improvement Act of 1982, a part of which accomplishes exactly what Judge Leventhal initally suggested.[65]

Judge Giles Rich worked on an idea to eliminate reasons for appeal in patent appeals from the U.S. Patent and Trademark Office for over twenty years before seeing its enactment as a technical amendment in a much larger bill.[66] Judge Aubrey Robinson, who proposed that civil filing fees for the District Court of the District of Columbia be the same as for federal district courts, recently achieved success in a much shorter time period, approximately one year.[67]

Judges often write opinions finding that a statute is constitutional but not well drafted, in that the statutory language does not achieve ostensible policy purposes. The judge notes, unhappily, that a correction of the statute is strictly within the province of the legislature. The opinion is then shared with the litigants, and often sent for publication in the proper reporter. Congress

64. *Investment Company Institute* v. *Board of Governors of the Federal Reserve System*, 551 F.2d 1270, 1283 (D.C. Cir. 1977); followed by an exchange of correspondence between Judge Leventhal and Robert W. Kastenmeier, reprinted in *Judicial Housekeeping*, Hearing before the Subcommittee on Courts, Civil Liberties, and the Administration of Justice of the House Committee on the Judiciary, 95 Cong. 2 sess. (GPO, 1978), pp. 372–89.

65. 96 Stat. 25, 55.

66. Letters of January 16, 1984, from Judge Rich to Robert W. Kastenmeier, reprinted in *Technical Amendments to the Federal Courts Improvement Act of 1982*, Hearing before the Subcommittee on Courts, Civil Liberties, and the Administration of Justice of the House Committee on the Judiciary, 98 Cong. 1 sess. (GPO, 1984), pp. 151–58.

67. *Federal Judicial Improvements—1985*, Hearing before the Subcommittee on Courts, Civil Liberties, and the Administration of Justice of the House Committee on the Judiciary, 99 Cong. 1 sess. (GPO, 1985), p. 237.

never hears about the opinion. A failure to communicate stifles the movement of an idea at its birth.

Judge Frank Coffin and Professor Leo Levin have suggested that all judicial opinions containing suggestions to the legislative branch could be collated "and the wheat winnowed from the chaff so that the unimportant ones were not sent on to the Congress."[68] The short list would be examined by a committee of the Judicial Conference and then forwarded to the appropriate committees and officials of the House and Senate. The conference might even provide advisory notations explaining if there is a problem with obsolescence, inconsistency, or language. Then, as explained by Judge Coffin:

> . . . Staffs of congressional committees would be able to include many of these ideas almost as a matter of course in general legislation. Suggestions that are of more major import would attract the interest of individual representatives and senators who are always interested in trying to improve things. This would be a systemic way of communicating without treading upon the independence of the legislative branch or of the judiciary.[69]

This is a capital idea in its own right.

Some ideas succeed and others do not. The only risk in sharing ideas between branches of government is that dreams of successful implementation and execution may exceed reality. What is the alternative? If the judicial and legislative branches fear the sharing of ideas, the endurance of their own institutions could be jeopardized.

Structural Weaknesses

A broad spectrum of institutional contacts exists between Congress and the courts. For the most part, relations between the two branches are better than one might expect. But certain structural weaknesses need reinforcement to avoid a potential calamity.

When Congress is engaging in a legislative activity such as oversight, appropriations, or program authorizations, it hears from the judiciary mainly on two occasions. First, legislative or appropriations committees formally (in writing) ask for the views of the Judicial Conference of the United States. Second, the committees request the personal testimony of a federal judge or high-level administrator.

As to the former, the Judicial Conference does not take a position on

68. Interview with Judge Frank M. Coffin, *The Third Branch*, vol. 14 (June 1982), p. 6.
69. Ibid.

legislation unless specifically requested to do so by a congressional committee. This unwritten rule, which is not statutorily required, is indisputably an attempt by the judiciary's policymaking arm to avoid the appearance of meddling in legislative affairs. The rule, however, is sometimes circumvented by verbal petitions from judicial branch personnel, who state that the conference would like to receive a written solicitation for views. In response, a letter is drafted. Armed with the "fictional" request letter, the conference then formulates a response. From a congressional perspective, certain questions are unavoidable. Why have the written request rule in the first place? Are members of Judicial Conference committees aware of the different forms of request?

Other worrisome developments abound, of which three will be mentioned. The first is the tendency of the courts to seek authorizations for experimental programs directly through the appropriations process. To date, programs involving arbitration in ten pilot districts and the creation of the office of district executive are in existence without express authorizing legislation. The entire staff attorney program in the circuit courts was established through the appropriations process and authorized many years later. If a particular project is sound on its merits, what possibly can be feared about seeking a program authorization (perhaps with a sunset provision) through the House and Senate Judiciary committees? If judicial review occurs involving an unauthorized government program, such as binding arbitration, then what will be the final outcome?

A second bothersome tactic, used occasionally, is the effort by legislative representatives of the judicial branch to play off the appropriations and authorizing committees in order to obtain maximum leverage on statutory proposals. This legislative forum shopping sometimes meets with short-term success, but, as in the case of a child who asks both parents for an ice cream cone and receives a positive answer from only one, any ensuing success is likely to be short-lived.[70]

Third, the Judicial Conference sometimes recommends legislative reforms in its report on its proceedings, but then never submits draft implementing legislation to Congress. The rationale for withholding draft proposals is that "timing" is an integral part of the political process. Properly timed amendments offered at an opportune time in the process have a greater likelihood of

70. An illustration of this strategy is the statutory augmentation of civil filing fees from $60 to $120—supported by the Judicial Conference—which was attached to the continuing resolution for fiscal year 1987 by the House and Senate Appropriations committees. Members of the House and Senate Judiciary committees were not aware of this major fee hike and would probably have opposed the amendment if there had been full and fair hearings.

success than proposals that have to run the gamut of procedures in both houses of Congress. However, a political plan designed to avoid introduction of a bill in order to rely on a last-minute amendment is not really justifiable for a branch of government that promotes due process and fairness in decisionmaking—unless it can be shown that there are no other means to the desired end.

Opinions are mixed as to whether judges should testify before congressional committees in their individual capacities, but the debate is not as heated as it once was. Since congressional hearings are now open to the public and, in theory at least, are designed to foster learning and stimulate debate, there should be little fear of knowledgeable judicial officers presenting their views to Congress in person or by correspondence. After all, the donning of the black robes does not signify the forfeiture of all civil rights to formulate views about the delivery of government services. Indeed, a relatively select group of federal judges has testified about issues relating to this nation's justice system and also questions affecting various substantive areas of the law, including copyrights and patents, antitrust, and criminal law. A private nonprofit organization—the Federal Judges Association—has also provided valuable input to Congress on the subject of pay and perquisites.

As a general proposition, the testimony of federal judges who appear in their personal capacities is well received, respected by members of Congress, and considered to improve the quality of the hearing process. Nonetheless, significant questions are raised by this sort of participation in the political process. Should judges lobby on questions of constitutional import? Is it wise for judicial officers to suggest legislative language that might one day be the subject of litigation? How far should judges go in terms of their political activities: should they hire lobbyists, contribute to campaigns, and engage in three-martini lunches?

Unsurprisingly, many more questions than answers are raised on this topic. It is to be hoped that responses might be forthcoming from members of the judicial branch, who are better able to assess the resiliency of their institutions and any structural flaws that might exist. In this regard, Congress can benefit by hearing more.

The Need for Information

The judiciary's analytical components need strengthening, in our view. Substantial resources—in the Administrative Office of the U.S. Courts—have already been devoted to the accumulation of data about the federal courts. This statistical information can be of enormous use to congressional committees in their quest to identify problems and to prove the existence of those problems with empirical information. The Administrative Office's statistics, however, can be frustrating because—like fine cuisine—there is never enough. Although the Administrative Office has not extended great effort in the past to evaluate the data to identify long-term trends and needs, it has recently taken steps to create a policy-planning component. This step should contribute to better evaluation of data and communication of the conclusions within the judiciary and ultimately to Congress.

The role of research and study of the operation of the judicial branch is assigned to the Federal Judicial Center. Much excellent work is accomplished by the center, but again the lack of quantity, rather than quality, of research can be a source of concern. The center is also statutorily assigned the role of providing both recommendations for improving court administration and management to the Judicial Conference and planning assistance to the conference and its committees. In this latter regard, the center appears to be somewhat underutilized.

Judge Richard Posner has suggested that law schools offer three new courses (opinion writing, judicial administration, and legislation) as a way of heightening understanding of the problems of the federal judicial system.[71] This suggestion, laudatory as it is, could be taken further. Might not the Federal Judicial Center teach new judges a course in legislation, which could include discussion of the legislative process, the role of congressmen and their staffs in drafting legislation, and the understanding of legislative history? Similarly, might not Congress offer—in its educational program for new members—courses on the judicial process or institutional structure of the federal judiciary?

Last, Congress and the judicial branch might work in concert to promote structured experiments. Historically, experimentation has proven to be an effective tool in improving the administration of justice. The results of program experiments, as evidenced with empirical data, can be quite useful initially to the Judicial Conference and ultimately to Congress in making final decisions on whether an experiment should be replicated systemwide. The appropriate boundaries and legislative barriers of experimentation are subjects unto themselves. Judges and legislators should recognize, as Judge Jon Newman has, ". . . the irony of the progress that the medical profession has made experimenting with matters of life and death, while we in the law shun experimental ways of deciding matters of property."[72]

71. Richard A. Posner, *The Federal Courts: Crisis and Reform* (Harvard University Press, 1985), pp. 317–40.
72. Jon Newman, "Rethinking Fairness: Perspectives on the Litigation Process," The Thirty-

Conclusion

From our Capitol Hill perspective, we wish to reiterate several points that might be further pondered, with no harm to the independence of the judicial branch or to the autonomy of the legislative branch, but rather with great promise for improving relations between the two coordinate branches.

Most important, the legislative branch sometimes does not have an adequate understanding and working knowledge of the Constitution. Not only judges but also members of Congress should have an independent and affirmative obligation to assess the constitutionality of legislation. When article III is implicated by legislation, Congress should consider constitutional questions and, indeed, might formulate a constitutional impact statement as an integral part of legislative history.

Judges, law professors, students, and even political representatives should seek a far better understanding of the institutional features of the federal judiciary. Familiarity with historical developments and institutional changes can lead to greater recognition that parts of the structure are currently laboring under great stress; that the federal judiciary cannot be expanded indefinitely without impairing its high quality; and that the judicial pyramid has been flattened by continuous additions to its base and slopes.

The administrative structure of the federal court system, which did not exist at all one hundred years ago, is today throroughly professional and modernized. Elected political representatives or their staffers who need assistance or information, for themselves or for constitutents, can fruitfully seek the advice of court supporting personnel. Knowledge of court administration and friendship with administrators, especially within a member's home district, can be a useful tool in the constant quest for better constituent services.

Channels of communication abound in the areas of oversight, appropriations and the budget, investigations, program legislation, rules of procedure, judicial confirmations, pay and perquisites, and impeachment, judicial discipline, and ethics. More thought should be given to each of these channels by those who seek better understanding between the courts and Congress. And of course personal friendships should not be ignored.

Virtually all legislation, certainly that affecting judicial machinery, where there is not a clamoring constituency for change, is based on compromise. Beyond the need to make wise compromises lies the greater need to foster cooperation and communications between the legislative and judicial branches.

Ninth Annual Benjamin N. Cardozo Lecture (Association of the Bar of the City of New York, 1984), p. 27.

As one examines the problems and opportunities confronting legislative and judicial branch relations, six broader points should be kept in mind.

First, one of our society's great laws is the inevitability of change, technological and social. Congress and the courts are vastly different than they were two hundred years ago, one hundred years ago, or even twenty short years ago. Institutional growth and complexity are a mixed blessing: more work can be accomplished, but coordination and organization become infinitely more arduous tasks.

Second, the judiciary and the national legislature depend on a basic ingredient for their effective operation: leadership. Despite the fact that the courts are more individualistic and Congress is more attuned to group dynamics, their need for strong leaders is exactly the same. Open and honest communication between the two branches requires consistent and clear thoughts enunciated by respected individuals empowered with authority to speak.

Third, ideas provide the substance for communications. Building upon existing institutional mechanisms that promote communications between the legislature and the judiciary, the creation of new channels to share ideas, such as those expressed in judicial opinions, would add to better understanding between the two branches and concrete improvements to the statutory law.

Fourth, the most important political message is that success is possible. There is strong latent support for judges, even though individual members may complain from time to time about judges for various reasons. Improvement proposals, even those involving job conditions, should not be withheld for fear of rejection by the House or Senate.

Fifth, even though interbranch relations can safely be characterized as good, several minor structural weaknesses in the relationship can be identified. One flaw relates to the policy arm of the federal judiciary (the Judicial Conference) and how it initiates recommendations for legislation. Another pertains to the authorizing of judicial branch programs or the amending of current law through the appropriations process. A third revolves around the failure of the conference to submit legislation to Congress after recommending amendatory changes.

Sixth, Congress has an ongoing need for precise information about the federal judiciary. Annual reporting requirements oblige the judiciary to share statistical data, the fruits of research, and experimentation results. Currently, there is not interbranch cooperation on educational programs potentially of interest to both judges and members of Congress and their respective staffs. In addition, in the past lack of a policy-planning apparatus within the judicial branch has inhibited the judiciary from formulating solutions to its own problems and preparing for the future.

We have raised questions and offered suggestions in the same spirit as family members give advice to each other. All ideas are offered with the realization that there is an unfinished agenda and there always will be. Members of Congress, their staffs, federal judges, and judicial personnel really have no choice: they must learn from and understand each other.

What Judges Ought to Know about Lawmaking in Congress

Roger H. Davidson

→→X←←

Making laws and making sausage, so the saying goes, are two processes so messy that they should never be watched. Perhaps it is just as well, then, that the details of the legislative process are a mystery to all but the closest observers of the process. Not that lawmaking is hidden from the public's view. But Capitol Hill can be a confusing place: the procedures are many and time-consuming, the rules complex and sometimes contradictory, the key players numerous and often shifting. And everything seems to happen at once. The mass media have long since abandoned detailed coverage of Congress; even a careful perusal of the written record can leave interested observers mystified about what is really happening. In contrast to the president, who embodies governmental action in a deceptively simple and direct way, Congress remains to most Americans a puzzling blur. "We are a hydraheaded monster compared to the president," House Speaker Jim Wright has complained.[1]

Judges, more than most people, need a sophisticated knowledge of how Congress works and what its lawmaking procedures are like. Judges are left to interpret legislative products that are often deliberately vague and open to refinement. Part of the interpretive challenge is to fathom the lawmakers' intentions, to uncover those clues strewn along the legislative path that may suggest what the provisions were intended to convey and what Congress expected the courts to resolve.

This paper offers general guidelines for understanding today's senators and representatives and the procedures they have devised for processing legislation. It is not designed as a primer in legislative draftsmanship, or even a guide to statutory interpretation. Rather, it assumes a broader and more

---

1. Quoted in Richard E. Cohen, "Presidential Election Could Determine Shape of House Democratic Leadership," *National Journal,* vol. 16 (June 2, 1984), p. 1080.

elementary task. I start from the premise that in order to understand today's congressional enactments, one must first know something of today's lawmakers—their objectives, their working conditions, and their procedures for processing bills and resolutions. What I attempt is a kind of critical tourist's survey of the legislative process.

Who Are the Lawmakers?

This very exercise would doubtless have seemed puzzling to officials of past generations. After all, judges are lawyers; so, historically, have been a large majority of House and Senate members. Thus there ought to be an affinity between the lawyers who make the laws and the lawyers who interpret and evaluate them. As it turns out, things are not so simple. Despite their common legal training, judges and lawmakers, at least at the federal level, display very different career patterns. And the two professions are probably farther apart today than ever before.

Lawyers on Capitol Hill

The legal profession, to be sure, is much in evidence in Congress. Ever since 1789, from 40 to 65 percent of Congress's members have been lawyers.[2] Typically they outnumber all other professions in the House of Representatives; the same is true in the Senate, of which Donald R. Matthews reported that "no other occupational group even approaches the lawyers' record."[3] Little wonder that a humorist has proposed that our government "of laws and not men" is really "of lawyers and not men."

Law and politics are closely linked in our culture. (Other cultures exhibit the same phenomenon, though to a lesser extent.) The legal profession stresses personal skills, such as verbalization, advocacy, and negotiation, that are useful in seeking and holding public office. Lawyers also can move in and out of their jobs without jeopardizing their careers—a characteristic that Max Weber called "role dispensibility."[4] Such mobility would be difficult and risky in medicine, engineering, or other high-status professions. Thus in the One-hundredth Congress there were only four physicians, four CPAs, five engineers, and three members of the clergy. In contrast, many lawyers seem to regard forays into electoral politics, even when unsuccessful, as a form of professional

2. Allan G. Bogue and others, "Members of the House of Representatives and the Processes of Modernization, 1789–1960," *Journal of American History*, vol. 63 (September 1976), p. 284.

3. Donald R. Matthews, *U. S. Senators and their World* (University of North Carolina Press, 1960), p. 33.

4. Max Weber, "Politics as a Vocation," in H. H. Gerth and C. Wright Mills, eds., *From Max Weber: Essays in Sociology* (Oxford University Press, 1946), pp. 77–128.

advertising. Of critical importance, too, is lawyers' monopoly over jobs that serve as stepping stones to Congress—especially elective law enforcement offices.[5]

There are fewer lawyer-legislators in Congress now, however, than in the past. By the 1830s lawyers represented at least 60 percent of the members of the House of Representatives; during the later years of the nineteenth century, the proportion sometimes went as high as two-thirds.[6] The numbers drifted downward in this century and since the mid-1960s have dropped sharply. When the One-hundredth Congress convened in 1987, 246 of its members—or about 46 percent—were lawyers (down a percentage point from the preceding Congress). The proportion in the House was lower than in the Senate. While law remains the most typical postgraduate training for senators and representatives, many of them enter elective office early in their careers and therefore have practiced little or no law. Business is the next most prevalent occupation among legislators, followed by such verbalizing professions as public service, teaching, and journalism.

What difference does it make that so many lawyers serve in Congress? Not very much, if one is to believe the scholars who have investigated the question. In terms of quantifiable measures of behavior—such as votes, role perceptions, or internal career patterns, lawyers and nonlawyers in Congress are virtually indistinguishable.[7] This may be explained by the fact that lawyers, more than most professionals, engage in a wide range of career activities. Some members of Congress have had extensive legal careers (especially as prosecutors), but many others with law degrees have practiced little or not at all. One suspects, just the same, that social scientists may have missed the more subtle effects of legal training upon the legislative process. Oral debates and written reports display lawmakers' intense fascination with legal procedures, concepts, and terminology. And members often reveal a knack for turning substantive issues into matters of legal or procedural detail—perhaps a belated manifestation of legal training.

Does it make any difference, conversely, that more nonlawyers now serve in Congress? Again, the answer must be speculative. No doubt, formal measures of legislators' behavior would reveal little alteration that could be traced to this development. Yet an observer notices that, while members

5. Joseph A. Schlesinger, "Lawyers and American Politics: A Clarified View," *Midwest Journal of Political Science,* vol. 1 (May 1957), pp. 26–39.

6. Bogue and others, "Members of the House of Representatives and the Processes of Modernization," p. 284; and Roger H. Davidson, *The Role of the Congressman* (Indianapolis: Bobbs-Merrill, 1969), pp. 37–49.

7. Heinz Eulau and John D. Sprague, *Lawyers in Politics: A Study in Professional Convergence* (Indianapolis: Bobbs-Merrill, 1964).

retain a fascination for legal aspects of the issues they deal with, they increasingly regard themselves as clients of the staff who work for them. Hardly any representatives or senators these days, for example, do their own legislative drafting. Rather, they rely on committee counsels (who sometimes, in turn, rely on drafters from the Office of Legislative Counsel). How much of this is due to the increased numbers of nonlawyer legislators, and how much to frantic schedules and skilled staff resources? No doubt all these factors are at work. However, it is noteworthy that, whether from lack of time or lack of detailed expertise, today's lawmakers rely heavily on the legal skills of others.

Diverging Career Paths

Looking beyond occupational training to actual career patterns, legislative and judicial careers are rarely combined, at least at the federal level. Studying House members from 1789 to 1960, Bogue and his colleagues concluded, "The judiciary has never been a major element in the prior political experience of representatives."[8] Today, the two career paths diverge more than ever before. In the first decade of the Republic, about 15 percent of all entering representatives had prior judicial experience; this figure remained steady for two more decades. Thereafter, the percentage stabilized at about 10 percent and remained there for the rest of the nineteenth century. In this century, judicial experience has tended to be even rarer on Capitol Hill. In the One-hundredth Congress, only seven representatives and five senators had held prior judicial posts of any kind.

On the other side of the fence, few of those serving in the federal judiciary have significant legislative experience. One in five district court appointees during the Johnson and Ford administrations had a background in politics or government (excluding the judiciary), but the figures dropped to 4.4 percent in the Carter administration and 7.4 percent in the early Reagan years.[9] The figures for appeals court nominees were much lower. Of all the justices of the Supreme Court (106 as of 1988), only eight were senators and four were representatives at the time of their appointment.[10] The last former legislator to serve on the high court was Hugo Black, an Alabama senator who was nominated in 1937 and served for thirty-four years.[11]

8. Bogue and others, "Members of the House of Representatives and the Processes of Modernization," p. 290.

9. Sheldon Goldman, "Reagan's Judicial Appointments at Mid-Term: Shaping the Bench in His Own Image," *Judicature,* vol. 66 (March 1983), pp. 338–39.

10. Henry Abraham, *The Judicial Process,* 5th ed. (Oxford University Press, 1986), p. 63.

11. Other modern-day Supreme Court appointees with congressional experience include

Judges with legislative experience were more common in the nineteenth century, when members of Congress frequently moved in and out of office. Relatively few lawmakers, in fact, stayed in Washington for extended periods of time. After serving one or two terms, they retired to their home state or district, undoubtedly relieved to escape the Washington climate. Not until 1900, in fact, did the average representative's service reach three terms (six years). A number of those short-term lawmakers presumably went on to fill state or federal judicial posts.

Few former legislators today, however, accept public positions of any sort after leaving Congress. The trend away from postcongressional service in the judiciary is even more striking. From these facts Bogue and his colleagues observe that "apparently the barriers between the judiciary and the legislative branch have risen somewhat."[12]

The same career barriers do not seem to affect state legislators, who are less apt than members of Congress to regard their posts as a career. One study of the later careers of state lawmakers found that more than a quarter of those who were lawyers went on to hold public offices open to their profession—that is, judges, prosecuting attorneys, and public attorneys.[13] So the bench, mainly at the state level, does benefit from the experience of former legislators. The researchers also found that, while lesser "lawyers-only" posts (including judgeships) were stepping-stones to the state legislature, the higher "lawyers-only" posts taken by retiring legislators did not lead to other public jobs, except to still higher "lawyers-only" positions. This suggests that the judiciary, no less than Congress, is a profession with substantial boundaries that discourage easy switching back and forth.

Whatever the practice in earlier times, career shifting occurs rarely today at the federal level. The reason is the rise of congressional careerism, a twentieth century phenomenon. Extended service on Capitol Hill is now the norm, not the exception. Career-minded lawmakers have few incentives, and little time, to consider a judicial career. It may be, too, that the general public, not to mention bar association panels, frowns on mixing political and judicial careers. Whatever the reason, the two public careers are increasingly "professionalized"—which also means distinct and isolated from one another.

Senators James M. Byrnes (South Carolina) and Harold Burton (Ohio), both appointed in 1941; former Senator Sherman Minton (Indiana), appointed in 1949; and former Representative Homer Thornberry (Texas), whose 1968 nomination was later withdrawn.

12. Bogue and others, "Members of the House of Representatives and the Processes of Modernization," pp. 300–01.

13. Paul L. Hain and James E. Piereson, "Lawyers and Politics Revisited: Structural Advantages of Lawyer-Politicians," *American Journal of Political Science,* vol. 19 (February 1975), pp. 44, 45.

Capitol Hill Careerists

The major characteristic of modern legislators is that they tend to be careerists. In the 1980s the average representative has served a little more than 10 years, or 5.3 House terms. The average senator has served about the same length of time—10.5 years, or 1.7 Senate terms. After each election, somewhere between 10 and 20 percent of the members of the two chambers are newcomers.

This profile contrasts sharply with Congress before the twentieth century. "In the beginning," writes Price, "all American legislative bodies were quite non-professional."[14] Legislative tenure was short, part time, and nonrecurring. Legislative careerism was suspect, and local rotation agreements limiting the length of service in Congress to one or two terms were not uncommon. The writer of *Federalist* number 53 (Madison or Hamilton), for example, viewed frequent turnover in office as the best means of ensuring responsible public officials. On the other hand, the author of the essay acknowledged the benefits of long tenure.

> A few of the members, as happens in all such assemblies, will possess superior talents; will, by frequent reelections, become members of long standing; will be thoroughly masters of the public business, and perhaps not unwilling to avail themselves of those advantages.

Among the momentous trends in Congress is surely the rise of members "not unwilling to avail themselves of those advantages" conferred by long service.

Several factors brought about the professionalization of Congress in the latter years of the nineteenth century and the early years of the twentieth.[15] One was the decline in party competition after the realignment of 1896, which produced vast numbers of one-party districts. Another was the heightened attraction of congressional careers, caused by expansion of the federal government and the advent of internal leadership posts conferred by seniority. Finally, the use of voluntary rotation agreements declined in House districts as voters and lawmakers discovered ways of keeping in contact with one another.

Careerism is made possible, of course, by the sufferance of the electorate.

14. H. Douglas Price, "Congress and the Evolution of Legislative 'Professionalism,'" in Norman J. Ornstein, ed., *Congress in Change* (Praeger, 1975), p. 3.

15. Samuel H. Kernell, "Toward Understanding 19th Century Congressional Careers: Ambition, Competition and Rotations," *American Journal of Political Science,* vol. 21 (November 1977), pp. 669–93.

More than a few congressional careers are cut short by the voters—especially when strong political tides flow in favor of one party or another. But such tides normally threaten only the minority of members who have marginal seats. In the twenty-one elections held since World War II, an average of 91 percent of all incumbent representatives and 75 percent of incumbent senators running for reelection have been returned to office.[16] Many reasons are cited for incumbents' success at the polls: perquisites of office, constituent outreach and casework activities, visibility advantages over possible challengers, and the ability to raise large campaign war chests. The upshot of these incumbent advantages is that most reasonably diligent officeholders can choose to remain in office for an extended period of years. And large numbers of them do so.

The prevalence of careerists on Capitol Hill has several consequences for the making of laws. Most important, a large proportion of the members working on a given piece of legislation will be veterans, with experience concerning the issue at hand. This is especially true of committee and subcommittee leaders. In this they stand in marked contrast to their counterparts in the executive branch: the average presidential appointee remains in his or her post for only about two years.[17] Another consequence of careerism is stability: the House and Senate are relatively stable institutions with strong traditions and elaborate procedures. The presence of sizable numbers of senior members means that sudden or drastic change is usually resisted. Observers and newcomers alike soon learn that the two houses of Congress must be accepted on their own terms, and that their habitual ways of doing things can be altered only with difficulty.

The Work Environment

The work habits of senators and representatives are affected by the fact that there is no single formula for serving in the U.S. Congress. The job consists of different facets, or roles, and incumbents themselves have varying priorities. Uppermost in the minds of most members are the twin duties of lawmaking and representation. Senators and representatives, after all, live and operate in two quite distinct worlds: the world of Capitol Hill, with its emphasis on legislative policies and processes, and the world of their home states or districts, which may be thousands of miles apart, not only in distance but in outlook as well.

16. Roger H. Davidson and Walter J. Oleszek, *Congress and Its Members,* 2d ed. (Washington, D.C.: CQ Press, 1985), p. 62; and author's calculations.

17. John W. Macy, Jr., Bruce Adams, and J. Jackson Walter, *America's Unelected Government: Appointing the President's Team* (Ballinger/Harper & Row, 1983).

Lawmaking versus Constituency Demands

Some members stress the formal aspects of Capitol Hill business: legislative work, investigation, and committee specialization. These may include such tasks as mastering rules and procedures, gaining information and expertise on issues, and plunging into the process of drafting and negotiating bills and resolutions. As late as the 1950s, Speaker Sam Rayburn counseled young colleagues to take care of their office work and visitors early each morning so they could attend committee meetings at ten o'clock, and at noon go to the House floor to observe and listen.[18]

Rayburn's advice assumed that members would have a single morning committee meeting and plenty of time to witness an entire afternoon's floor proceedings—a leisurely pace that has gone the way of the Edsel and the Hula-Hoop. Even in Rayburn's time, diligent attention to the legislative side of Capitol Hill life was a luxury that could be indulged in mainly by members who, like Rayburn, came from safe (and unreapportioned) districts, often rural and sparsely populated, that made few demands on their elected representatives. Less fortunate colleagues from competitive districts had less time to devote to the intricacies of legislative business. In the quarter century since Rayburn's death, more and more legislators have moved into this latter category. No matter that incumbents' reelection rates are high; members know that inattention to constituents can spell disaster.[19]

Today's members therefore cannot slight the second role, that of representative or constituency servant: communicating with constituents, reflecting their views, trying to solve problems they face in dealing with federal agencies, and making certain that they get their fair share of federal programs and funds. Some members invest in constituency outreach to win breathing room for legislative goals they want to pursue. Others do it because they realize it is essential for reelection. Whether or not they relish constituency tasks, members regard them with a strong sense of duty. As they see it, if they do not stand up for local interests, no one else is likely to do so.

One of the most vexing dilemmas members face is how to balance pressures to remain in Washington against those to be in the home state or district. They tend to view their choices as a zero-sum game: time spent in the constituency means giving up certain tasks in Washington and vice versa.[20]

18. Sam Rayburn, *Speak, Mister Speaker,* ed. H. G. Dulaney and Edward Hake Phillips (Bonham, Texas: Sam Rayburn Foundation, 1978), p. 466.

19. Thomas E. Mann, *Unsafe at Any Margin: Interpreting Congressional Elections* (Washington, D.C.: American Enterprise Institute for Public Policy Research, 1978).

20. Richard F. Fenno, Jr., *Home Style: House Members in Their Districts* (Little, Brown, 1978),

In the Ninety-sixth Congress (1979–80), the average representative spent nearly 120 days each year in the home district; the figure for senators was about 80 days.[21] The figures have risen steeply in both chambers since the 1950s. Members travel home more frequently than ever before, and the two chambers have added to the incentives through scheduling and travel allowances.

The Daily Merry-Go-Round

Even when the lawmaker remains in Washington, there are numerous distractions. Time is the lawmakers' most precious commodity; lack of it is their most often-voiced complaint.

Senators' and representatives' daily schedules are long, fragmented, and unpredictable. Studies dating from the mid-1970s indicate that on average members work an eleven-hour day. Little of this time is devoted to serious or sustained study of the legislation they are working on. As recently as 1965, representatives spent almost a full day every week on "legislative research and reading"; by 1977 the time spent on reading was down to an average of eleven minutes per day.[22]

Legislators spend only about a third of their time in the House or Senate chamber or in committee or subcommittee meetings.[23] "We're like automatons," one senator said. "We spend our time walking in tunnels to go to the floor to vote."[24] Nowadays members spend even less time on the floor, since the advent of televised sessions, first in the House (1978) and then in the Senate (1986). Members can follow the floor action from their offices or cloakrooms, going to the chamber when they want to speak or vote.

Scheduling of committee activities is complicated by the large number of committees and subcommittees—in the One-hundredth Congress, 105 in the Senate and 172 in the House, not counting joint panels. Taken together, these units offer almost 3,000 seats or positions for members in the House

---

p. 34; and Glenn R. Parker, *Homeward Bound: Explaining Changes in Congressional Behavior* (University of Pittsburgh Press, 1986), p. 10.

21. Parker, *Homeward Bound,* pp. 17–18.

22. Donald G. Tacheron and Morris K. Udall, *The Job of the Congressman,* 2d ed. (Indianapolis: Bobbs-Merrill, 1970), p. 303; and *Administrative Reorganization and Legislative Management,* H. Doc. 95-232, House Commission on Administrative Review, 95 Cong. 1 sess. (Government Printing Office, 1977), vol. 2, pp. 17–20.

23. *Final Report,* H. Doc. 95-272, House Commission on Administrative Review, 95 Cong. 1 sess. (GPO, 1977), vol. 1, pp. 630–34; and *Toward a Modern Senate,* S. Doc. 94-278, Senate Commission on the Operation of the Senate, 94 Cong. 2 sess. (GPO, 1977), p. 27.

24. Ross A. Webber, "U.S. Senators: See How They Run," *The Wharton Magazine* (Winter 1980–81), p. 38.

and more than 1,000 in the Senate. The average senator holds 10 committee and subcommittee seats and the average representative 7 seats. Leadership posts abound: almost all Democratic senators and more than half of all Democratic representatives chair a committee or subcommittee. Minority party members are not left out: most Republican senators and about 80 percent of the GOP representatives are ranking minority members of these same committees and subcommittees. These leaders have separate staff assigned to assist them, and they have special responsibilities to voice their party's interests in the legislative business before their panels.

With so many assignments, lawmakers are hard pressed to cope with their crowded schedules. Scheduling problems are endemic, especially in the Senate. Committee quorums can be hard to achieve, and members' attentions are often directed elsewhere. During peak times—midweek (Tuesdays through Thursdays) and midsession (March through July)—members constantly face scheduling conflicts among two, three, or more of their committees. Even within committees, scheduling is sometimes haphazard. Working sessions are not infrequently composed of the chairman, perhaps the ranking minority member and one or two other colleagues, and a bevy of staff aides.

Members' schedules are splintered into so many tiny bits and pieces that effective, simultaneous pursuit of lawmaking, oversight, and constituent service is hampered. According to a management study of several senators' offices, an event to which the senator or the chief aide must respond personally occurs every five minutes, on the average.[25] Unpredictability is another attribute of daily schedules. Sometimes members have scant notice that their presence is required at a meeting or a hearing. Carefully developed plans can be disrupted by changes in meeting hours, by unexpected events, or by sessions that run longer than anticipated.

Most members say they want to devote more time to legislation. In a 1977 House survey, members were asked to compare the tasks that should be very important with those that actually take a great deal of time. The pursuits that received the shortest shrift were studying and legislative research; overseeing executive agencies, either personally or through formal committee work; debating and voting on legislation; negotiating with other members to build support for proposals; and working in committees to develop legislation. Members were also asked about the gaps between what others expected of them and what they themselves thought they should be doing. The most commonly cited problem, mentioned by fully half the members, was that

25. Ibid., p. 37.

"constituent demands detract from other functions." A second complaint, cited by 36 percent of the legislators, was that "scheduling problems [and] time pressures detract from the work of the House."[26]

The dilemma legislators face in allocating their time is more than a matter of daily scheduling. It is also a case of clashing role expectations. Members are pulled in opposite directions by the two Congresses—the Congress of lawmaking and the Congress of representation. There are no pat formulas for striking a balance. If members concentrate too much on legislative work in Washington, they are accused of getting "Potomac fever" and neglecting the home folks. If they spend too much time at home, they are accused of neglecting their committee work and floor attendance.

Members' frustrations continue to surface in a variety of ways. During the Ninety-ninth Congress a number of senators, dubbed the "quality of life" group, gathered informally to discuss ways of tightening up Senate procedures and easing scheduling problems. And retiring Speaker Thomas P. O'Neill, Jr., told a *New York Times* reporter that members want power on Capitol Hill to be less dispersed. "They say there are too many subcommittees out there, too many," O'Neill said. "And too many staff people."[27]

Lawmaking by Staff?

The ambivalence expressed by many senators and representatives toward their staffs is a revealing commentary on the bureaucratizing of Congress. Like the White House—and, for that matter, the federal courts—Congress is no longer simply a collection of individual decisionmakers. Rather, it is a collection of officials who manage small entrepreneurial "firms" of people who work for them.

The congressional bureaucracy is impressive in its size and diversity, even though the 1980s have brought stabilization and even some cutbacks in the number of staff. Some 11,000 people serve in the personal (as opposed to committee) offices of senators and representatives. Increasingly, these are located in state or district offices rather than in Washington. House committees employ nearly 2,000 staff members, Senate committees about 1,000. In addition, information and analysis are supplied by four support agencies: the Congressional Research Service, the General Accounting Office, the Office of Technology Assessment, and the Congressional Budget Office. Finally, there are employees—counsels, clerks, secretaries, and others—who expedite the

26. *Final Report,* vol. 2, p. 875.
27. Steven V. Roberts, "Watching the Pendulum of Powers of Congress," *New York Times,* October 23, 1986, p. B10.

business of the two chambers and who participate in drafting and processing legislation.

Many factors explain the rapid growth in staff that has occurred since World War II. Among them are the complexity of issues, expanding work loads, competition among committees and members, election of activist members, diffusion of power, constituency services, and legislative-executive conflicts.

This spectacular staff growth has profoundly and irrevocably altered the operation of Congress. Whereas once members dealt with each other directly on a daily basis when Congress was in session, they often interact today through staff aides and organizational arrangements.[28] In the House of Representatives, members tend not to know one another very well, and sometimes not at all. The same is true of the Senate, though to a lesser degree. Members and staff aides working on a given problem may be unaware of what others are doing along the same or parallel lines. In short, Congress has shifted from a small, unified, corporate body to one that has a bureaucratic character—with all the trappings of size, complexity, specialization, and routinization.

The Capitol Hill bureaucracy has, however, grown in ways peculiar to the character of Congress as a decentralized, nonhierarchial institution. Congress has begotten not one bureaucracy but many, clustered about various centers of power and in a sense defining their power. Efforts to impose a common framework upon the staff apparatus have thus far been stoutly resisted.

For those who are charged with interpreting and passing judgment on congressional legislative products, the advent of this sizable staff apparatus poses vexing problems. For the staff growth has occurred at the same time, and for many of the same reasons, as has the relaxing of members' own control over the details of legislative drafting and processing. Not too many years ago, a large number of representatives, and even some senators, actually did their own legislative research and drafting. Today it is a rare member who does not delegate these tasks to legislative assistants, committee aides, lawyers from the Office of Legislative Counsel, or experts from one of the support agencies.

This inevitably poses the question: to what extent do provisions in statutes—much less reports and statements—reflect the considered judgment of the legislators, and to what extent do they embody the objectives of unelected staff members? Staff politics, after all, are as complex as member-

---

28. Michael J. Malbin, *Unelected Representatives: Congressional Staff and the Future of Representative Government* (Basic Books, 1980), p. 245 ff.

to-member politics; and staff differ widely in the amount of latitude or supervision they receive from those who hire them. A great number of legislative decisions, not all of them minor or technical, are delegated to, or assumed by, staff aides. In his study of transportation policy for the disabled, Katzmann relates how staff-drafted report language went far beyond the provisions of the Rehabilitation Act of 1973, creating confusion in the courts and the administrative process.[29] Staff influence is at its peak in low-visibility products—technical language, provisions of lengthy omnibus bills, committee reports, correspondence, and verbal communications with executive agencies.

Concern over staff power focuses not merely on the possibility of irresponsible policymaking, but also on its effects on Congress as a collegial body. Staff enable legislators to cope with burgeoning personal and institutional demands—to follow more issues and process more legislation. But at what cost to the collective body of Congress? Insofar as staff carry on the negotiations leading to enactments, Congress sacrifices the advantages of direct deliberation by its elected members. Insofar as staff are delegated the mechanics of legislative drafting and report writing, it becomes difficult for outsiders to gauge the extent to which Congress stands collectively responsible for its products. Thus staff may "make deliberative behavior less likely and make it difficult for the legislature to act with collective responsibility."[30] Coupled with the division of labor embodied in the committee system, the staff system may lead administrators and judges to wonder what is really the will of Congress.

Handling the Legislative Agenda

Demands on the contemporary Congress are no less varied than the concerns of the American people. In the earliest days, the government in Washington was, as Alexander Hamilton had feared (*Federalist* number 22), "at a distance and out of sight." Lawmaking was a part-time occupation. As John F. Kennedy was fond of remarking, the Clays, Calhouns, and Websters of the nineteenth century could afford to devote a whole generation or more to debating and refining the few vital controversies at hand.

Once limited in scope, small in volume, and simple in content, Congress's work load has today grown to huge proportions. Historically, the long-term trends have been upward in almost every indicator of work load or activity:

29. Robert A. Katzmann, *Institutional Disability: The Saga of Transportation Policy for the Disabled* (Brookings, 1986).
30. Ibid., p. 193.

measures introduced, reported, and passed, committee and subcommittee meetings; hours in session; and floor votes.

Elements of the Committees' Work Loads

In the years since World War II, the overall work load trend has been marked by a gradual buildup, then an era of extraordinary legislative activity, and most recently a rather sudden and striking contraction. The number of measures introduced in the two chambers has followed roughly this pattern. The average senator introduced about 33 bills per Congress at the beginning of this period, reaching a peak of nearly 50 in the early 1970s, then falling to 34.5 in the mid-1980s. Comparable House figures, though distorted somewhat by changes in cosponsorship rules, fluctuated more widely. In the 1980s the average member introduced 16.3 bills, less than a third of the figure in the late 1960s and early 1970s.[31]

Another work load element consists of presidential messages and executive reports of various kinds. President Truman transmitted seven messages to the Republican-controlled Eightieth Congress (1947–48) and only four to the Democratic Congress that followed it. In 1985–86, President Reagan sent 302 messages to Capitol Hill. Executive messages and reports to Congress more than doubled over the same period. Because of its special constitutional duties, the Senate receives more of these than the House, although the gap is closing. In the Ninety-ninth Congress, Senate committees received significantly more executive communications than legislative proposals of all kinds.

Executive communications are a far from negligible category of committee business. Of course, many messages are routine and require no action. Others are reports requested by Congress on questions major or minor. Some may require detailed review by the committee staff or even hearings or legislative action by the committee members.

The Senate also has the time-consuming task of confirming presidential appointments. A total of 1,642 presidential nominations were received by Senate committees during the Ninety-ninth Congress (1985–86); of these 1,488 were reported to the full Senate.[32] Among the committees faced with exceptionally large numbers of nominations is Judiciary, which must process and confirm nominees for the federal bench and U.S. attorney. Individual

31. Roger H. Davidson and Carol Hardy, "Indicators of House of Representatives' Activity and Workload," Report 87-136S (Congressional Research Service, June 8, 1987); and Davidson and Hardy, "Indicators of Senate Activity and Workload," Report 87-497S (CRS, June 8, 1987).

32. The source for these numbers is the Senate's computerized LEGIS files, in which "nomination" means any separate transmittal to the Senate, whether an individual name or a batch of names. While the numbers thus do not represent separate nominees, they give a fairly accurate picture of the work load demands generated by such transmittals.

nominations are especially numerous at the beginning of a new administration, tapering off at the later stages.

Virtually all measures, once introduced, are referred to the appropriate committee of jurisdiction. Referrals are made by the chamber's presiding officer—the Speaker of the House or the president pro tem of the Senate. In most cases the actual referral is performed by the parliamentarians, in accord with chamber rules and precedents. For legislative committees, the bills and resolutions referred to them constitute the bulk of their agenda.

Trends in referrals obviously follow bill introduction patterns. Most committees experienced a surge of demand in the post–World War II years, then a period of high activity, and more recently a downturn in activity. Committees vary widely in their legislative work loads: some receive hundreds of bills and resolutions, others only a handful.

The Judiciary Committees

The two Judiciary panels receive more bills and resolutions than any other committees in the House and Senate. The Senate Judiciary Committee had 23.8 percent (1,038) of all measures referred in the Ninety-ninth Congress, while House Judiciary had 14.2 percent (1,288) of the bills in that chamber. The Judiciary committees' broad and oftentimes controversial jurisdiction attracts numerous proposals pertaining to constitutional amendments, the criminal code, administrative procedures, claims against the government, and the federal court system. Moreover, the committees often process or review legal issues raised by measures falling mainly within other committees' jurisdictions. The two panels also account for a large proportion of the measures reported—that is, brought to the floor—by committees. Senate Judiciary accounted for 34.5 percent of all bills reported to that chamber in the Ninety-ninth Congress, while the House Judiciary figure was 13.8 percent.[33]

The Judiciary committees have a history of partisanship and ideological conflict. They were the arenas for the civil rights battles of the 1950s and 1960s; more recently, they have been the scene of conflicts over such social issues as abortion, school prayer, and criminal law. The House panel in 1974 voted articles of impeachment against President Richard Nixon.

The two panels often deviate from the ideological center of gravity in their respective chambers. The conservative oligarchs who dominated Congress before the 1960s tried to maintain the committees as vetoers of civil rights legislation; fierce opposition in the Senate committee was the reason that early civil rights bills were steered through the Commerce Committee by

33. Davidson and Hardy, "Indicators of Senate Activity," pp. 60, 61; "Indicators of House Activity," pp. 29, 30.

focusing on discrimination in interstate commerce. Increasingly, however, liberals were attracted to Judiciary by the prospect of working on civil rights and other liberal legislation. In recent years, the House committee especially has been a killing ground for constitutional amendments and other measures desired by conservatives on such subjects as school prayer, abortion, and budget procedures.

Taken as a group, House Judiciary members in 1987 scored 48.4 on a "liberalism" scale derived from *Congressional Quarterly* voting indices.[34] The average for all House members was 40.3. Senate Judiciary committee members scored 51.1 on this liberalism scale, compared with 40.5 for the full Senate. In both chambers, Judiciary ranked among the most liberal committees in 1987, as indicated by the combined liberalism scores of their members. The Senate committee was exceeded in the average liberalism scores of its members by only two other panels (Labor and Human Resources, Veterans Affairs); House Judiciary ranked fifth among all House committees.

Members of the Judiciary panels are deeply divided ideologically along partisan lines. Judiciary Democrats tend to be more liberal than their fellow partisans, while Judiciary Republicans are to the right of their GOP colleagues. Self-selection may partially account for this phenomenon: ideologically committed members are drawn to arenas that allow them to voice their views and pursue their goals. Party leaders may add to the situation by ensuring that "reliable" partisans are given seats on Judiciary. When Republicans took over the Senate in 1980, for example, they made a concerted effort to recruit conservatives and reverse the committee's liberal tendencies.[35]

"The Dim Dungeons of Silence"

However many bills and resolutions may be drafted, introduced, and referred, congressional practices strictly limit the number that emerge successfully from the process. The winnowing is mainly done by the committees, whose major task is seeing to it that the vast majority of proposals never see the light of day. That is why Woodrow Wilson called committees "the dim dungeons of silence."[36]

Of the nearly 10,000 bills introduced in the two chambers in 1985–86,

---

34. The "liberalism" figures cited here are calculated by the author from *Congressional Quarterly's* "Opposition to Conservative Coalition" scores, recomputed to remove the effect of absences. Individual scores were averaged by committee and by party to provide comparisons within the two chambers. Joseph A. Davis, "Conservative Coalition No Longer a Force," *Congressional Quarterly Weekly Report,* vol. 46 (January 16, 1988), pp. 110–17.

35. Roger H. Davidson and Walter J. Oleszek, "Changing the Guard in the U.S. Senate," *Legislative Studies Quarterly,* vol. 9 (November 1984), p. 649.

36. Woodrow Wilson, *Congressional Government* (New York: Meridan Books, 1956), p. 63.

only about 6 percent found their way into the statute books. It is easier to halt than to pass legislation. Measures reaching the latter stages of the process invariably command a certain level of support but can still fall victim to concerted opposition, interchamber differences, or simple lack of time at the end of the session. At each stage, the number of successful measures becomes smaller and smaller.

Within the committees, bills and resolutions generally pass through four stages between the time they are referred and the time they emerge to the full chamber. (The vast majority of measures, of course, receive no action at all.) First is the *research* phase, conducted largely by the staff. Background material is collected concerning the issue at hand—including readings, investigative reports, background studies, comments from executive agencies, and lists of experts and potential witnesses. Committee leaders may then decide to proceed to *hearings*, the second stage. Held ostensibly to gather information, hearings have many other purposes; they are designed to permit members to air their views, to allow witnesses their "day in court," to probe the reactions of relevant lobby groups, to lay the groundwork for subsequent committee action, and perhaps to throw the public and media spotlight on the issue. If the hearings uncover support for legislative action, *markups* may be scheduled to work on the bill or resolution and perfect its provisions. If agreement is reached, the measure is *reported* by a formal vote in the full chamber.

One or more of these four stages may be duplicated at the subcommittee and full committee level. Many measures, in fact, are rereferred within committee to the appropriate subcommittee. House rules even require every standing committee with twenty or more members (except Budget) to have at least four subcommittees that have stated jurisdictions and must be referred bills within their boundaries. Many Senate subcommittees are also strong. What Woodrow Wilson called "committee government" has now become in many instances "subcommittee government."

The Legislative Paper Trail

At each stage of the committee's work, public documents may emerge that form part of the measure's legislative history and help illuminate the lawmakers' intentions and expectations. In view of members' heavy work loads and the staffs' domination of these operations, however, it would be a mistake to assume that such documents necessarily embody the considered judgment of the committee's members.

From the initial research phase may emanate documents, called committee prints, that include background studies, investigative reports, and relevant readings. Although valuable for clues as to why the issue was brought to the committee's attention, these items are rarely helpful in interpreting the resulting piece of legislation.

More important for legislative interpretation are the hearings, usually published by the committee. No history or policy analysis of a statute would be complete without careful study of these documents, even though the task may be formidable. Hearings leading up to a major enactment may cover thousands of pages, involve two or more committees, and stretch over many years. The attributes of hearings, moreover, dictate care in interpreting them. Because hearings are political events, members and witnesses alike are apt to view them as stages for sermonizing or making political points. There are procedural problems as well. Because of schedule overlaps, hearings are not always well attended, especially in their later stages. Members come and go; sometimes only a single member is on hand. Supplementary questions and answers are sometimes inserted after the fact; members and witnesses may "revise and extend" their remarks.[37]

The records emanating from all-important markup sessions are even more variable. Markups are usually not published, and the unpublished transcripts may not be complete. House and Senate rules require committees to record all "actions"—including votes on any question on which a record vote is demanded (Senate Rule XXVI (7)(b) and House Rule XI (2)(e)(1)). The Senate also requires its committees to keep "a complete transcript or electronic recording adequate to fully record the proceeding" of each meeting, whether open or closed (Rule XXVI (5)(e)). A majority of the committee may vote to forgo such a record, however.

The committee's final product, the report on the bill or resolution, is the key document setting forth the committee's formal action. It is important to distinguish between the committee's action in reporting the bill or resolution, and the report *document*, typically drafted by the staff, that accompanies most but not all measures. House and Senate rules specify that when reporting an action to the full chamber, a committee quorum (that is, a majority of the members) must be present and the vote must itself be reported.

The committee report—that is, the document embodying the committee's recommendation—may be only a page or two or may run to hundreds of

---

37. On rare occasions this evokes complaints. When minority members of the House Committee on Science and Technology complained that their words had been altered by a committee staff member, the committee revised its rules to require publication "in verbatim form," the only exceptions being "errors in transcription" or "disputed errors in transcription." *Rules Adopted by the Committees of the House of Representatives,* Committee Print, House Committee on Rules, 99 Cong. 1 sess. (GPO, 1985), p. 229. Other committees, however, have not followed suit.

pages. Chamber rules require that the document contain such information as the votes of members favoring or opposing the action; minority or supplemental views of members; cost and revenue estimates; comparison of the text of existing and proposed statutory provisions (if a current law is to be amended); a regulatory impact statement (Senate); an inflationary impact statement (House); and relevant oversight findings and recommendations (House). In addition, reports usually, although not always, include explanations of the committee's recommendations and arguments for a favorable vote on the floor.

The report is the committee's chance to marshal evidence on its behalf from hearings, expert reports and studies, and other sources. It is also an opportunity to explain or underscore the committee's reasons for writing the measure as it did. It also affords members and staff a chance to influence subsequent implementation of the measure by explaining what the bill leaves unclear or unstated. Such passages must be approached with full awareness of their intent and function.

Congress is quintessentially a political body, a fact reflected by all of these types of committee documents. They are used by committees, factions, or even individual members to advance their particular views of what the committee has done, what it might have done, or what it should have done. Given Congress's decentralized character, it would be inaccurate to assume that committee documents represent the members' collective judgment. Some committees take care to circulate draft reports to all their members and to label documents that do not have members' express endorsement.[38] Not all committees are careful to maintain this distinction, however; even if they were, members' schedules preclude detailed review of the mass of documents that is produced.

One Bill, Many Committees

When one thinks about how legislation is processed by Congress, it is natural to visualize a single measure referred to a single specialized committee, which considers and perhaps reports it. This remains an accurate picture for a majority of bills and resolutions. In the past decade, however, measures have increasingly come to be considered jointly or in sequence by two or more committees. Multiple referrals were not formally sanctioned by the House

38. The House Judiciary Committee, for example, specifies that "no report . . . which does not accompany a measure or matter for consideration by the House shall be published unless all Members of the Committee or subcommittee issuing the report shall have been apprised of such report and been given the opportunity to give notice of intention to file supplemental, additional, or dissenting views as part of the report." Members have at least three days to file such views. Ibid., p. 163.

until 1975, but since then more than 7,000 bills and resolutions have gone to two or more committees.[39] The Senate, which permits multiple referral of legislation through unanimous consent motions resulting from private negotiations among the interested committees, now refers 200–300 measures to two or more panels during each Congress. In the Ninety-ninth Congress, more than a quarter of the work load of House committees and about a tenth of the work load of Senate committees, on average, consisted of bills and resolutions shared in some way with one or more other panels.

The two Judiciary committees share a large number of measures with other panels, but these represent relatively small portions of their total work load. Their jurisdiction, while broad, is well bounded and rarely overlaps with other committees. Among the committees with which they most frequently share bills are Energy and Commerce (for example, restraints of trade, patents, copyrights, and trademarks); Ways and Means (bankruptcies, claims); Rules (apportionment of representatives, meetings of Congress); and Education and Labor (civil rights and certain civil and criminal proceedings).

The use of multiple referrals has changed lawmaking, especially in the House. First, measures referred to two or more committees are less likely to succeed than those referred to only one committee. The more committees, in general, the more difficult it is for the measure to survive. This flows not only from the complexity of such measures, but also from the sheer procedural barriers involved in dealing with multiple committees.

Second, multiple referrals encourage intercommittee coordination. Alert committee staff keep an eye on bills that are introduced, in order to protect their turf and assert claims of shared jurisdiction if need be. In many cases, moreover, committee cooperation makes possible a better or more complete measure than would otherwise be possible. A joint-venture bill (the National Cooperative Research Act of 1984, P.L. 98-462), for example, was successfully crafted because the principal committee, Science and Technology, shared the bill with Judiciary, which drafted the antitrust provisions.

Finally, multiple referral procedures add potentially to the scheduling powers of House leaders—the Speaker and the Rules Committee. This is paradoxical. The multiple referral device was originally pushed as part of the 1970s trend toward decentralization—permitting more members and committees policy leverage for shaping particular measures. And yet its ultimate effect may well be to encourage centralized planning and scheduling of complex measures.

39. Roger H. Davidson, Walter J. Oleszek, and Thomas Kephart, "One Bill, Many Committees: Multiple Referrals in the U.S. House of Representatives," *Legislative Studies Quarterly*, vol. 13 (February 1988), pp. 3–28.

Although committees continue to dominate the processing of legislation, they no longer monopolize it. Reaction against the power of the "barons" who ran the committees during the 1940s and 1950s, mostly on behalf of the conservative coalition, succeeded in the 1960s and 1970s in democratizing the distribution of power in both chambers. Within the committees, power was decentralized to the subcommittees, which in some cases became the real centers of action, holding the hearings and marking up the bills. Outside the committees, new opportunities were opened up for noncommittee members to have a hand in shaping legislation through floor amendments, party task forces, informal caucuses, and the like.

All of this dispersion of influence means that it is harder than ever to fix responsibility for the authorship of specific statutory provisions. Many hands, staff as well as member, may have been at work to shape a given bill. With fragmented responsibility and overlapping jurisdictions, the drafting process is far more open and porous than in years past. This means that "legislative purpose" is increasingly hard to discern.

Legislative Packaging

Packaging is another element that has altered legislative products. In 1955–56, when Congress produced more than a thousand public laws, the average enactment took less than two pages in the statute books. By the 1980s, the average law took up more than nine pages. Some of these measures are very long indeed: the 1986 tax reform bill was 1,500 pages long, and the funding bill (continuing resolution) the same year ran to 690 pages. This reflects not only growing sophistication in drafting, but also the tendency to write omnibus, multititle bills.

Congress now tends to package large numbers of policy decisions in a relatively few broad-spectrum vehicles—authorizations or reauthorizations, omnibus tax measures, appropriations bills, continuing resolutions, and budget resolutions. Critics contend that members are forced to vote on wide-ranging measures that embrace major policy changes on a variety of issues with little time to learn, much less understand, all of the provisions. Defenders maintain this is the only way to achieve consensus, especially when unpleasant policy alternatives (like cutbacks) must be accepted. Senate Appropriations Chairman Mark O. Hatfield explained in 1982, for example, that he would "hold [his] nose and do certain things here for the purpose of getting the job done, but certainly not with enthusiasm or anything other than recognizing . . . that we are doing things under emergency conditions."[40]

40. Dale Tate, "Use of Omnibus Bills Burgeons Despite Members' Misgivings; Long-Term

Legislative packaging further blurs responsibility for explicit legislative provisions, which is sometimes exactly what is intended. Such packages are especially popular in an era of fiscal stagnation, when many programs face freezes or cutbacks. Rather than alienating the clients or beneficiaries of such programs, lawmakers find it easier to vote for omnibus measures that embody across-the-board cutbacks. As long as all are taking their lumps, it is easier to accept damage to one's favored programs.

Yearly Cycles of Legislative Activity

In each new Congress, legislative activity follows a distinctive and predictable annual pattern. Committee hearings tend to be held in the first year of a Congress (that is, odd-numbered years). Hearings rise to a peak in March and April, dropping off as the year progresses. The drop-off is gradual in nonelection years, precipitous in election years.

Floor activity follows quite a different cycle. It begins very slowly and intensifies as the year proceeds, peaking just before scheduled recesses. The most frantic floor activity takes place just before the Congress adjourns *sine die*. Legislators intensify last-ditch efforts to get a floor vote on their legislation before adjournment. At the same moment, the dwindling time makes it easier to delay or kill the measure. Bills that are passed under these last-minute conditions may be hastily put together, and members may be ill informed about the provisions they are voting upon. As the 1986 session came to a belated end, for example, members complained that they had no time to read, much less understand, the provisions embedded in such huge documents as the tax reform bill or the continuing funding resolution. Hundreds of technical corrections were left to the staffs to work out; a hefty bill incorporating these had to be prepared in the wake of the tax reform measure. As for the funding resolution, Representative Henry Hyde said days after the bill passed that he still didn't know what was in it. "The whole legislative session is wrapped up in that torn and tattered pile of papers on the desk," he complained.[41]

The hectic end-of-session pace not only exacerbates the difficulties members face in comprehending the legislation they must approve. It also heightens the difficulty outsiders have in interpreting and evaluating the statutes' provisions.

Impact Is Disputed," *Congressional Quarterly Weekly Report,* vol. 40 (September 25, 1982), p. 2379.

41. Jonathan Rauch, "One Big, Big Bill," *National Journal,* vol. 18 (November 1, 1986), p. 2654.

The Impact of Bicameralism

Another influence on legislation is the existence of two separate chambers, each with its special character and dynamics. Several differences between the House and Senate powerfully shape their approach to policymaking: among others, their terms of office, the size and character of their constituencies, and the size and character of the legislative bodies themselves.

The different constituencies unquestionably pull in divergent directions. Smaller, more homogeneous House districts often promote clear, unambiguous positions on a narrow range of questions, whereas senators must weigh the claims of many competing interests. Representatives tend to specialize more in the topics covered by their committees and to delegate less to their staffs. With broader constituencies and more committee assignments, senators are more apt to be generalists and to delegate legislative matters to their staffs. These distinctions between senators and representatives are fading, but they remain.

The size of the chambers, moreover, dictates distinctive procedural biases. House rules are designed to allow majorities to work their will and to resolve matters by floor votes. In contrast, Senate rules give individual senators great latitude in influencing decisions, by protecting the rights of small minorities or even individual senators.

Procedurally, bicameralism adds to the complexity of lawmaking and offers new opportunities for ambiguity in legislative products. A single enactment will normally be accompanied by hearings, reports, and floor debates in both chambers, and these are not always consistent. Because the measures themselves must pass the two houses in identical form, conferences between the House and Senate may be required to negotiate an acceptable compromise. Indeed, many actions in the two chambers are taken in full knowledge that they will be modified, compromised, or even negated in conference. Despite the critical role played by conferences, their decisions are not always well documented, and subsequent debate in the two houses is often abbreviated. Thus bicameralism underscores Congress's pluralistic approach to lawmaking.

The Character of Congressional Enactments

As a lawmaking machine, Congress displays the traits and biases of its structure and constituent parts. It is bicameral, with divergent electoral and procedural traditions. It is representative, especially where geographic interests are at stake. It is fragmented, with many components and few mechanisms for integrating its policy decisions. And it is reactive, mirroring prevailing current perceptions of problems.

Congressional enactments may be binding upon all citizens, but they manifest Congress's character as a collection of emissaries from geographic areas. Sometimes the results are geographically explicit. A 1979 aviation noise control bill required construction of a control tower "at latitude 40 degrees, 43 minutes, 45 seconds north and at longitude 73 degrees, 24 minutes, 50 seconds west"—the exact location of a Farmingdale, New York, airport in the district of the representative who requested the provision.[42] More commonly, programs are directed toward states, municipalities, counties, or metropolitan areas.

Rather than refer to the beneficiaries by name, statutes commonly define them in general phrases or in terms of formulas. Arnold explains that "typically there is little consensus on [the policy's] fundamental purposes or long-term goals, but only short-term agreement on how benefits are to be allocated. In the absence of any unity of purpose, it becomes legitimate to break open the allocational formulas now and then and relaunch the fight for local advantage."[43] Eligibility requirements, then, may be written to embody compromises over the policy's purposes or to cover specific groups or geographic areas.

Legislative products mirror Congress's scattered and decentralized structure. Policies are typically considered piecemeal, reflecting the patchwork of committee and subcommittee jurisdictions. Sometimes policies are duplicative or even contradictory: one committee sponsors acreage allotments and agricultural research to promote tobacco production, another funds research on lung cancer. An authorizing committee drafts an expansive charter for a program and its mission, while the relevant appropriations subcommittee approves dwindling dollar amounts. Even strictly judicial matters are overseen by at least six panels—two Judiciary committees, two Appropriations subcommittees, and two Budget committees.

The approach and wording of a given measure often depend on which committee or committees have reported it. Working from different jurisdictions, committees can approach the same problem in widely diverging ways. A policy from the revenue committees will feature tax provisions, from the appropriations committees a fiscal approach, from the banking panels a financial approach, from the commerce panels a regulatory approach, and so

42. Judy Sarasohn, "Noise Bill Amended," *Congressional Quarterly Weekly Report*, vol. 37 (May 12, 1979), p. 916.

43. R. Douglas Arnold, "The Local Roots of Domestic Policy," in Thomas E. Mann and Norman J. Ornstein, eds., *The New Congress* (Washington, D.C.: American Enterprise Institute for Public Policy Research, 1981), p. 277.

forth. If the measure passes through more than one panel, a combination of approaches might well result. The approach may be well or ill suited to the policy objective—it all depends on which committee was best positioned to promote the bill.

Once it surmounts all the hurdles within Congress, the resulting measure may be internally vague, confusing, and inconsistent. Indeed, the very looseness of the statute may be the price paid for its passage. Former Representative Abner J. Mikva recalled a controversial strip-mining bill managed by Interior Chairman Morris K. Udall:

> They'd put together a very delicate coalition of support. One problem was whether the states or the feds would run the program. One member got up and asked, "Isn't it a fact that under this bill the states will continue to exercise sovereignty over strip mining?" And Mo [Udall] replied, "You're absolutely right." A little later someone else got up and asked, "Now is it clear that the Federal Government will have the final say on strip mining?" And Mo replied, "You're absolutely right." Later, in the cloakroom, I said, "Mo, they can't both be right." And Mo said, "You're absolutely right."[44]

In his study of the Clean Air Act, Melnick put the situation this way:

> The majorities that support major pieces of legislation such as the Clean Air Act are uneasy coalitions, not unified armies. Ambiguities in statutory language often indicate the coalitions' failure to reach agreement. . . . The legislative history of most important statutes reflects this coalition building and shadowboxing. It contains conflicting pieces of evidence that can be interpreted in many different ways by agencies and courts.[45]

Members and staff are quick to shape legislative histories to buttress their policy goals. "Recognizing that the courts may pick up on suggestions inserted in committee reports, floor debate, and hearings," writes Melnick, "committee members and their staff lace these parts of the record with their interpretations of ambiguous sections of the statute."[46] Although the courts can not escape grappling with these problematic documents, they should be fully aware of

44. Marjorie Hunter, "On Leaving Capitol Hill for the Bench," New York Times, May 12, 1983, p. B8.
45. R. Shep Melnick, Regulation and the Courts: The Case of the Clean Air Act (Brookings, 1983), p. 374.
46. Ibid., p. 375.

the risks they encounter. It is easy enough to discover expressions of the views of Congress's subgroups and factions; it is far more difficult to discern the will of Congress as a collective body.

It is little wonder that judges and administrators often react in dismay and amazement when confronting a statute's vagueness or incompleteness. Congress, unable to resolve its differences, may leave the matter in the courts' or executive agencies' hands; equally often, the legislative record includes conflicting views about how the issue is supposed to be resolved, placed there by competing forces within the legislature. So the legislative struggle is transferred to other arenas.

Conclusion

In this brief travelogue about Capitol Hill, I have tried to survey those attributes of lawmakers and the lawmaking process that must be taken into account in reading and interpreting laws passed by Congress. All the factors I have discussed shape the content of measures that must be interpreted, administered, and evaluated by judges and executive agents. The overall picture is not tidy or coordinated, for Congress is not a tidy or coordinated body. Nonetheless, the information I have presented about members of Congress and how they work allows a number of generalizations to be made about the legislative process.

The legislative and judicial branches share an affinity—prevalence of legal training—but barriers between the two are formidable and are widening. The number of lawyer-legislators in Congress is dwindling, and in any event lawmaking and judging careers seem to be on divergent paths. This makes it even more urgent that legislators and judges take greater pains to communicate with one another.

It is well to recall the leading characteristics of lawmaking in today's Congress. First, lawmakers are torn, as always, between the conflicting demands of Capitol Hill and their home constituencies. Second, rising demands upon their time make it virtually impossible for members to devote sustained attention to legislative problems. Third, senators and representatives have responded to burgeoning work loads and scheduling problems by delegating the mechanics of lawmaking to staff aides. Fourth, while committees are the main processors of legislation, they are more likely these days to combine their efforts to produce legislative packages or omnibus bills. Finally, ideological conflict—especially prevalent in the "divided government" era of the 1980s—produces legislation that is full of compromises and ambiguities.

The bills and resolutions passed by Congress, not to mention the reports and other documents, bear the markings of Congress itself—decentralized, dispersed, constituency-oriented, bicameral, slow, and prone to obfuscation and compromise. To gain the votes for passage, a bill's sponsors may agree to compromises and contradictory passages and may sanction ambiguities or postponements of resolution of the issues. Indeed, lawmakers and their staffs are fully aware as they are working on legislation that administrators and judges will continue to shape the policy long after it has been sent to the president and signed into law.

Bureaucrats and judges, in other words, must often pick up the pieces that Congress has left scattered. Members of Congress and their staff aides will not remain silent as their legislative products are reshaped and adjusted in administrative or judicial arenas. They may play roles of lobbyists or claimants, calling upon the legislative record they have created to buttress their interpretations. Or they may stand on the sidelines, waiting for administrators or judges to reach tough decisions that have been fuzzed over by the lawmakers. In either case, the legislative process is transferred to arenas in other branches of government. But circumstances or constituency reactions may force senators or representatives to recapture their initiative and take further legislative action. The resulting process may very well resemble a continuing dialogue between the branches of government—a dialogue that would be better informed if each branch understood the other's ways of doing things.

Observations of a State Court Judge

Hans A. Linde

-»>X<<-

These remarks offer a perspective on relations between judges and legislators in one state capital. I make no pretense of speaking about state legislators generally. In fact, I believe that what happens in state capitols is a function of different political cultures in each state, more than of legal arrangements and formal standards.

I do, however, suggest that there are certain characteristics common to state courts and state legislatures that distinguish their problems from those of federal courts and Congress and that color the interaction between them. Practices in the states cast doubt on some generalizations and shibboleths about judicial involvement in legislation at the national level. I seek to discuss those features of the state environment, offer a framework for examining the role of the judge with respect to different kinds of legislative matters, explore some of the norms that apply to judicial communications to the legislature, and provide some thoughts about possible improvements.

Distinguishing Characteristics of the States

The active participation of state judges in the policy process is much more taken for granted and much less controversial than the involvement of federal judges in the national government. A variety of factors account for this view in the states.

First, the state judiciary has always had broad jurisdiction over a wide range of subjects, most prominently the traditional responsibility for common law doctrine. The public accepts—indeed, expects—the courts to be responsible for much of the substance of the law as well as for day-to-day decisions. Nothing is more important in the public's perception of and reaction to the judiciary than the courts' role in criminal law. It is the essential issue in judicial elections, and candidates feel compelled to address it. The responsibility of state supreme courts to regulate the legal profession gives the judiciary an added visible public role.

Second, the judiciary is perceived as being a more professional and permanent institution than state legislatures, which meet only intermittently and have relatively weak institutional structures or traditions of pursuing a complex subject, either during or between sessions. Adding to this sense of relative weakness is the perception that legislators in many states are even more driven by special interests, partisanship, and personal ambitions than members of Congress.

Third, most state judges are elected to or retained in office by popular vote, either competitively or in retention elections. As elected representatives, like legislators, they feel less hesitant to offer their policy views than do appointed judges. The manner of their selection gives state judges a defense against being regarded as a "bevy of platonic guardians." Also, many state judges, by dint of prior political experience as legislators or prosecutors, are quite familiar with the legislative branch and feel comfortable interacting with it.

Fourth, the smaller geographic distance of state judges from their state capitals makes it relatively easy for them to stay in touch with legislative activities. In contrast, I would think that it would be hard for federal judges across the nation to monitor events in the U.S. Congress.

Fifth, in at least a dozen states justices can render advisory opinions to the legislative and executive branches.[1] That kind of interaction is constitutionally prohibited at the national level.

Sixth, many governors have an item veto that proponents or opponents can ask them to use on parts of legislation that have an effect on the courts. This has implications for judicial communications with the legislature as well as with the executive.

Finally, another feature of many state governments—direct popular legislation through the initiative and referendum—raises interesting questions about judges' relation to lawmaking. If it is appropriate for judges to testify

1. In Colorado, Delaware, Maine, Massachusetts, and Rhode Island, courts of last resort may issue advisory opinions in cases within their *mandatory* subject-matter jurisdiction (cases in which the court must reach a decision on the merits). In Alabama, Colorado, Florida, Louisiana, Michigan, New Hampshire, North Carolina, and South Dakota, courts of last resort may issue advisory opinions in cases within their *discretionary* subject-matter jurisdiction (cases in which a court can decline review on the merits). In Florida and South Dakota, the courts may issue advisory opinions in cases within their discretionary subject-matter jurisdiction only to the governor. National Center for State Courts, *1984 State Appellate Court Jurisdiction Guide for Statistical Reporting, Summary Tables* (Williamsburg, Va.: National Center for State Courts, 1985), pp. 34–45.

before a legislative committee, it must be proper for them to make a speech for or against an initiative, when the people themselves are the legislature. After all, the Constitution says that the legislative power is reserved to the people except insofar as the legislature has been given some of it—so that the people are the legislature in cases of direct popular election.

Diverse Judicial Relationships with the Legislature

Despite all of these differences, state judiciaries are similar to their federal counterpart in the kinds of institutional arrangements they have for interacting with the legislative branch. A 1985 study by the National Center for State Courts describes how state court administrators keep track of pending bills, inform judges of legislative developments, and propose measures of importance to court administration on behalf of the judicial system. Three states— California, New York, and Washington—have distinct legislative divisions within their administrative offices (with one planned in New Jersey). Although other state administrative offices may not have formal legislative departments, many are active in the process of legislative review of bills directly affecting judicial administration and employ staff persons to respond to the legislature. These include Connecticut, Georgia, Illinois, Iowa, Kentucky, Minnesota, Missouri, New Mexico, Oklahoma, Oregon, Pennsylvania, Texas, and Wisconsin. Most state court administrative offices have a role in the initiation of legislation dealing with judicial administration, typically working through the Judicial Conference of the state.[2] In Oregon, for example, two staff attorneys work for the state court administrator.

These institutional arrangements are concerned with "housekeeping" matters—questions of resources, such as the number of judges, staff, and facilities needed to maintain the judicial system. But this concern with "housekeeping" legislation obscures the diversity of judicial concerns and possible involvement with the legislature. I am not aware of any study that reaches further to examine how judges may influence substantive legislation for reasons other than its effect on judicial administration.

To go beyond what one might call housekeeping legislation, it is necessary to identify, first, different types of legislative and policy proposals; second, the position held by different judges in expressing views on these policies; and third, the formal or informal modes of expressing such views. The table on page 120 visualizes these different questions and suggests some tentative and not very surprising answers to them.

2. Memorandum, "The Role of the Administrative Office of the Courts in the Review and Initiation of Legislation," National Center for State Courts, January 14, 1985.

Subjects and Forms of Judicial-Legislative Communication at the State Level, by Role of Judge

Subject and form	Role of judge			
	Chief justice as statutory head of judicial branch	Chief justice or other spokesman for Judicial Conference	Judge as member of official reform agency	Judge as individual or as spokesman of minority view
Institutional concerns of court system (jurisdiction, procedures, resources, judicial selection, and institutional reform)	Communications dealing with resources (staffing, budget, space, court administration)	Communications dealing with jurisdiction and procedure, judicial selection methods, standards of judicial conduct	Communications dealing with jurisdiction and procedure, judicial selection methods	Communications dealing with minority views, special interests of one level or type of court
Professional standards of the bar	…	State supreme court	…	…
Personal concerns of judges as a class (salaries, pensions, and fringe benefits; working conditions)	Communications proper as an aspect of total available resources	Communications proper	Communications proper	Communications proper, if identified as a minority or individual view
Substantive law and policy	Communications not proper	Communications not proper	Communications proper	Communications proper when expressing personal views and avoiding (1) disqualification from a case, (2) doubts about judicial impartiality and nonpartisanship
Form and style of communication	Formal[a]	Formal[a]	Formal[a]	Formal if expressing dissenting or minority views; as individual, either formal or informal[a]

a. *Formal* means on the record, not avoiding attribution, whether addressing lawmakers directly or indirectly through addressing the profession or the public.

One should distinguish between (1) legislation that is of importance to the judiciary (meaning the institutional functioning of the court system or any part of it), (2) legislation that is of importance to judges as a class of public servants, and (3) legislation involving matters of substantive or general public policy. It oversimplifies matters to speak in terms of the judiciary to the exclusion of roles played by individual judges as proponents or critics of proposed legislation.

Institutional concerns include the provision of adequate numbers of judges and staff, courtrooms, and offices—in short, issues of budgets and money. They also include questions of jurisdiction and procedure, methods of judicial selection, and standards of conduct for judges and lawyers. Some of these are concerns for which a state's law may place responsibility in the chief justice alone. Some are placed in the responsibility of the Supreme Court. Some are concerns of all judges, often formally organized in a Judicial Conference. These concerns are expected to be communicated to legislators and are done so formally. In thirty-three of the fifty states, for example, the chief justice testifies before the legislature about the judiciary's budget.[3] In Iowa and Maine, other justices of the court of last resort assume this responsibility. In Virginia, although the state court administrator presents legislative testimony about the judiciary's budget, the state's chief justice meets with key legislators to discuss budgetary concerns of the judiciary before the budget season.

The personal concerns of judges as a class have to do with salaries, pensions, fringe benefits, and working conditions. Judges, collectively or individually, feel free to express their views on the subject, on the record.

A more interesting question is how judges may contribute to general, substantive legislation that only indirectly affects the courts and where the institutional effect on the courts is not the point of the judges' contribution. Tort law is one of many good examples.

For at least sixty years, since the flowering of legal realism, state courts have been exhorted, not only by plaintiffs' lawyers, but also by most torts professors, to be "creative"—by which they mean to find theories of civil recovery for plaintiffs and to discard old defenses (for instance, charitable immunity, intrafamily immunities, contributory negligence, or the so-called

3. These states are Alabama, Arizona, Arkansas, Colorado, Connecticut, Delaware, Florida, Georgia, Illinois, Indiana, Kentucky, Louisiana, Maryland, Massachusetts, Michigan, Minnesota, Mississippi, Missouri, Nebraska, Nevada, New Mexico, North Carolina, North Dakota, Oklahoma, Oregon, South Carolina, South Dakota, Texas, Utah, Vermont, Washington, Wisconsin, and Wyoming. Marcia J. Lim, memorandum, "Appearance of Chief Justice Before the Legislature Regarding the Budget," National Center for State Courts, March 27, 1986.

fireman's rule). The great triumph for common-law torts buffs, of course, was to develop strict liability for injuries caused by defective products under court-made tort doctrine rather than under the commercial codes. Other areas of current activity include liability of employers for wrongful discharge, liability for psychic harm caused by injuring family members, liability for "outrageous conduct," and landlords' tort liability for injuries caused by conditions of leased premises.

The present point is not whether state courts have such authority or whether a particular innovation is desirable. The point is that practitioners and legislators as well as commentators assume that change in tort law is properly something to be left to judges. Proposals that the legislature actually legislate on tort issues such as product liability or professional malpractice are opposed on grounds that tort law should be left to judges for case-by-case development. These issues get into legislatures only as political battles between large interest groups, in which defendants and their insurers are perceived to have all the money. The legal profession routinely praises courts as being superior lawmakers to the legislatures, and often legislators are happy to leave politically unproductive areas of policy to the courts or to anyone who will deal with them.

So state judges are used to being regarded as experts on substantive legal policies. To the extent that they do comment about substantive law and policy in the context of proposed legislation, they do so as private citizens, with expertise in specific areas, and when an expression of views would not result in disqualification from a case or endanger confidence in judicial impartiality and nonpartisanship.

Norms

A variety of norms or provisions are invoked with respect to judicial communications to the legislature. They include separation of powers, petition for redress of grievance, codes of judicial conduct, and prudential constraints. Taken together, they suggest that the judiciary, or its judges, can exercise considerable discretion.

Separation of Powers

The discussion of judicial-legislative communications abounds with references to separation of powers. But is this a political slogan more than a legal obstacle? In many states, the answer is not derived merely from the affirmative allocation of powers to the separate branches; it is stated also as a negation. For example, the Oregon state constitution (article III, sec. 1) says:

The powers of the Government shall be divided into three separate departments, the Legislative, the Executive . . . and the Judicial; and no person charged with official duties under one of these departments shall exercise any of the functions of another, except as in this Constitution expressly provided.

Under this section, an Oregon trial judge was reprimanded for teaching a class in a state college (a function of the executive branch), and it took a constitutional amendment to make teachers and professors eligible to serve in the legislature.

But note that when it is examined as law, the separation-of-powers clause says nothing about judges speaking in favor of or against legislation of any kind, whether as witnesses or in public, when speaking for the judiciary or as individuals, as long as they have no vote in actually passing or rejecting legislation. Again, this distinction is questionable when a state constitution, like Oregon's, reserves the legislative power to the people by means of the initiative and referendum. Should judges refrain from voting in referenda on legislation? Should they not sign petitions to put a measure on the ballot? May they "advise" the public on the merits of legislation submitted to a plebiscite?

Another shortcoming of "separation of powers" as a reason for judicial silence on legislation is that the constitutional text applies equally to the executive branch, and no one would suggest that executive officials should be silent on pending legislation. Separation of powers becomes a real problem, rather, in devising systems in which judges join in making rules subject to legislative review and disapproval (as in Oregon's Council on Court Procedures) or promulgating sentencing guidelines; and there the problem is the familiar one of partial delegation with strings attached, a constitutional obstacle for the legislature, not for the judges. So "separation of powers" is only a label for a sense of the fitness of things, not a legal obstacle to communication between judges and lawmakers.

Petition for Redress of Grievances

Another constitutional provision that judges might invoke—although it is rarely discussed—allows them to petition for redress of grievances when they do so as individuals or groups. The judiciary is a part of the government and cannot as an institution invoke this provision. The distinction has significance when, for instance, judges disagree over the allocation of funds among levels of judges or among salaries, pensions, and fringe benefits.

Codes of Judicial Conduct

The canons of judicial conduct prepared by the American Bar Association and adopted by many courts address the conduct of judges when acting as individuals more than as a collectivity. Canon 4 expressly allows judges to "speak, write, lecture, teach, testify in public hearings, and participate in other activities concerning the law, the legal system, and the administration of justice" as long as this does not "cast doubt on [their] capacity to decide impartially any issue that may come before [them]."[4]

The canon specifies that judges "may appear at a public hearing before an executive or legislative body or official on matters concerning the law, the legal system and the administration of justice," and that they "may otherwise consult with an executive or legislative body, but only on matters concerning the administration of justice."[5] Note that the canon confines "consulting" with executive or legislative officials to "matters concerning the administration of justice." The distinction shows that judges are not obliged to remain silent on controversial issues of legal policy, since the canon lets judges speak, write, or testify on such issues; the point of the distinction seems to be that beyond "consulting" on the narrower matters of judicial administration, judges should express their views on the record.

In Oregon, judges acting collectively confine their recommendations to the facets of legislation that directly affect the courts; they avoid taking positions on issues of social policy. But individual judges sometimes are quite active in proposing or opposing legislation in areas of law in which they have expertise.

Prudential Constraints

Are there obvious and well-defined prudential constraints on judicial lobbying? Again, the answer may concern either the interests of the judicial branch as a whole or the interests of an individual judge.

From the standpoint of the judiciary, it is generally thought unseemly for judges, individually or in groups, to take positions contrary to that of the chief justice or of a majority of the Judicial Conference. It may also be counterproductive. To avoid this, subjects that are controversial among the judges themselves are likely to be taken off the agenda on which the Judicial Conference will take a position. A good chief justice also may gently dissuade individual judges from pursuing the issue in public appearances before

4. American Bar Association, *Model Rules of Professional Conduct and Code of Judicial Conduct* (ABA, 1983), pp. 140–41.
5. Ibid.

legislative committees if he thinks it might harm other objectives of the judicial branch, although he would be careful not to inhibit the judge from less visible advocacy.

In any case, I think it is important that judges who do not agree with the position of the Judicial Conference or the chief justice in his role as chief administrator have an opportunity to express their views to the legislature. They should be able to provide the benefit of their expertise in their capacity as private individuals. Although the Judicial Conference in Oregon maintains that the judicial branch will not involve itself in substantive law legislation, it permits individual judges to transmit their ideas to the legislature or take positions dissenting from that of the Judicial Conference.

The prudential considerations from the standpoint of the individual judge are more complex and can hardly be given systematic form. Individual judges differ as to expertise, background, friendships with political people, credibility as nonpartisan or impartial advisers on public policy questions, and ambitions for the future. As I have already indicated, federal judges are more likely to feel constrained about uttering public positions about controversial issues than are state judges who must stand for election and are expected to take public stances. The extent to which this is true could vary from state to state.

Possible Improvements

In assessing possible improvements, I think attention should be given to creating or strengthening mediating institutions. Before setting forth my views on this subject, I want to note some of the problems in definition surrounding improvements in law and judicial administration.

Judicial Contribution to Law Improvement

The literature on the role of judges in legislation speaks rather piously of "improvement in the law and in judicial administration," joining two concepts in a single phrase. Commingling the two ideas is good political cover in a delicate area, but it should not obscure the fact that law reform and improvement in the administration of justice can be quite different agendas. Often the way to improve the administration of justice is to change substantive laws, but the fact that a change helps courts to decide cases better or faster does not mean that the change is good public policy.

The Oregon Supreme Court has used opinions to exhort the legislature to state explicitly whether a change in the law is to apply retrospectively. It has encouraged reducing different statutes of limitation to a single period or two periods in order to stop turning good but stale tort claims belatedly into bad contract or property claims. It has recommended clarification of an obscure formula for comparative fault. These all affect substantive interests as well as, one hopes, reducing needless litigation and appeals. But what about statutory attorney fee provisions? Codification of standards for exemplary or other statutory damages? Changes in immunities, or in the law of employee rights against purely discretionary discharge? Any use of law to provide new protections (for instance, for the environment) or new remedies (for instance, for consumers) brings new burdens and costs rather than "improvements" to judicial administration.

Major illustrations of the interplay between substantive law and judicial administration occur in any field that involves a massive caseload. Workers' compensation and family law are examples. As I have already mentioned, however, the central political concern in many state courts tends to be criminal law.

The most important recent example is the choice between two policies for dealing with driving under the influence of intoxicants. In Oregon a few years ago, the official Commission on the Judicial Branch recommended emphasis on obligatory suspension or revocation of drivers' licenses. This could be administered by administrative due process without jury trials or assigned counsel, and it could be followed by vigorous enforcement and greater penalties for driving while suspended, which does not leave room for many defenses. Other groups recommended heavy penalties for driving under the influence, an offense that does lend itself to defenses and is far costlier in judicial and public defender resources. The legislature politically preferred the punitive approach.

In short, when one thinks about "law improvement," it should be remembered that what is at issue is not simply administration or resources but also changes in the substantive law. The battle is over what the law should be in the courts, which can involve a clash of basic values not captured by the term "law improvement."

Mediating Institutions

Are there existing or potential institutions through which judges can offer both their critical insights about the shortcomings of existing laws and their suggestions for improvements to the legislatures? Some nonofficial organizations are familiar: for instance, the bar associations (in which, however, the experts also have clients), and the American Law Institute (which may be more scholarly but does not have open membership). The more challenging question is how and where to locate an ongoing, systematic interest in the quality of the legal order as a whole in an official body that can also get proposed reforms on the legislative agenda.

Whatever might be true of ministries of justice in different parliamentary democracies, the Department of Justice and its state equivalents under state attorney generals are probably not the best bodies as presently organized. They are too political and too preoccupied with the law enforcement function to be accepted by the bench and bar as the chief agency for reform in general civil law. Their present organization and focus could, of course, be changed, but that would mean a major shift in the American tradition. And the judiciary certainly would not want its institutional concerns mediated through any executive department, least of all the one that represents the executive branch before the courts.

When the federal government has wanted to place other long-term policy areas at some distance from the immediate political administration, it has found alternative institutions for doing so, such as the National Institutes of Health.

One might take a look at the way legislation is prepared in Sweden. It is my impression that Swedish ministries are rather small and expert commissions are assembled to draft legislation. Similar bodies are used in Germany and of course in the form of Royal Commissions in the United Kingdom. Most of these, however, are assembled ad hoc, after a problem has made it onto the political agenda. What is needed is a permanent, ongoing forum.

Many states, possibly half of them, have some form of permanent statutory law revision commissions.[6] So far as I know, only Louisiana's has judges among its members.[7] I earlier mentioned Oregon's temporary Commission on the Judicial Branch, which also included judges. These bodies offer an accepted and respectable official forum in which judges individually or collectively can present proposals for legislative consideration, along with the bar association committees and other informal channels previously mentioned.

But the question of whose expertise or wisdom is accorded official status is inescapable in any official advisory body. It is not peculiar to the participation of judges. I suggest a few safeguards. First, the subject on which their advice is sought should be one on which genuine expertise, rather than mere policy preference, is important. Second, the body's advice should be given in a form

6. In California, for instance, two legislators and seven executive appointees serve on the California Law Revision Commission. There seems to be no official bar against judicial appointees. *California Government Code,* sec. 8281 (West Supplement, 1988). In New York, the commission consists of four legislators and five executive appointees. *New York Legislative Law,* sec. 70 (Consolidated Laws Service, 1979).

7. Louisiana has five judges, two executive officers, and many practitioners and law professors. 24 *Louisiana Revised Statutes Annotated,* sec. 202 (West, 1975 and Supplement, 1986).

and at a time that leaves it open for public as well as expert scrutiny, criticism, and the formulation of alternative views—before a proposal is taken up for debate in the legislature, the forum ultimately responsible for the policy decision.

If the federal judiciary wants to create its own body of "wise men" through which judicial suggestions for legislation might be channeled to Congress without necessarily representing the official position of the chief justice or the judiciary, might it not find a pool of experienced and respected volunteers for such a panel among the senior judges who no longer are obliged to hear cases? It must be recognized, of course, that given the divergent policy perspectives of any body of judges, the selection of the members of such a group would have to be carefully conceived.

To sum up, the relationships of judges to state legislators and to members of Congress have much in common, despite important differences in the respective legislative institutions and in community expectations of the role of judges. There are no insurmountable legal obstacles to useful interaction between judges and legislators in the development of good policies with respect to the judicial institution or to substantive law. What is important is to maintain clear distinctions as to whether a judge speaks for the institutional concerns of the judicial branch, for the personal interests of judges as a group, or as an individual citizen expressing his or her own policy views.

Judicial-Legislative Relations in England

Patrick S. Atiyah

->>X<<-

To understand the nature of judicial-legislative relations in England, it is first necessary to grasp that the constitutional and institutional arrangements in Britain differ so greatly from those in the United States that the very nature of the judicial role in England differs in essential respects from that role in America.[1] Indeed, the nature of the executive and legislative functions also differs very greatly in the two countries, but there is a sense in which the different role of the executive is the key to the different roles of the other two branches.

Putting it bluntly and briefly, in Britain the government *is* the executive, which in modern times has had sufficient control of the legislature to secure the passage of whatever legislation it wishes. Given also the absence of any constitutional constraints on the legislative powers of Parliament,[2] it follows that the judicial role has come to be of less and less political significance in England. The judiciary has become a more professional and a less political body precisely because the executive has little reason to control the political composition of the judiciary. At the same time, and no doubt partly because there is little political tension between the judiciary and the executive (or

This paper draws heavily on a book by the present author and Robert S. Summers, *Form and Substance in Anglo-American Law: A Comparative Study in Legal Reasoning, Legal Theory, and Legal Institutions* (Oxford University Press, 1987). I am grateful to Professor Summers for allowing me to draw on some joint materials for this paper.

1. I refer in this paper to "England" because England has a distinct legal system and judiciary, and it is with England that I am concerned; but I also often refer to "Britain" because England has no separate political institutions, and it would sound distinctly odd to refer to the "English" Parliament or cabinet. Even "Britain" is inaccurate in regard to some political institutions that are those of the whole United Kingdom, but this usage is common.

2. The general consensus remains that Parliament has unrestricted legislative authority, though there are today academic doubts about its legislative authority with respect to two matters: Scotland and the European Economic Community. For an introduction to these two issues, see Patrick S. Atiyah, *Law in Modern Society* (Oxford University Press, 1983), pp. 60–64.

legislature), the executive (and the legislature) can afford to treat the judiciary handsomely in such matters as salary, status, and protection from public criticism.

In addition, relations between the judiciary and the executive are, in a sense, mediated in England by the lord chancellor, a person who embodies in his official duties a profound violation of the fundamental American constitutional doctrine of the separation of powers. The lord chancellor is a judge, a cabinet minister, and a member of the legislature, and there is no doubt that relations between the judiciary and legislature revolve around his position to a very substantial degree. I will therefore begin this paper with a short account of the key role of the lord chancellor; I shall then say something of the nature of the judicial role in modern Britain; and I shall then show how the institutional differences between Britain and the United States influence the relationship between judge and legislature even in such matters as lawmaking and the interpretation of statutes.

The Lord Chancellor

Institutionally speaking, the lord chancellor is a very anomalous figure.[3] He is first a politician and a member of the cabinet. In that capacity, he plays a full political role and is in no sense expected to behave differently from other politicians simply because he also has other nonpolitical functions. For instance, in his political capacity, he is expected to abide by the general convention of collective responsibility, which means that he must be prepared publicly to support government policy once it has been decided upon by the cabinet.

As a cabinet minister, the lord chancellor is, of course, in the same position as all other cabinet ministers, which means that he is appointed by and may be removed by the prime minister and also goes out of office if the government resigns or is defeated in an election. Some past lord chancellors have played a relatively minor political role, concentrating on their judicial and other nonpolitical work, but Lord Hailsham, lord chancellor from 1970–74 and 1979–87, had a long political career before becoming lord chancellor for the first time. He was a contender for the Conservative party leadership in 1963 and continued to play a vigorous political role.

As a politician, the lord chancellor is also head of a department of state,

3. The lord chancellor's office has surprisingly been very little studied or written about in modern times, so citations here are sparse. What is written here is largely common knowledge in English political and legal circles. Some idea of the range of the lord chancellor's functions in modern times can be gleaned from R. F. V. Heuston, *Lives of the Lord Chancellors, 1885–1940* (Oxford University Press, 1987); and Heuston, *Lives of the Lord Chancellors, 1940–1970* (Oxford University Press, 1987).

and in that capacity, he has responsibility for overseeing a number of administrative and executive functions, for example, the legal aid scheme, law reform bodies, and the administrative side of the work of the courts. He also has general oversight of the workings of the legal professions, insofar as their work impinges on government or legislation. In addition, the lord chancellor is responsible for legal aspects of many international treaties and conventions, especially those which impinge directly on the work of the courts, for instance, the many modern conventions on reciprocal enforcement and recognition of judgments of the courts of foreign countries and foreign arbitrations.

Another small department of which the lord chancellor is the responsible minister and political head is the immensely important Office of the Parliamentary Counsel. This office (which until recently was nominally under the Treasury) is responsible for the drafting of all government legislation (which in Britain means nearly all legislation that is actually passed), and it has an iron grip on the shape and form of the statute book. I shall, however, postpone discussion of the role of this office until a later point. At this point I merely stress the crucial importance of the lord chancellor in his mediating capacity between judges and legislature. For example, if there is anxiety about the judicial workability of some proposed legislation, the lord chancellor can consult senior members of the judiciary and use his influence, on the basis of such consultation, to influence the shape of the legislation.[4]

Above all, the lord chancellor is responsible for most judicial appointments. He appoints virtually all judges in England, including lower judges, part-time judges, and magistrates, and he can also remove many of them. High Court judges are nominally appointed by the queen, but the appointments are (by standard constitutional convention) made on the recommendation of the lord chancellor. In only a few cases of appointment to the highest judicial offices the queen acts on the advice of the prime minister rather than the lord chancellor, but even in these cases the prime minister would undoubtedly consult the lord chancellor. Except for appointments of this last character, there is no control or oversight of the lord chancellor's powers of appointment, although it is evident that wide consultation among the judiciary and the senior bar takes place before all higher appointments.[5]

4. Thus the lord chancellor consulted the judges as to whether they felt that the rather broad judgments of public interest required of them in the bill that became the Restrictive Trade Practices Act of 1956 could be handled "judicially" within the British judicial tradition, that is, "nonpolitically." The judges responded that they could be. See R. B. Stevens and B. S. Yamey, *The Restrictive Practices Court: A Study of the Judicial Process and Economic Policy* (London: Weidenfeld and Nicholson, 1965), esp. chap. 3.

5. See *Judicial Appointments* (Her Majesty's Stationery Office, May 1986), setting out some

In addition to being a cabinet minister, the lord chancellor is actually a judge; indeed, he is the head of the English judiciary. He is expressly designated by statute as president of the Supreme Court (though, confusingly, the English Supreme Court is not supreme, nor one court, comprising only the High Court and the Court of Appeal).[6] He also presides over the House of Lords, sitting in both its legislative and its judicial capacity (when it actually sits today as a committee of the house). Because the office has so many other duties, not all lord chancellors sit frequently in the judicial committee of the House of Lords, and some recent ones have sat quite rarely; but Lord Hailsham did seem to make an effort to sit regularly, if not very frequently. In one or another of his many capacities—it is not always possible to say in which—the lord chancellor also exercises a potent influence over the practice and procedures of the judicial committee of the House of Lords, for example, by inviting retired law lords to sit in particular appeals. In recent years, the lord chancellor has also played a particularly influential role in securing the agreement of the other judges in the House of Lords to the Practice Statement of 1966, by which the house asserted its power to overrule its own previous decisions, and more recently, to the change of practice that has resulted in a single opinion normally being given in decisions where there are no dissents. He has also formulated, in agreement with the judges, bodies of informal rules (known as the Kilmuir rules) concerning appropriate standards of behavior for the judiciary in relation to such matters as media appearances or writing for the press.

Finally, the lord chancellor is a member of the legislature. He will usually have been, before his appointment, a member of the House of Commons, and although he must then move to the less important House of Lords, he remains an important legislative figure. As he presides over the House of Lords, he is one of the government's chief representatives in that house and must, in that capacity, defend government policy, assist in carrying bills through the house, and, if need be, defend the role of the judiciary against criticism.

Another important facet of the lord chancellor's unique constitutional role is that by convention, if not by strict law, nobody is eligible for appointment to the office unless he has been a barrister of considerable experience and would therefore have been regarded as eligible for ordinary judicial office. This means that the lord chancellor has gone through the same sort of apprenticeship as other English judges and is a real member of "the club."

---

of the practices and procedures followed by the lord chancellor in relation to judicial appointments, esp. p. 6.

6. Supreme Court Act, 1981, 11 Halsbury's Statutes, 4th ed. 760, sec. 1(2).

Despite his political role, therefore, he identifies with the judiciary, and the other judges feel able to call on him privately to discuss issues concerning their relationship with the executive or the legislature.

One role the lord chancellor fulfills, which has not received any official recognition but is of particular relevance to this paper, is that of mediator between the judiciary and the other two branches of government. As head of the judiciary, the lord chancellor is able, and usually is anxious, to present the judicial point of view to the government and the legislature, whenever occasion demands. The last lord chancellor (Lord Hailsham) did this very successfully in relation to a number of important issues. For example, judicial salaries were not allowed to fall significantly behind the rate of inflation, and indeed in 1985 were raised to exceptionally high levels. Judicial salaries can be increased (though not reduced) by the lord chancellor with the concurrence of anther minister,[7] and in 1985 the salary of High Court judges was raised to £60,000 under this procedure. By English standards, this was an exceptionally high salary (at the equivalent of over $100,000, it would be high even compared with most American judicial salaries). The increase provoked such a political storm that it was only very narrowly carried in a vote in the House of Commons, despite the government's normally huge majority.[8]

There are many other issues concerning the law and its administration on which the lord chancellor can exercise a powerful influence by virtue of his extraordinary position. In particular, he is able to use his considerable weight to see that the views of lawyers and judges prevail over what may be a lay opinion widely popular in Parliament. The importance of this is doubled by the fact that the smallness and homogeneity of the English judiciary (and sometimes the bar) mean that there is often an almost unanimous "legal" opinion on some issue that may not always be shared by nonlawyers. One example of this is the way in which demands for minimum sentences for certain crimes have always been successfully resisted by the government. The view of lawyers and judges in England is almost always against minimum sentences on the ground that it is impossible to eliminate the ultimate discretion of the trial judge without risk of serious injustice. The lord chancellor is able to present this view in the cabinet and (if necessary) in the House of Lords. Similarly, when the Roskill Committee on the trial of fraud offenses recently recommended abolition of the defense's right of peremptory challenge to members of the jury, the government accepted this recommendation, supported (presumably) by the lord chancellor in the knowledge that

7. Ibid. at 769, sec. 12.
8. See Hansard (Commons), 6th ser., vol. 83 (1985), cols. 990–1012.

this reform would be desired by the judges, even if opposed by many members of Parliament, where of course the trial bar is well represented.[9]

Then again, the lord chancellor is always quick to defend members of the judiciary against uninformed, and sometimes unreasonable, public or parliamentary criticisms. Occasionally in England, as no doubt elsewhere, judges catch the headlines with unfortunate or discourteous remarks or strange exercises of discretion, for instance in sentencing. To some extent, judges are already protected against unfair criticism in Parliament by the rule of procedure that the conduct of a judge can only be criticized on a substantive motion, and not by way of side comment on different issues.[10] But such a rule can never wholly restrict questions or comments on judicial behavior, and therefore the lord chancellor is well placed to defend the judiciary against such criticism in the House of Lords and to ensure that other members of the government defend it in the House of Commons. The last lord chancellor made it clear that he might privately write to a judge drawing his attention to public reports of apparent discourtesy or other ill-considered remarks, but it is all the same helpful to the judiciary to have a spokesman in the cabinet and in Parliament to defend it against unfair criticism and more generally to represent its viewpoint.

Of course the role of the lord chancellor, and his ability to carry so much influence in Parliament and in the cabinet, is itself intimately linked with the fact that in modern times the judiciary in England is seen by most people, including lawyers and politicians, to be fundamentally a nonpolitical body with nonpolitical functions. It is therefore now necessary to say something of the judicial function and of the judges themselves.

The Judicial Function

The function of an English court, and especially an appellate court, differs in certain fundamental respects from the function of an American court, and these differences are important to an understanding of the judicial-legislative relationship. In particular, English courts accept unquestioningly their subordinate status to Parliament. Parliament can give orders, and the judge— like everyone else—must obey. There is no such thing as an unconstitutional statute in English law, and even though the courts can declare executive

9. See *Fraud Trials Committee Report* (HMSO, 1986), p. 130. The government has decided that the abolition of peremptory challenges should apply to all offenses: see *The Times*, July 9, 1986, p. 1. Legislation will, of course, be needed, but once a firm government decision has been made, the legislation is almost certain to be carried in due course.

10. See Erskine May, *Treatise on the Law, Privileges, Proceedings and Usage of Parliament*, 20th ed. (London: Butterworths, 1983), pp. 430–31.

action to be unlawful, such action can easily be legalized for the future. It is even possible, in extreme circumstances, to secure the passage of retrospective legislation to indemnify executive officials or ministers against illegalities. Furthermore, the English political machine is very efficient in production of ordinary legislation needed for updating the law. Much law reform that would be carried out in the United States by courts has been enacted in England by the legislature.[11] Thus the fact that the legislature is so active means that the judiciary needs to be less active—although some critics would maintain that English judges could nevertheless play a more vigorous role than they do. Moreover, this activity on the part of the legislature is not the spontaneous activity of legislators themselves: it nearly always stems from the executive, which exercises a general oversight and control of the lawmaking process in England quite unknown in the United States. What is quite clear is that the entire constitutional-political role of the legislature and the executive determines the role of judges and courts.

American courts of last resort are in general far more activist than English courts and also far less technically rulebound or formal in their approach to legal rules and other sources of formal legal reasoning such as judgments, precedents, and statutes. Further, the functions that the courts of last resort play in the two countries differ in significant ways. For instance, English courts, including even the House of Lords, take *stare decisis* much more seriously than do many judges in American courts of last resort. Even though the House of Lords now asserts the power to overrule its own decisions, it does this very sparingly indeed compared with the practice of the U.S. Supreme Court or even federal appeal courts.[12] One reason for this, in all probability, is the English judge's conception that he has a duty to apply the law, and that previous decisions in the courts of last resort *are* the law. English judges do recognize, of course, that they have a secondary lawmaking function where there are no statutes or prior decisions,[13] but these gaps in the law are relatively few and far between, in the English view.

Nearly all serious commentators in England agree that judges should avoid "political" decisions. In the United States, on the other hand, a large body of legal opinion holds that "judicial opinions are inescapably and rightly

11. For example, the Law Reform (Contributory Negligence) Act, 1945 (23 Halsbury's Statutes, 3d. ed. 789) introduced comparative negligence; the Crown Proceedings Act, 1947 (8 Halsbury's Statutes, 3d. ed. 844) abolished governmental immunity in tort; and the Unfair Contract Terms Act, 1977 (47 Halsbury's Statutes, 3d ed. 84) restricted the availability of contractual exculpatory clauses.

12. See Alan Paterson, *The Law Lords* (University of Toronto Press, 1982), chap. 7.

13. For one recent statement of this view, see Lord Roskill, "Law Lords, Reactionaries or Reformers?" 37 *Current Legal Problems* 247 (1984).

political."[14] The English position may be criticized as theoretically incoherent or indefensible: how can judges take account of policy factors in exercising their secondary function of lawmaking (as most English judges now admit must sometimes be done), if they are not to be "political"?[15] Clearly, the two positions are inconsistent unless a narrow meaning can be given to the term "political," and there may be serious difficulties in trying to do this. Since value choices underlie nearly all policy choices, and since selection of values is the essence of political controversy, it is hard to avoid the conclusion that all policymaking is a political activity.

If judges could claim that they only chose uncontroversial policies, where the underlying values would be widely or almost universally accepted, it might be argued that judicial policy decisions were nonpolitical; and the somewhat "positivist" nature of much English contemporary morality may lend support to the belief, or at least the appearance, that judges are not making controversial value choices when they decide policy questions. On the other hand, detailed examination of a number of areas of case law has led to the view that policy decisions in England cannot be explained in this way.[16] But however theoretically weak the position of the judges may be on this question, what matters for present purposes is that English judges believe that it is possible to make policy decisions (on the rare occasions when this is necessary) in a neutral way without seriously impinging on the general, formal, rule-oriented nature of the legal system. These beliefs are important, however ill-founded they may be, because they influence the judicial view of the proper function of courts of last resort and hence also the way they decide cases.

Constitutional Differences

There are constitutional factors in England that are notably absent in America and help explain why English judges perceive their own role in this rather narrow apolitical way. The difference in the constitutional positions of the courts of last resort in the two countries means that there are many political

14. Ronald Dworkin, "Political Judges and the Rule of Law," 64 *Proceedings of the British Academy* 259 (1978), noting that this is not a unanimous view in America. See also Richard A. Posner, *The Federal Courts: Crisis and Reform* (Harvard University Press, 1985), pp. 18–19, noting that "American law is inherently more political than English."

15. See, for example, *McLoughlin* v. *O'Brian* [1983] Appeals Cases 410, though note the view of Lord Scarman that judges should stick to principle and eschew policy, ibid., at 430. See also Roskill, "Law Lords," p. 258 (judges have a "policy" but not a "political" role). Also see John Bell, *Policy Arguments in Judicial Decisions* (Oxford University Press, 1983), pp. 4–7. There are signs that Lord Hailsham was more aware than most of his colleagues that policy judgments and politics are inseparable (see p. 5.)

16. See the conclusions of John Bell's study, ibid., chap. 9.

issues on which the judges have the last word in the United States, but this is not the case in England. In particular, there is the striking phenomenon of judicial review in the United States, which is unknown in England. This has been the subject of so much discussion in the literature of lawyers and political theorists that emphasis on it may have obscured a number of other equally important points.

First, there is a crucial, and indeed symptomatic, difference between the final appeal courts in the two countries. The U.S. Supreme Court is one collegial court, in which all the judges participate in all the decisions (unless a judge is disqualified from sitting in any particular case). But the House of Lords is not a collegial court; it is composed of about ten judges who are qualified to sit, rather than one single court. In practice the House of Lords sits in two panels, usually of five judges each, and the choice of which judges are to hear which appeals is usually made by administrative personnel, although occasionally the lord chancellor may invite a particular judge to sit in a particular appeal. This difference between English and American practice is highly significant, because it reflects the English belief that it is largely immaterial which judges hear which appeals; all American lawyers know that the Supreme Court could not possibly sit in panels without a radical change in its functions. Given the highly political nature of many of the decisions that court is called upon to make, the composition of a panel would frequently determine the outcome of the appeal. Moreover, given the case selection procedure of the Court, the body that selected the cases and allocated them to the different panels would become more important than the Supreme Court itself, clearly an impossible state of affairs.

Second, it is not only in constitutional adjudication that the relative position of the judiciary differs in the two countries. The American judiciary often has in practice the last word in statutory interpretation and in the resolution of common law disputes, because the legislative overturning of such decisions often requires a degree of legislative consensus that cannot be attained. The situation is very different in England. Any House of Lords decision with serious political implications is open to subsequent modification or reversal by Parliament. To be sure, it is rare for a judicial decision to be retrospectively overturned by Parliament—even the supreme and omnicompetent British Parliament rarely does that—but it is far from unknown.[17] But other decisions are very readily reversed. And in the British political system, this is no mere ritual phrase on the lips of judges anxious to disclaim ultimate

17. See, for example, War Damage Act, 1965 (38 Halsbury's Statutes, 3d. ed. 745) retrospectively overturning the decision of the House of Lords in *Burmah Oil Co.* v. *Lord-Advocate* [1965] Appeals Cases 75.

responsibility for the long-term state of the law. It is a reflection of political reality. A decision with serious political implications will inevitably be studied by the government, and if the government does not like it, proposals to modify or reverse it will be laid before Parliament and passed. It may occasionally happen that for some political reason the government feels unable to reverse a judicial decision which it would have preferred to see go the other way, but in the British political system this will be a rare event.[18] Of course, the urgency with which the government seeks legislation to reverse a decision of the courts will depend on the distaste the government feels for the decision and the degree to which it interferes with government policy or the proper functioning of the administration. It can sometimes be done with considerable haste.[19] In principle, the same is true for decisions that are not overtly political in their implications but simply cut across the policy of the government or a government department, even in matters of routine administration.[20]

Of course, even in the United States, judicial interpretation of legislative enactments and ordinary common law judicial decisions are in theory subject to legislative change. But it is often far more difficult to overrule decisions of courts of last resort than it is in England. The reasons for this have much to do with the basic role of the judiciary and its relationship to the executive and the legislature. Compared with England, the U.S. executive branch has far less influence over Congress (which may indeed be controlled by a different party), party lines are anyhow much less strongly observed in practice, and legislative procedure often gives disproportionate influence to the chairmen of committees and subcommittees. In short, the U.S. Congress seems less efficient in the production of legislation than the British Parliament. This gives the U.S. appellate courts greater freedom and a greater responsibility to pursue their own policies and values, even in those cases in which they are in principle subject to legislative reversal. This freedom is of course exercised vigorously by many U.S. courts, but the comparison with England suggests that one of the principal reasons that U.S. courts legislate so much is that U.S. legislatures legislate so little.[21]

18. A point not appreciated by Dworkin in his "Political Judges and the Rule of Law."

19. See, for example, the Trade Disputes Act, 1965 (37 Halsbury's Statutes, 3d. ed. 72) overturning the decision in *Rookes* v. *Barnard* [1964] Appeals Cases 1129.

20. See, for example, sec. 72 of the Supreme Court Act, 1981 (11 Halsbury's Statutes, 4th ed. 827), which overturned the decision in *Rank Film Distributors Ltd.* v. *Video Information Centre* [1981] 2 Weekly Law Reports 668 (restricting availability of orders requiring defendants to give information regarding pirated copyrights, etc.) decided only a few months previously.

21. Particularly when the failure of legislatures to act is due to procedural obstacles, something

The fact that U.S. courts are willing to perform many functions that in other countries would fall to the legislature naturally affects other members of the legal world. Law reformers, lobbyists, and political pressure groups are encouraged to turn to the courts for legal change in America, where in England they would always turn to Parliament, the government bureaucracy, or the political parties. It has been suggested that legal change in America is both more speedily and more cheaply obtained through the judicial than through the legislative process, which seems astonishing to the English lawyer.[22] Lobbyists and pressure groups rarely turn to the courts in England for political change, first because the courts are much less likely to respond, and second because any success obtained in the courts may easily prove short-lived, given the willingness of Parliament to reverse judicial decisions.

Because courts of last resort in the U.S. system know that their decisions are not likely to be subject to legislative reversal even when they are not immune from it, U.S. judges are much more free than their English colleagues to decide cases in accordance with their own personal value systems and predilections. There is much in American traditions and institutions to encourage them to do just that. In England it would be largely pointless for judges to try to forward political or policy values; their political role is so small compared to Parliament's, and the likelihood of legislative reversal of unpalatable political decisions so strong, that judges can only give policy the occasional nudge in this or that direction. Because many of these nudges are likely to be inconsistent with other judicial decisions, and the total effect of judicial decisions on public policy is so small, the whole exercise would seem futile to most judges. Besides, judges in England today are not in general politically oriented; if they were, they would not become judges. People who want to have a significant effect on policy in England go into politics. Both the function and the personal backgrounds of U.S. judges tend to be far more overtly political than those of their English counterparts. Almost by definition politicians tend to be either goal oriented or power ambitious; such people are more likely to decide questions of law in legal disputes on the basis of desired results in the legal system or in society at large. Judges who see their

that still seems common at least at the state level. Many American state judges seem to be influenced by the poverty of the legislative process and the consequent necessity for judicial activism. Mary C. Porter, "State Supreme Courts and the Legacy of the Warren Court: Some Old Inquiries for a New Situation," in Mary C. Porter and G. Alan Tarr, eds., *State Supreme Courts: Policymakers in the Federal System* (Westport, Conn.: Greenwood Press, 1982), pp. 3, 8–9.

22. Maurice Rosenberg, "Anything Legislatures Can Do, Courts Can Do Better?" 62 *American Bar Association Journal* 587 (1976); and Richard Neely, *How Courts Govern America* (Yale University Press, 1981), pp. 30, 71.

role as more professional and less political (and who may have no political background, like most modern English judges) may be less likely to decide cases in accordance with their own private beliefs and desires.

Case Selection

Case selection procedures are also an important part of this picture. The extent to which an appellate court can control the cases it will decide may not only facilitate but even encourage a court to see its role in more substantive terms, as that of carrying out various judicial innovations and reforms, rather than in more formal terms, as that of merely applying rules to correct errors of law. A court with a large number of cases to choose from can select those that will afford the most opportunities to advance desired policies rather than those in which formal law may have been most egregiously misapplied. Here again, practice differs in English and U.S. courts. Many U.S. appellate courts have acquired power to choose their own dockets, in the same way as the Supreme Court. This enables these courts to select the cases that they regard as the most suitable vehicles for making policy pronouncements designed to have a significant legal or social impact. Indeed, it is quite easy for such a court virtually to invite appeals on certain issues and then to select them for decision when they are presented. Thus one of the traditional restraints on the political powers of courts—that they cannot *initiate* policy decisions—is today much less operative in many U.S. courts of last resort. That some of these courts do actually use their power of selecting which cases to hear for political purposes seems indisputable.[23] Indeed, in the case of the Supreme Court, this seems not only an evident fact, but one whose legitimacy is now largely taken for granted.[24] The Supreme Court can be extremely selective in the cases that it chooses to hear and perhaps use in order to make policy decisions. In 1982, for instance, the Court agreed to hear only 3 percent of the cases for which petitions for certiorari review were filed.[25]

23. Doris M. Provine, *Case Selection in the United States Supreme Court* (University of Chicago Press, 1980), cites on p. 34 the statement of one (anonymous) justice who said he would vote not to take a case he thought "outrageously wrong" if he believed the court would affirm it. "I'd much prefer bad law to remain the law of the 8th Circuit or the State of Michigan than to have it become the law of the land." No English judge would behave in this way.

24. See, for example., the remarks of Chief Justice Vinson in 1949, cited in Joel B. Grossman, *Lawyers and Judges* (Wiley, 1965), p. 12. It is widely believed that the failure of the Freund Study Group's report (on reducing the burden of cases on the Supreme Court) to secure general support was due to the group's lack of appreciation of the importance of case selection to the role of the Supreme Court.

25. Francis J. Flaherty, "Inside the 'Invisible' Courts," *National Law Journal,* vol. 5 (May 2, 1983), p. 1.

It seems no exaggeration to conclude that—whatever the judges may say publicly—most (or at least many) U.S. courts of last resort see their primary function not as that of correcting errors in the lower courts, nor of overseeing the functioning of the lower courts, but of making law for the future. As long ago as 1927, even so moderate a judge as Cardozo expressed the view that the state's highest court existed not for the "individual litigant, but for the indefinite body of litigants."[26] Today, although the trend has its critics,[27] it is widely accepted that American appellate courts have a broad social function as innovators. Thus even though litigants may have a right of appeal to federal circuit courts, there seems an increasing tendency for those courts to grant the fullest consideration only to those cases offering opportunities for innovative decisionmaking. This approach has wide implications for the legal system as a whole. In particular, a legislature may feel that law reform is the business of the courts, rather than itself, even when the issues are strongly political.

In all these respects, the position in England differs quite fundamentally from that in the United States. In the first place, English courts would certainly reject the idea that courts ought to introduce social change. One recent extrajudicial pronouncement on the judicial role in England makes it clear that the primary function of the courts is still to determine disputes, and although "the decisions of the courts ought to reflect change which has been taking place," it is not the function of the courts to *initiate* or *prevent* social change.[28] This last view would almost certainly be noncontroversial among English lawyers and judges. What controversy there is concerns the degree to which the courts, as opposed to Parliament, have the responsibility for changing the law to keep pace with existing social change.

Regarding case selection, the position in England is that all appeals to the House of Lords come from the Court of Appeal, and either that court or the House of Lords' appellate committee has to grant leave to appeal.[29] Only applications to the House of Lords' appellate committee are comparable with

26. Robert A. Kagan and others, "The Evolution of State Supreme Courts," 76 *Michigan Law Review* 961, 973 (1978).

27. See Jerome Frank in *Aero Spark Plug Co.* v. *B. G. Corp.*, 130 F. 2d 290 (2d. Cir. 1942), cited in Jerome Frank, *Courts on Trial: Myth and Reality in American Justice* (Princeton University Press, 1949), pp. 286–88.

28. Sir Sydney (now Lord) Templeman, "An English View of the Judicial Function," in Harry W. Jones, ed., *Legal Institutions Today: English and American Approaches Compared* (American Bar Association, 1977), p. 6.

29. Administration of Justice (Appeals) Act, 1934 (25 Halsbury's Statutes, 3d. ed. 750); see generally Louis Blom-Cooper and Gavin Drewry, *Final Appeal: A Study of the House of Lords in Its Judicial Capacity* (Oxford: Clarendon Press, 1972), chap. 7.

appeals to the U.S. Supreme Court, and the total volume of applications for leave to appeal is very low compared with the number of cases heard.[30] There is nothing at all resembling the immense ratio of rejected to granted certiorari applications in the U.S. Supreme Court. The grounds on which leave to appeal is granted by the House of Lords' appellate committee are not always clear, and no doubt vary from case to case.[31] Dissent in the Court of Appeal is usually a sufficient ground. Other cases are taken because of their public importance (for example, tax cases or cases challenging the validity of some important governmental action), but given the general nature of the English judicial role and the apolitical background of the judges, it is almost unthinkable (as well as pointless) for leave to appeal to be granted by judges with the aim of furthering their own policy views. The only policy that seems to be clearly followed is to grant leave to appeal where lower court decisions appear to be aberrational or to depart from established law. It is also unthinkable for the House of Lords not to hear an appeal where conflicting decisions have been rendered by lower courts of equal authority (which anyhow rarely happens in England), for this would leave the law in a state of uncertainty unacceptable to the English legal profession.

Thus correcting errors in lower courts remains the major function of the English House of Lords, and is seen to be such by most judges of the House of Lords.[32] Although the broader public importance of their decisions is not irrelevant in the selection of cases for appeal, this public interest is usually seen to lie in clarifying the law or eliminating confusion following from lower court decisions. These are formal "rule of law" values.

Institutional Differences

Of course there are other institutional differences between England and the United States that also help account for the very different roles of the judiciary and their relationship to the legislature. In particular, the immense size of the United States and the limited nature of federal jurisdiction mean that the federal judiciary cannot operate in the same tight, hierarchical way that the English judiciary does. In England the smallness of the judiciary and the hierarchical structure of the courts mean that innovative judges may have

30. For instance, in 1982 there were only 110 applications for leave to appeal made to the House of Lords, of which 34 were allowed and 74 refused (two were withdrawn). See *Judicial Statistics: England and Wales 1982* (HMSO, 1983), p. 11. For earlier years, see Blom-Cooper and Drewry, *Final Appeal,* pp. 42–43.

31. As to applications to the Court of Appeal for leave to appeal from that court to the House of Lords, see Blom-Cooper and Drewry, *Final Appeal,* p. 140. The grounds for granting leave by the Court of Appeal are more easily discerned. Ibid., pp. 146–48.

32. Paterson, *The Law Lords,* p. 10.

great difficulty in having much impact on the legal scene. English judges who do not conform to the usual behavior are apt to be reversed by appeal courts or find themselves dissenting in multijudge courts.[33] This too discourages judicial activism and encourages the tendency to leave serious political issues to Parliament.

Another set of institutional factors may help explain some of the differences between the workings of the English and the American judiciary, and hence their relationship with the legislatures, though it is sometimes difficult to disentangle cause from effect. The procedure of appellate courts in the two countries is now very different indeed. In particular, the proceedings in English appellate courts remain almost entirely oral. Legal argument is presented in oral form, often at great length; argument before the House of Lords may last for several days. Very little is written down in the form of legal argument either in the Court of Appeal or the House of Lords.[34] In practice most appeal judges will read the papers filed with the court in advance, so that they are familiar with what the case is about when they take their seats. Nevertheless, to hear an argument in court, one might often suppose that the judges knew nothing about it when they first came into the courtroom. Counsel takes them through everything orally in open court, sometimes reading at length from documents, or opinions in cases, or the transcript of evidence. Much of this seems inefficient and time wasting, but it may have an effect on the way judges perceive their role. It probably makes English judges especially conscious of the facts of the particular case under appeal,[35] and may encourage them to see their function as the relatively narrow one of determining a dispute between two contending parties, rather than of attempting to settle the law to be applied over a wide range of similar cases.

This narrow focus of counsel and judges on the facts of the case and the immediate points at issue tends to make judges anxious about the possible effects of the decision on surrounding areas of the law if they stray too far.[36] The anxiety is compounded by the fear of creating uncertainty, which affects

33. Lord Denning's career sufficiently illustrates the difficulties facing an innovative English judge. He voluntarily stepped down from the House of Lords to become master of the rolls (president of the Court of Appeal) because he felt himself unable to influence decisions in a court of five members. See generally J. L. Jowell and J. P. W. B. McAuslan, eds., *Lord Denning: The Judge and the Law* (London: Sweet & Maxwell, 1984).

34. See Practice Note [1983] 1 Weekly Law Reports 1055.

35. See Sir Robert (now Lord) Goff, "The Search for Principle," 69 *Proceedings of the British Academy* 169 (1983) (commenting on influence of facts on decisions on points of law).

36. Lord Simon especially makes this point in *Miliangos v. George Frank (Textiles) Ltd.* [1976] Appeals Cases 471–72.

so many English lawyers and judges. American judges seem less worried by the specter of uncertainty and are more willing to leave new problems thrown up by the instant case to future cases.

Similarly, English appellate judges, when deciding questions of law, rely more heavily on the arguments of counsel and much less heavily on their own research.[37] In part this is forced on English judges by the lack of any research assistance and even of adequate secretarial help. English judges have no clerks to do research for them; if they want to research a problem, they must do it themselves. Moreover, little time is available for research, given the traditional English view that decisions (except in the House of Lords) ought to be handed down on the conclusion of the argument if at all possible. In the English Court of Appeal—the final appellate court for the vast majority of cases—most appeals are still decided at the conclusion of the oral argument and extempore oral opinions are delivered immediately. Furthermore, English Court of Appeal judges sit continuously during the legal term so that most research and writing have to be done in the evenings or on weekends.[38]

It is true that in the House of Lords, where judgment is never given until the law lords have had a chance to consider the case, there is more time for reflection and research and consultation with colleagues. Nevertheless, there is not a great deal of such research or consultation, partly because the facilities are scarcely adequate, but partly because of tradition.

These traditions encourage the judge to see himself in the role of a passive arbitrator who decides which of the rival contentions offered by opposing counsel is the better.[39] This discourages judges from setting off on voyages of discovery of their own, rejecting the views of both parties and fashioning their own result to match some private vision of the public good or the rights of the parties. Indeed, most English judges regard it as improper for a judge to rely on precedents or arguments that have not been canvassed by counsel.[40] English lawyers would be astonished at the way in which the U.S. Supreme Court, uninvited and without argument, overruled *Swift* v. *Tyson* in *Erie R.R. Co.* v. *Tompkins*.[41]

37. A majority of counsel who regularly appear before the House of Lords expressed the view that the Lords should "restrict the propositions of law in their speeches to matters covered by counsel in argument. . . ." Paterson, *The Law Lords,* pp. 20–21.

38. See Delmar Karlen, *Appellate Courts in the United States and England* (New York University Press, 1963), esp. pp. 152–54. There has been some relaxation of late with a view to providing Court of Appeal judges with more time to write opinions. Personal communication with various judges.

39. See Goff, *The Search for Principle,* pp. 182–84 (commenting on the "fragmented" nature of judges' vision of the law).

40. See Paterson, *The Law Lords,* p. 46.

41. 41 U.S. (16 Peters) 1 (1842); and 304 U.S. 64 (1938). To be fair, probably many

The fact that all higher judges in England have spent twenty years or more as successful barristers is also important as an indicator of the kind of person who becomes a judge, and therefore helps to explain the way the courts behave. Moreover, the judges and the senior members of the bar form a professional group of exceptionally homogenous background and values. It is thought important that members of this group should hold "moderate" views and "conventional" values and be traditional if not downright conservative in manner, deportment, and dress, and in general, shy of publicity, flamboyance, and eccentricity.

An English judge writing an opinion is doing something very similar to what he has been doing for perhaps twenty years as a barrister, writing large numbers of "counsel's opinions." He will have become highly expert at this task, which is conceived to be almost exclusively a technical inquiry into what the law is and not what it ought to be. This, together with other factors discussed above, helps to explain the more formal vision of law prevalent in England. Thus substantive policy and moral arguments are taken to be largely irrelevant to counsel seeking to determine what the law is, except insofar as he perceives how they may sway the judge in doubtful cases. Mostly, counsel concentrates on what he takes to be "the law" as laid down. What can be more natural for the judge who now finds himself writing judicial opinions to carry on in the same style? But the perspective is obviously different: counsel is performing a predictive exercise. He does not, like the judge, have to *decide* about political or moral considerations, and it is therefore to be expected that counsel will address such issues in a more neutral way. So it does not seem surprising if English judges, who have spent many years performing this sort of exercise as counsel, do not always appreciate that the neutral perspective may not be wholly appropriate for the judge, and tend to carry on in the same way.

These attitudes naturally encourage a "law is law" formal approach to rules and principles and discourage the activist judge who seeks to venture into the waters of policy, purposes, and instrumental lawmaking. Lower court judges are likewise unlikely to be candidates for promotion to appellate courts if they display deviant tendencies to reject or disregard appellate court precedents, just as barristers are unlikely to be candidates for appointment to judicial office if they have given any indication that they reject conventional ideas of *stare decisis* or embrace radical views of the judicial role. Appellate court judges—at least in the House of Lords—are free from such constraints,

---

American lawyers were astonished at this too, but the same thing happened in *Mapp* v. *Ohio* 367 U.S. 643 (1961).

but the conventional requirement for prior experience as a trial judge means that few judges reach the House of Lords under the age of sixty. By that time an English judge will have been exposed to at least thirty-five years of socializing pressure in the conventions of the judicial role. At such an age, an inclination for radical innovation is apt to wane. Over several centuries, only one judge—Lord Denning—can be said to have retained such tendencies. This does not mean that English judges—especially in higher courts—believe that they have no proper role in developing or modifying the law. Most of them believe that there is such a role, though many of them also believe, perhaps inconsistently, that judges should not meddle in "policy."

Of course, within the parameters of the English judicial tradition, levels of activism vary with the individual judges (as no doubt they do in America) and also with the times. But for present purposes, these variations in England are indeed "interstitial" if not glacial in comparison with the degree of policy orientation displayed by the more adventurous American judges. With very rare exceptions, English appellate judges for at least the past century have been professional lawyers whose main loyalty has been to the profession and to the law as a nonpolitical institution, as they thought it to be.[42]

In the long run, much of this mosaic fits together. English judges tend to be professional lawyers, apolitical, nonactivist, and more concerned with the case at hand than with laying down the law for the future. It is a fundamental principle of their faith that adjudication differs from legislation. This in turn encourages the executive to assume responsibility for keeping the law under review and to make regular proposals for change to Parliament, which in turn is not slow to respond.

The Making of Legislation

Parliament speaks to the judges in a very formal way: through statutes. Officially, it does not speak to the judges in any other way. No doubt informal discussions sometimes take place between senior judges and executive ministers, although (as I have already suggested) such communications will normally occur through the mediation of the lord chancellor. And no doubt, judges read the newspapers and learn what members of Parliament are

42. On the whole, the further one goes back, the more signs there are of occasional involvement of some judges in political controversy and political issues. The tradition of total political neutrality (which is of course seen as a myth by many) is perhaps no older than World War II, and even today the office of lord chancellor is a permanent embodiment of the relationship between the political and the judicial function. For the earlier periods, see Brian Abel-Smith and Robert Stevens, *Lawyers and the Courts: A Sociological Study of the English Legal System, 1750–1965* (London: Heinemann, 1967), chaps. 5, 11.

thinking and saying in the same way that other informed persons do, and what they learn in this way may occasionally influence the way they decide cases—although probably only by strengthening their resolve never to make decisions on "political" grounds. But legislation remains the way in which Parliament's instructions are officially conveyed to the judges; thus the way in which legislation is made has a profound bearing on the relationship between the two bodies.

Institutional Differences

An analysis of the institutional differences in the constitutional and political arrangements of the two countries helps to explain why England uses legislation so much more readily to resolve questions that in America are left to the judges. There are two fundamental reasons for this. First, England has strong centralized political institutions, while in the United States both federalism and the separation-of-powers doctrine lead to a fragmentation of political power and hence to much weaker government. And second, for similar reasons, the English judiciary is a relatively weak body with a very minor political role compared with the centralized executive-legislative machinery, while in America the judiciary is immensely powerful in comparison with the other branches of government. I have dealt with the position of the judiciary, so I now look at the relationship between executive and legislative bodies.

The greater relative strength of British governments is most visible in the relationships between executive officials and the legislatures. Britain has never had the strict American separation-of-powers doctrine. In Britain, the ministerial heads of the executive departments are all members of, and exercise a powerful control over, the legislature; the British parliamentary system, through the party system, to a large extent actually combines the executive and legislative powers in one central governing body, the cabinet. Thus statute lawmaking in England is subject to strong centralized control.

Similar differences affect nonstatutory legislation, what in England is called delegated legislation, and in America administrative regulations. Most such legislation in England is made by ministers (that is, political heads of executive departments) and is therefore subject to the same sort of centralized control as other legislation.

Although statute making in England is done by Parliament, even Parliament's legislative powers are in practice almost completely controlled by the executive. In the first place, the executive controls what legislative proposals should be put before Parliament or made by ministers. The cabinet (backed by the entire civil service machine, as well as the noncabinet ministers) constitutes a body of persons with continuous responsibility for overseeing the management of the entire body politic. It is their responsibility, among other things, to oversee the law, to study social problems, and to bring forward proposals for change.

In modern times, it is less and less common for any legislative proposals approved by the cabinet not to secure passage through Parliament.[43] Legislation can be amended during its passage through Parliament, but the cabinet, through the party system, exercises such control over the legislative machine that amendments can rarely be *forced* on a government by an adverse parliamentary vote.[44] The most that is likely to happen is that the pressure of speeches from government supporters may persuade the minister in charge of a bill that it is necessary or at least expedient to make concessions. If he feels the concessions cannot be made without threatening the essence of the proposal, he will resist them, probably explaining in more detail why he does so in a private party meeting, and the government will ultimately impose a "three-line whip," which requires all party members to support the government.

In this system of government, minor amendments to the law and the administrative machinery of the state are common and easily obtained. If the matter is small and likely to be relatively uncontroversial, there will be little or no difficulty in having the necessary legislation prepared and introduced into Parliament. There may be delay, of course, because Parliament is busy and has limited time for legislation. But every department has its annual opportunity to demand a place in the legislative timetable, though not all will succeed every year.

Furthermore, once this kind of routine legislation is introduced, there is little difficulty about securing its enactment more or less in the form desired by the minister and his executive officials. Because the minister is both head of his executive department and a member of the legislature, he feels responsible for getting these minor reforms carried through, for explaining to the legislature why they are required, and for persuading his colleagues that any necessary finance should be provided. When the bill is introduced,

43. A very rare example occurred in 1986 when the Shops Bill (to remove restrictions on Sunday trading) was defeated in the House of Commons. See Hansard (Commons), 6th ser., vol. 95 (1986), cols. 584–702. This may well be the only example since World War II of a government bill being defeated while the government had an overall majority in the House of Commons. But defeats on less important issues (especially in the House of Lords) have become more frequent recently.

44. On the extent to which bills are amended during their passage through Parliament, see J. A. G. Griffith, *Parliamentary Scrutiny of Government Bills* (Oxford: George Allen & Unwin, 1974).

a minister will be in charge of it as it goes through the houses of Parliament. The minister will always be fully briefed for this job by his civil servants, including the draftsman of the bill. These officials know exactly what each provision is, what it is intended to do, and how it is supposed to dovetail with other bodies of law. Members of Parliament will not usually appreciate these niceties, but the minister will.

Richard Posner has recently argued that many of the canons of statutory interpretation used by the U.S. courts display ignorance of the legislative process. A realistic understanding of the legislative process is, he says, "devastating to the canons of construction."[45] In turn, he charges that legislators do not know anything about these judicial canons of interpretation and it is farcical to attribute such knowledge to them. For example, the presumption that implied repeals are not intended is based on the wholly unreal implication that legislators comb the statute book before passing a bill to see what previous legislation may be inconsistent with it.[46] Much of this critique of methods of statutory interpretation may be valid in the United States, where it is often assumed that the canons of interpretation do not mean very much anyhow. But this is not true in Britain. Although members of Parliament may not know much about the rules of statutory interpretation, the draftsman of bills does, and the minister who pilots the bill through Parliament will be taught as much as he needs to know about them by his draftsman and public officials. Here again, it is the executive in Britain that mediates between the judiciary, which has to interpret statutes, and the legislature, which passes them.

Of course, everything does not always work as well as this. More complex legislative proposals may have to take their place in the queue for parliamentary time. The government's legislative timetable is invariably congested, and Parliament can deal with only so much at a time, even when it is largely the government that determines how Parliament's time is to be allocated. Seriously controversial proposals may also need much political activity and discussion before the cabinet is prepared to approve the legislation and allow it to be introduced in the government's name.

The British parliamentary and party system also operate negatively. Very little private members' legislation is ever passed in Britain, and when it is, it tends to be on nonpolitical and nonparty issues.[47] A private member of

45. Posner, *The Federal Courts*, p. 276 ff.

46. Richard A. Posner, "Statutory Interpretation—in the Classroom and in the Courtroom," 50 *University of Chicago Law Review* 800, 812 (1983).

47. That is not to say that private members' legislation deals solely with uncontroversial issues. In recent years a convention has grown up of leaving sensitive "liberal" or "conscience"

Parliament can, as a senator or representative can, introduce a bill as a gesture, as a symbolic act, to draw attention to some issue. But such bills cannot be passed, or usually even secure any significant debating time, if the government opposes them. So any proposal for legislation emanating from a private member of Parliament will be examined by the civil service, and it would be a rare civil servant who could not find plenty of good reasons for advising that the proposal is a bad one that should not be supported by the minister. Any proposal, for instance, that seems to emanate from some special interest group and fails to take account of the public interest would simply be scotched and killed in the civil service machine. Any legislative proposal that is going to cost money is particularly subject to scrutiny because of the procedural rule of the House of Commons that such a bill cannot be introduced without the support of a government minister.[48] This rule is designed to ensure that those who are responsible for collecting taxes—or for putting forward proposals for the collecting of taxes—must approve a measure that is going to require additional taxes.

Effects of the Party System

The control exercised by the British cabinet over the legislature derives, of course, from the party system.[49] It is today very difficult for anyone to be elected to the House of Commons without the support of one of the major political parties; in return for party nomination, money, and support at election time, the party expects and exacts a high degree of loyalty from its members. Members of Parliament, especially those on the government side, are expected to vote as their party requires, although they may speak against the party (with moderation, and not too often) or at least ask ministers for concessions or variations to their policies. Thus it is common to see many government supporters speak against some proposal and then dutifully vote for the government. Of course, government supporters are not sheep and their views must be taken into consideration; but rebellions are usually settled behind closed doors at party meetings and ultimately nearly all toe the line. Members may be allowed a few "votes of conscience" against their government (and more freedom is usually allowed opposition members), but if they repeat

---

issues to be dealt with by private members' bills. Thus the laws relating to obscenity, homosexual offenses, capital punishment, and abortion were all liberalized as a result of private members' bills.

48. May, *Treatise on the Law,* p. 760 ff.

49. On the party system in England, see generally Vernon Bogdanor, *The People and the Party System: The Referendum and Electoral Reform in British Politics* (Cambridge University Press, 1981); and for a comparative study, see Bogdanor, ed., *Parties and Democracy in Britain and America* (Praeger, 1984).

the process too often they are likely to jeopardize any chance of being selected for office by the prime minister. "Voting against one's party [in Britain] is like a Bostonian in the stands at Fenway Park rooting vociferously for the Yankees. One can do it, but it is dangerous."[50]

In the last resort a member of Parliament may be expelled from his party, and recent experience has shown that the chances of his losing his seat at the next election are then high, even if he should stand as an independent without party support. This is still true even if he has been a popular member, well liked in his constituency, and with a distinguished political record behind him. The chief reasons for this are that it is very difficult for a private member to build up any sort of campaign organization, and contributions to election funds have traditionally been funded through the parties and not to individual members.

But although the British party system thus exacts loyalty and imposes discipline on its political supporters, it also tends to insulate them from some of the extremes of populism. A very large proportion (perhaps as many as four-fifths) of parliamentary constituencies are so dominated by one party that the party's nominee has little to fear from the electorate itself.[51] So long as he retains the support of the party itself (or at least of the local party officials), he can normally be confident of being continually reelected. This helps to give members of Parliament a degree of independence from the electorate that few elected American politicians appear to enjoy. And this in turn means that the British political process does not conform to the model of the democratic process in which elected representatives of various interest groups simply compete for power and distribution of goods. British members of Parliament are often free to support and vote for proposals which the majority of their constituents would reject if they had the opportunity. Thus it was possible for Parliament to abolish capital punishment in 1959 and several times since then reject proposals for its reintroduction, even though opinion polls nearly always show a majority in favor of its use.

The party system, as it operates in modern Britain, also has another, more subtle, effect on political and legal debate, and ultimately on the nature of the legal system and therefore the role of the judges. The party system tends to lead to a polarization of opinion on most political issues. This stems partly

50. Anthony King, "How to Strengthen Legislatures—Assuming That We Want To," in Norman J. Ornstein, ed., *The Role of the Legislature in Western Democracies* (Washington, D.C.: American Enterprise Institute for Public Policy Research, 1981), p. 88.

51. In British general elections, the number of members of the winning party who lose their seats is usually negligible; and the number of the losing party who lose their seats is rarely more than 50 or 60 (out of a total House of Commons membership of 650).

from the fact that British politics has for long been dominated by two major parties, but there are other factors involved. For instance, the absence of electoral primaries means that the British voter is usually offered a choice between two or three candidates representing the main political parties, and he has to accept or reject the party packages *en masse*. He cannot split his vote between candidates of different parties as the American voter can.

The polarization of opinion in England has two results that are important for present purposes. First, it facilitates the passage of legislation, because it is easier to secure a majority for a proposal; and second, it tends to make political (and to some degree, even moral and social) debate and discourse less pluralistic than it is in America. Thus British political debate tends to be highly adversarial. Issues tend to be sharpened, and legislation can take a much more precise and consistent approach, once a majority exists for the principle.

A further aspect to this polarization of political opinion is that coalitions are largely unnecessary in modern British politics. For many years most British governments have had absolute majority control of the House of Commons, and the governments have been of a single party without the need for formal coalition support. This allows governments and ministers to formulate clear policies and to instruct their officials to produce bills to give effect to them. There is very rarely any need in the British political system for a government deliberately to choose a legislative provision that obfuscates a troublesome point, fudges a confusing compromise, or ducks an issue altogether by passing the buck to the judiciary. Of course parties themselves are sometimes built on their own internal coalitions, and varying opinions within a party may need to be respected. But the unifying effect of a strong party system is powerful.

These features of the British parliamentary system lead to a number of results with important implications for the role of the judiciary and therefore for judicial-legislative relations. First, hasty and ill-considered legislation is unlikely to be introduced, let alone passed. Similarly, legislation drawn up to further the wishes of one interest group is unlikely to get far, unless that interest group happens to be the majority parliamentary party or closely associated with it.[52] On the other hand, necessary and useful legislation is very easy to pass, even over the dissent of minority groups. Further, legislative policy is usually clear. Any obscurity in modern English legislation results not from political compromises, nor from failure to face up to necessary

52. Of course some would say that the trade unions, on the one side, and commercial-industrial interests, on the other, are such minority groups whose interests are regularly preferred by one party or the other over those of the nation at large.

decisions, but from drafting techniques and the inherent difficulties of language.

What has been said above may to some degree be an idealized rather than a realistic version of the British political legislative process. In practice, things do not always work in this fashion. Needed and useful reforms are sometimes postponed for lack of ministerial interest or energy; the problem of not antagonizing an important section of party supporters may sometimes prevent legislation on some topic; the need to maintain party support, or to appear to comply with electoral promises, may occasionally require some fudging of legislative policy. And it cannot be denied that one of the fundamental threats posed by the British system of government, which the American system was designed to avoid—the threat of a tyrannical majority party bulldozing through legislation in the sole interest of a small segment associated with the majority party—has reared its head from time to time in recent years. But this does not alter the fact that the British Parliament operates in a very different way indeed from the U.S. Congress, and that one result is to relieve the English judiciary from the responsibility for making many political decisions of the kind American judges often have to make.

Features of the U.S. System

It is hardly necessary here to do more than draw attention to certain basic features of the U.S. political system in order to make the contrast with Britain. The essential point for present purposes is that there is no body in the United States which performs the functions of the British executive. There is thus no single institutional force which controls the content of American federal statutes, and when statutes are enacted they may be watered down or adopted in compromise form. As a result they are often less sharp and precise in their policy and are less likely to contain hard and fast rules embodying clear-cut legislative policy decisions. Although they may include considerable detail, that detail will often incorporate open-ended concepts that defied precise compromises. Thus, as Judge Posner has recently said, "Federal statutes often emerge from the legislative process radically incomplete, and the courts are left to complete them by a process that is only formally interpretive."[53] This does not happen in Britain.

While British political institutions help to polarize opinion on most issues, producing highly adversarial politics and hence clear-cut policy decisions that translate into formal statutes, American politics is much less polarized.

Occasions for compromise and the fudging of issues tend to arise constantly

53. Posner, *The Federal Courts,* p. 19.

in the U.S. legislative process because political power is so fragmented that without compromise it would often be difficult to achieve anything at all. The American use of primaries, for example, militates against polarization because primaries enable the public to choose between political packages in a more fragmented way. And within the federal Congress itself there are many factors that tend to prevent polarization of opinion.[54] Many political issues in America tend to become polycentric, where in Britain they would become adversarial. In the absence of powerful executives and party leaders in the legislative bodies themselves, there is a lack of "organizing issues or lines of battle. . . . In place of identifiable, consistent voting blocs, there is a multitude of floating, ever-changing coalitions around specific issues."[55]

The constitutional powers of the U.S. courts must also be remembered in considering the way in which the U.S. legislative process differs from the British. The fact that the courts have the power to strike down legislation as unconstitutional may sometimes make legislatures less hesitant to pass laws about which some members have qualms. Why risk political controversy by standing up for minorities or espousing unpopular causes when one can vote for a bill with a clear conscience, knowing that if it is found to be seriously offensive to traditional liberties, the courts can strike it down? Some commentators believe that there is a strong temptation for American politicians to pass unpleasant political issues to the courts for this reason.[56] Indeed, it is argued by some writers that the American political system encourages legislatures to refuse to face up to controversial issues that demand a clear answer,[57] and that they fudge political compromises that will end up with the courts, designedly or undesignedly.[58] Some see the explosion of litigation as due in part to the failure of the legislatures to resolve fundamental value conflicts and the resulting tendency to take these conflicts to the courts.[59]

54. See generally Malcolm E. Jewell and Samuel C. Patterson, *The Legislative Process in the United States,* 4th ed. (Random House, 1986), p. 11.

55. Roger H. Davidson, "The Two Congresses and How They Are Changing," in Ornstein, *The Role of the Legislature in Western Democracies,* p. 19.

56. Thayer long ago noted the tendency of judicial review to make legislators less responsible. James B. Thayer, "The Origin and Scope of the American Doctrine of Constitutional Law," 7 *Harvard Law Review* 129 (1893); see also Alexander M. Bickel, *The Least Dangerous Branch: The Supreme Court at the Bar of Politics* (Indianapolis: Bobbs-Merrill, 1962), pp. 21–23, 35–44.

57. John H. Barton, "Behind the Legal Explosion," 27 *Stanford Law Review* 567, 576 (1975); and Ruggero J. Aldisert, "An American View of the Judicial Function," in Jones, ed., *Legal Institutions Today,* p. 77.

58. Louis L. Jaffe, "An Essay on Delegation of Legislative Power: I," 47 *Columbia Law Review* 359, 366–67 (1947).

59. Maurice Rosenberg, "Devising Procedures That Are Civil to Promote Justice That Is Civilized," 69 *Michigan Law Review* 797, 810 (1971).

Thus American judges are frequently called upon to deal with novel, deep moral issues that in England would be legislated upon, perhaps after some committee of inquiry had first studied them and published a report. Recent examples relate to experimental research on embryos and the problems of "surrogate mothers."[60]

One result of the lack of centralized control over the legislative process is the ease with which Congress can be "hijacked" into passing legislation without a full appreciation of its implications. More accurately, this would be even easier if the legislative machinery were not designed to make the passage of legislation exceedingly difficult.[61] In Britain, of course, the legislative process is designed to make it very easy for the government to secure the enactment of its proposals, but very difficult—indeed almost impossible— for anybody else to secure the passage of legislation.

This sort of obstacle course to the passage of legislation in U.S. legislatures results in the failure of many legislatures to pass not only bad legislation, but also necessary and desirable legislation. It also prevents the repeal of obsolete statutes when they have become an encumbrance. All this throws a heavier burden on the courts to introduce such reforms themselves and explains why there is constant pressure on the courts to become even bolder and, for instance, declare statutes to be obsolete, leaving it to the legislature to reenact them if it wishes.[62] Although obsolete statutes can occasionally cause problems in English law, routine governmental legislation now updates and repeals obsolete statutes as part of the regular work of the political machine.

The Drafting of Legislation

The drafting of legislation is much more professionalized in England than it is in the United States. All parliamentary legislation in England is drafted in the Office of Parliamentary Counsel, a very small office of highly skilled and dedicated professional draftsmen with great technical proficiency and strong

60. See Surrogacy Arrangements Act, 1985 (12 Halsbury's Statutes, 4th ed. 55), following the report of the Warnock Committee of Inquiry into Human Fertilisation and Embryology, Cmnd. 9314 (1984), also published as Mary Warnock, *A Question of Life: The Warnock Report on Human Fertilisation and Embryology* (Oxford: Basil Blackwell, 1984).

61. "Normally legislation has to work its way slowly through multiple decision points. One congressional report identified more than 100 specific steps." Walter J. Oleszek, *Congressional Procedures and the Policy Process*, 2d ed. (Washington, D.C.: CQ Press, 1984), p. 14. In the Ninety-fifth Congress (1976–77), 1,027 bills out of 15,587 introduced became law, a 6 percent success rate. William J. Keefe, *Congress and the American People*, 3d ed. (Prentice-Hall, 1988), p. 27.

62. See Guido Calabresi, *A Common Law for the Age of Statutes* (Harvard University Press, 1982), p. 190.

traditions of methodology and technique. The British government's control over the legislative process is so great today that it is almost impossible for any bill, or even an amendment to a bill, to be passed by Parliament unless it has been drafted by (or in some rare cases, approved by) the Parliamentary Counsel.[63] These counsel (it must be stressed) are employees of the executive, not of Parliament itself.

The Office of Parliamentary Counsel is a very powerful one in the British governmental machine because the draftsmen have a monopoly over the production of legislative bills. Thus their views as to the needs of their work are largely respected by successive governments. A draftsman who says he needs six months to prepare a major bill will not be pressed to produce it earlier without compelling reasons. Equally, departmental lawyers and policymakers have learned that the draftsman expects to be given very detailed instructions before he starts to draft. Thus the preparation of legislation is an exceptionally thorough exercise in modern Britain, at both the preliminary and the drafting stages.

English parliamentary counsel know and understand the way in which English judges interpret statutes, and they draft bills in this knowledge. Because of the uniformity of approach of English judges, this aspect of the work of parliamentary counsel is greatly simplified. The judges respond by interpreting statutes in the way parliamentary counsel expect because the uniform style of drafting facilitates such an approach. Interpretation and drafting are thus reciprocal functions, each of which is affected by the uniformity of technique of the other.

Thus it is not absurd to assume that an English act should be read in light of the canons of interpretation; acts are *designed* to be interpreted in this way by the draftsman, and although his views are not those of Parliament at large, his views are (where necessary) transmitted by the minister in charge of the bill to the relevant house.

Private members' bills (that is, bills not introduced by or on behalf of the government) are occasionally passed, if they relate to nonpolitical subjects (though usually not more than five or six a year), but no modern British government would permit even a bill of this kind to be passed unless it had been properly drafted. Similarly, amendments to government bills are referred to the Office of Parliamentary Counsel for their views on the amendments' technical legal soundness.

63. See generally Reed Dickerson, "Legislative Drafting in London and Washington," [1959] *Cambridge Law Journal* 49; and Noël Hutton, "How the English Meet the Problem," in Dickerson, ed., *Professionalizing Legislative Drafting: The Federal Experience* (American Bar Association, 1973), pp. 110, 113.

This does not mean that the British legislative process is beyond criticism. Many lawyers today find the style of parliamentary drafting obscure and tortuous; it is often impossible to get a general idea of the intent of a statute from a casual reading; and of course, occasional mistakes, ambiguities, and inconsistencies inevitably occur. Moreover, draftsmen often complain that bills (or more usually amendments) sometimes have to be drafted with inadequate time for preparation.[64] But the ability of British governments to control the form and substance of statutes passed by Parliament, and to ensure that they are drafted by lawyers of high professional competence, means that the onus is firmly on Parliament to make the political choices, and ambiguities and obscurities are reduced to a minimum. The control of legislation by the executive also means that time is not wasted in the drafting of hundreds of bills that are unlikely to be passed. Most bills introduced by the government in Britain are passed, and few bills are drafted which are not introduced.

The style and competence with which legislation is drafted is bound to have a considerable impact, not only on the detailed methods of interpretation adopted by the courts, but on the whole relationship between the legislature and the courts. If the legislature chooses to give its instructions in the form of exceptionally precise and detailed commands, drafted with great technical skill, those who have to apply and interpret such commands may well find that the sensible course is to interpret them at face value and not to look too deeply for underlying purposes or the spirit of the legislation. This tendency will be reinforced if, as is also the case in England, Parliament tends to update statutes with relative frequency and to correct promptly errors thrown up by legal cases.

The drafting of federal legislation is very different in the United States. There is, for instance, no single centralized office where all congressional legislation is prepared and where control of methodology, technique, and on-the-job training can be undertaken. American legislative counsel also have to contend with difficulties not faced by English parliamentary counsel. For example, American legislative draftsmen have to recognize that their bills will be interpreted by a judiciary quite unlike the compact, homogeneous English judiciary. This is bound to make drafting more difficult, because the draftsman cannot count on the judges to understand the particular styles and methods he uses.

In addition, American legislative counsels' instructions come not from the

---

64. See George Engle, "Bills Are Made to Pass as Razors Are Made to Sell: Practical Constraints in the Preparation of Legislation," [1983] *Statute Law Review* 7, at 14, 15–20.

government, but from the individual members of the two houses. This means that they have many taskmasters and they may spend a great deal of time preparing bills that will never be passed.

Yet another difference is that, even if the legislative counsel's bill is well drafted initially, once the bill reaches the committee stage significant changes are likely to be made, and the draftsman loses control of the bill in a way that does not happen in Britain. Much of the initial draft may be rewritten, usually under difficult conditions for even the most expert of draftsmen. These obstacles to the satisfactory drafting of U.S. statutes are encountered even when a bill has been initially drafted by the expert draftsmen of the Office of Legislative Counsel. But "less than half of all federal legislation originates in Congress," according to George Galloway.[65] A substantial amount of legislation derives initially from the executive branch. Proposed legislation is drafted by personnel within each particular agency, who may not be well trained and experienced in drafting legislation.[66] Still worse are legislative proposals originating in the private sector—in labor or civic groups, public interest associations, or professional, business, or agricultural organizations. Here the proposals may be tendered in the form of bills prepared by lay draftsmen, and the legislative counsel cannot supervise or revise the drafting of all these bills.

One final point is worth making about this comparison of drafting techniques. England has a long tradition of narrow, detailed drafting; English draftsmen have for at least two centuries tried to produce language that is capable of neutral, nonpurposive interpretation. An English statute has traditionally been drafted in such detail that it can be said to be a catalog of rules. It is not a set of principles that the judges can be left to apply to a variety of situations, or that they can be encouraged to build on, as though they were common law principles. By contrast America has a tradition (which goes back to Jefferson) of drafting legislation in broader language,[67] using it to state wide general principles, such as in the federal Constitution itself. To be sure, not all modern American legislation is drafted quite as tersely as the Constitution. The federal Internal Revenue Code, for instance, is scarcely less detailed than the corresponding English legislation. Nevertheless, the tradition

65. Quoted in John M. Kernochan, *The Legislative Process* (Mineola, N. Y.: Foundation Press, 1981), p. 8. A further difference between English and American institutional arrangements that probably contributes to the much greater power exercised by the English Parliamentary Counsel's Office arises from the American practice of treating senior public service appointments as political offices that change with each administration.

66. Dickerson, *Professionalizing Legislative Drafting*, p. 171.

67. See *The Writings of Thomas Jefferson*, vol. 2, ed. Paul L. Ford (Putnam's, 1893), pp. 103–29.

of broad statutory language is not dead in America, as it is in England, and the Constitution is a permanent and living reminder that written law can be expressed in the language of principle, rather than detailed rule.

A few illustrations will suffice to show how the factors discussed above can affect the kind of legislation produced in the two countries, and hence the nature of the tasks thrown on the judges. One obvious example of how Congress sometimes enacts broad principles rather than detailed legislative codes is the various antitrust statutes enacted since 1890, which are typically brief and ambiguous. By contrast, this subject has been dealt with in England by many detailed statutes of great complexity, beginning with the Restrictive Trade Practices Act of 1956, a statute of thirty-eight sections and almost thirty printed pages in length. Since that act was passed, the special court established under it to hear cases concerning restrictive agreements has delivered a number of lengthy and complex judgments, but the initiative in relation to the policy issues involved has remained firmly in the hands of Parliament, and much further legislation has been passed.[68] This legislation is entirely in the British tradition: it is detailed, complex, and leaves a minimum of discretion or policymaking to the courts.

Another example concerns a more modern congressional statute, the Education for Handicapped Children Act of 1975, which requires all states receiving federal funds under its provisions (which means all the states) to adopt a policy of ensuring "all handicapped children the right to a free appropriate public education." Nowhere does the act spell out precisely what this means, nor does it even explicitly delegate to the states the task of deciding what is a "free appropriate public education" for handicapped children. This question therefore becomes a matter for the courts to decide.[69] But the question is a fundamental political one, raising obvious financial implications, and no guidance is given to the courts as to how these issues are to be resolved.

A directly comparable statute in Britain is the Education Act of 1981, which appears at first sight to be somewhat similar to the congressional act of 1975. It deals with the "special educational needs" of children who have a "learning difficulty." But the act operates in a very different way from the congressional statute. The broad effect is to confer discretion on local education

68. See, for example, Restrictive Trade Practices Act, 1976 (46 Halsbury's Statutes, 3d. ed. 1955); Resale Prices Act, 1976 (46 Halsbury's Statutes, 3d. ed. 2033); Fair Trading Act, 1973 (Halsbury's Statutes, 3d. ed. 1618); and Competition Act, 1980 (50(2) Halsbury's Statutes, 3d ed. 2555).

69. See, for example, *Board of Education* v. *Rowley*, 458 U.S. 176 (1982); and Katherine T. Bartlett, "Educational Decisionmaking for the Handicapped Child," *Law & Contemporary Problems*, vol. 48, no. 2 (1985), p. 7.

authorities, and it is their responsibility to make the fundamental political choices involved in, for example, considering the question of cost and resources available. The function of the courts in relation to such an act is the purely supervisory one of ensuring that local authorities act in accordance with the statute. The court may be compelled to interpret particular statutory provisions, but it has no general power to decide the broad issue of what is a "special educational provision" or what ought to be provided in particular cases. It is in fact inconceivable that a statute imposing such a responsibility on the courts would be passed in modern times in Britain. Nor would any British government allow legislation to pass through Parliament similar to the congressional act of 1975, which neither makes the detailed political choices itself nor delegates those choices to the local governments. The way in which resources are spent on such matters as special education would always be regarded as a matter for elected bodies to decide within discretionary power, and never for the courts.

Another illustration of an American statute shows the difficulties that can ensue from legislative compromises when fundamental choices are not made in Congress. The Newspaper Preservation Act of 1970 was a highly controversial statute in which Congress attempted to balance the competing interests of threatened newspapers and the antitrust laws. Different versions of the bill were introduced in the two houses, and the ultimate act was the result of a legislative compromise: the effect of some of the House amendments that were agreed to by the Senate were apparently left vague quite intentionally. The result was that the meaning of the act was utterly ambiguous on one crucial and central element of the statute, leaving the ultimate decision to the courts.[70] This kind of legislative compromise would almost never be made in Britain.

Another example of the kind of problem that can be thrown at the courts in America resulted from a section being slipped into a congressional statute on the floor of the House in 1976. That provision, requiring that 10 percent of each federal grant applied for under the Public Works Employment Act of 1977 be expended for "minority business enterprises," arguably was contrary to the Civil Rights Act of 1964—which most members of Congress had no intention of repealing or modifying.[71] Here again, the fact that legislation in Britain is generally under the tight control of the executive

70. See *Newspaper Guild* v. *Levi*, 539 F. 2d 755, 761 (D.C. Cir. 1976), where these difficulties had to be resolved.

71. See *Associated General Contractors* v. *Sec. of Commerce*, 441 F. Supp 955 (D. Cal. 1977), *vacated*, 438 U.S. 909 (1978). The Supreme Court remanded to consider the question of mootness, 459 F. Supp. 766 (D. Cal. 1978).

means that a legislative mistake of such serious proportions could almost never happen.

Conclusions

The principal conclusion to be drawn from the above survey is that the relationship between the judiciary and the legislature is part of a highly complex and integrated mosaic. This relationship is influenced by innumerable factors such as the basic constitutional structure of a country, the way in which the legislature works, and the way legislation is prepared, drafted, and enacted; so also the relationship is profoundly influenced by the perception of the appellate and the judicial function, how the courts work, what kinds of people become judges, and how they operate. Behind them both extend the democratic process, the party system, and the way politicians behave in and out of their legislatures. But above all, it can be seen how it is the role of the executive that dominates the scene in Britain. In Britain the executive is the government, and the government governs. The nature of the relationship between the judiciary and the legislature, like almost everything else in Britain, is determined by the government.

Summary of Proceedings

Robert A. Katzmann

-»»X««-

With the preceding papers in hand, colloquium participants met on November 13, 1986, to launch this inquiry into judicial-congressional relations. Attendees represented a full cross section from the courts and Congress. The participants were asked to consider three principal issues: prudential and constitutional concerns affecting judicial-legislative interaction; the institutional capacity of courts and Congress to understand each other's processes and problems; and a preliminary examination of ways to improve relations between the branches. To address each question, a panel was created. What follows is a summary of the discussions of the three principal themes, drawing upon comments made throughout the proceedings.

Prudential and Constitutional Concerns

The Constitution is virtually silent about the character and form of relations between the judiciary and Congress. In the absence of such direction, judges and legislators are uncertain about what kind of interaction would be appropriate. At the same time, both sides recognize in principle the desirability of improved communications. All this became particularly clear as participants examined the general state of relations between the branches, the role of judges in communicating with Congress, the constraints on judges and the judiciary, the manner of judicial representation before the legislature, and the propriety of judges' assuming nonadjudicatory functions at the request of Congress.[1]

From the outset, a consensus emerged that the judiciary and the Congress often do not understand each other—indeed, as Judge Frank Coffin suggested, do not know how to communicate with each other on some of their most fundamental concerns. "One thing this discussion shows," commented Judge

---

1. Paul D. Carrington moderated the first panel. Panelists were Abner J. Mikva, Kenneth W. Starr, Irving Hill, Russell Wheeler, Chesterfield H. Smith, Thomas Railsback, Johnny H. Killian, and Louis Fisher.

Abner Mikva, "is that . . . both groups come in totally unaware of how each other's process works." Observed Representative Robert Kastenmeier, "We seem to be characterizing the Congress in a very unfavorable role—but I must concede . . . that it's pretty accurate, regretfully. . . . In some respect, the judiciary [for] the Congress is like the U.S. prisons—sort of tolerated by benign neglect. . . ." At times, the attitude is "close to being hostile." Justice Antonin Scalia observed that Congress may not "know the extent of the difficulties that it's imposing on the federal courts." Assessing the third branch's perceptions of Congress, Ralph Mecham of the Administrative Office of the U.S. Courts commented that "the difficulty is that many members of the judiciary don't understand some of the key issues. They're not aware of some of the nuances." Steven Ross, the general counsel to the Clerk of the House of Representatives, who represents the chamber in court, stated that there is "an incredible degree of ignorance as to how the legislative branch operates, and in the legislative branch as to how the judiciary operates."

As Russell Wheeler of the Federal Judicial Center noted, participants seemed far more interested in prudential concerns than in arcane constitutional questions or how the separation-of-powers doctrine constrains interaction between the branches. The heart of the inquiry, for Judge Irving Hill, should be an examination of the "proper role of a judge, the proprieties of communicating and being available to Congress for consultation about legislation." "In terms of the way life is lived on the bench these days," he continued, "there are certain inhibiting factors." Alluding to one such constraint, Mikva stated that "there's something unseemly about a judge appearing too often in legislative chambers offering his views on legislation." The real problem of communications between the branches, he asserted, was "just simply that we are not used to talking to each other."

Judges, the participants believed, have First Amendment rights to express their views. Citing the late Judge Harold Leventhal's declaration that separation of powers does not have to mean an isolation of the branches, Louis Fisher of the Congressional Research Service contended that judges can add much to legislative deliberations with their testimony about the judicial effect of legislation. If the Supreme Court wants to write a letter to the two Judiciary committees saying "give up mandatory jurisdiction," and "have all nine justices sign it, there's nothing objectionable about that at all." Because many judges come to their jobs with valuable prior experience in other branches, they should feel free to testify on matters pertaining to those spheres of activity—not perhaps in their capacity as judges, but as individuals who have worked in the executive, the agencies, or Congress. Mecham stated that he believed that it was "quite appropriate for judges to be in touch with their sponsor in

Congress and others. They have a First Amendment right to petition Congress
. . . along with everybody else." In his own state, at least, Justice Hans Linde
of the Oregon Supreme Court observed that "the active participation of state
judges in the policy process is much more taken for granted, is much less
controversial, is much less a matter of concern as to whether you're involving
yourself in something that isn't judicial business"—largely because they are
elected to office and thus are not perceived as a bevy of platonic guardians
imposed from outside upon the electorate.

If the participants agreed that judges have First Amendment rights of free
speech, they also believed these rights should be exercised prudently.
Chesterfield Smith, former president of the American Bar Association,
commented that individual judges ought to exercise self-restraint because
"they're not any wiser than a lot of other people." Hill said that he would
not hesitate to talk about legislative matters that are germane to his duties,
not only those dealing with judicial machinery, but also substantive legislation
in which he had discerned problems in drafting and interpretation. But he
would not discuss such public policy questions as whether to have a
constitutional amendment on abortion. "I just don't think it's proper, and
I'm willing to restrict my normal First Amendment rights because I am a
sitting judge, but I know some of my colleagues just don't agree with me."

Although he would "never even dream of volunteering advice" about the
selection of judges, Mikva noted that he responds on those rare occasions
when a senator asks for his opinion. Some judges, he stated, would think it
inappropriate for them to answer not only senators, but the American Bar
Association (ABA) as well. The danger, he observed, is that "if judges were
too influential in the selection of their colleagues, it would look like a self-
perpetuating branch of government." Mikva responds, not because he believes
he has "any superior wisdom," but because he may have some views about
the quality of performance of those candidates who have appeared before his
court.

The colloquium participants clearly believed that more thought needed to
be given to the medium through which judges' views were communicated.
As one of the factors inhibiting expression, Hill cited the perception that
judges could not speak for themselves but only through the unitary voice of
the Judicial Conference, and if individuals' views differed from the conference's,
then they felt constrained from publicly uttering them. Noting that "probably
most judges would like to be asked to testify," Kastenmeier offered the opinion
that "individual judges . . . ought to be able in their . . . individual capacity
to speak, to say no, they disagree. . . . After all . . . they are not bishops
responding to the Vatican." Linde declared that it is "essential" that judges,

acting as individuals, be allowed to present their ideas or testify before the legislature, contrary to the views of the majority of the Judicial Conference. That is, in fact, the position of the Judicial Conference in Oregon. Judges, asserted Smith, should filter their views through the ABA and let that organization, "as a voice of officers of the court," present proposals that are in the interest of the administration of justice. In other words, the ABA would serve as a surrogate for the judiciary. When judges come before Congress to address matters relating to the functioning of the judicial system, Johnny Killian of the Congressional Research Service suggested, they should speak through the Judicial Conference or other judicial organizations. But when they deal with subjects outside the judiciary, they should do so as individuals.

Thomas Railsback, a former member of Congress and currently a representative of the Federal Judges Association (an organization of federal judges seeking support for their compensation needs), has a different view. Asserting that there are some things that a judge is uniquely equipped to discuss, he argued that because members of the bench often have ties to particular legislators, they are in the best position to make the case for improving the health of the judiciary. To that end, the Federal Judges Association is "trying to organize a grass-roots involvement by the judges, just like virtually every other group in the country that wants to get something done."

More broadly, the discussion of communications between the judiciary and Congress led Hill to ask "whether our . . . 'stiff-necked and absolutist notion' about undertaking nonjudicial functions, even at the request of the other branches of the government, is right." In recent years, the President's Commission on Organized Crime was criticized for violating the separation of powers because its chair, Judge Irving Kaufman of the U.S. Court of Appeals for the Second Circuit, was an active jurist. Similarly, the Sentencing Commission is likely to be the object of a separation-of-powers attack. Dean Paul B. Carrington was concerned that if judges sat on commissions, they would "dilute, to some degree, the force of what they have to say when they are making decisions [in their adjudicatory capacity]." Judge Kenneth Starr declared that whether or not it was appropriate for a judge to serve on a commission depended upon the function of that body. If the commission's mandate was simply fact-finding outside the adjudicator's setting, then it would be proper to call upon a judge who could bring his or her skills to bear on the task at hand. But, continued Starr, if the charge of the commission is more in the nature of "policymaking or policy recommending," then considerations as to appropriateness become "much more severe and acute."

At the same time, judges, by dint of their experience with various areas of the law, may have special expertise that makes their participation invaluable.

When, for example, Congress creates a commission to make recommendations with sweeping ramifications for the administration of justice, the contributions of a judge could be most helpful to the commission in its development of those recommendations, to the legislature in its assessment of their judicial effect, and to the courts in their effort to implement the new policy. Mikva supported such participation, while expressing misgivings about judges serving on "high-profile, highly visible commissions," such as the Warren Commission. The first commission he served on in Congress, the Brown Commission, examined possible changes in criminal law. He recollected that it included three judges. "It was very important to have them, because here were academicians and congressmen sitting around and arguing about what we were going to do to the criminal law, and it was nice to have three people on it who knew . . . the impact of . . . what we were proposing to do."

Legislative and Judicial Capacity

Whatever the appropriate limits of interaction between the branches might be, institutional means will vitally affect the character of judicial-legislative relations. As Richard E. Neustadt has observed, in policymaking, means often matter as much as ends; they sometimes matter more.[2] It is thus important to look at the way each branch formulates its views and assesses the problems of the other. Participants examined such questions as how the structural characteristics of Congress affect judicial-legislative relations and the way members of Congress communicate with the judiciary (through such recent devices as court suits and amicus briefs). From the vantage point of the federal judiciary, panelists explored the judiciary's institutional difficulties in presenting its case to Congress.[3] A major theme emerged: the judiciary's use of legislative history in interpreting statutes. Summarized first is the discussion about institutional means; then the views about legislative history are presented.

Institutional Means

With respect to the institutional means by which Congress communicates with the judiciary, Kastenmeier pointed to the absence of informal "gateways" or "entry points." "My being able to go once or twice a year to speak to the Judicial Conference of the United States, or possibly to speak to a circuit

2. Richard E. Neustadt, *Presidential Power: The Politics of Leadership* (Wiley, 1960), p. 47.
3. A. Leo Levin chaired the panel. Joining him were Antonin Scalia, Stephen G. Breyer, Roger H. Davidson, Robert W. Kastenmeier, Kenneth Feinberg, Michael J. Remington, and Steven R. Ross. L. Richardson Preyer, both a former federal district judge and member of Congress, was a scheduled panelist, but was unable to attend.

conference somewhere else in the country, is not shared by most members and they virtually have no access to the courts," he continued. "The entrance of the Congress to forums of the judiciary is so limited" that unless some neutral forum offers to convene meetings on the basis of parity of the branches, legislators almost never communicate directly with judges.

Congress does have some formal means to express its views to the judiciary, if only in a fitful and time-delayed fashion. As Fisher noted, the legislature at times responds to Supreme Court decisions by enacting laws that seek to remedy a judicially recognized defect in legislation or statutes that effectively modify the Court's rulings. In discrete cases, Kastenmeier observed, the legislature transmits messages to the courts through the confirmation, impeachment, and judicial disciplinary process. And through oversight hearings, the House Subcommittee on Courts, Civil Liberties, and the Administration of Justice can communicate formally to the judiciary, although Kastenmeier asserted that such meetings are more illustrative of the access the judiciary enjoys to Congress than the reverse.

Still another method of communication, what Killian referred to as "a real sea change in the matter of congressional representation," involves legislators in litigation before the courts, either as parties or amicus curiae. With greater frequency, in cases of statutory interpretation members of Congress are using the legal process to press upon the courts their views of legislative intent. Among the colloquium participants, such strategies met with mixed reviews. In support, Mikva stated that if these activities are part of the public record and done through briefs so that all parties have an opportunity to "criticize and respond," he saw "nothing improper" about them. He would be far more "troubled by a phone call from a legislator saying that I know you've got that case up there and I'll tell you what I had in mind." For his part, Hill "frankly applaud[ed] Congress and groups of members who filed information and briefs to present their point of view to the courts. That's the kind of interchange we ought to foster and encourage, as far as I'm concerned." But for Kastenmeier, the filing of suits is "a questionable procedure," by which legislators "having lost probably on . . . policy grounds in the Congress . . . then pursue the matter in the courts."

Ross similarly objected to the filing of briefs for the purpose of "adding" to legislative history. "What I always tell members when they come to me and suggest such a brief is, 'You've already had your chance, your bite at the apple.' There's ample opportunity for members of the House to say what the law means during the legislative process." The amicus brief, commented Railsback, "may not represent the feelings of all of the other legislators, or all of the legislative participants." Characterizing such means of communication as "an entirely bad development," Killian remarked: "I would rather suspect that it's entitled to less weight by a court than the weight to be given to somebody else's interpretation of what the statute means, since if the difficulty is the ambiguity or the imprecision of the statute, the assumption is that the members really meant that at the time, they should have written it better, and they shouldn't be heard on it at this point."

With regard to how Congress assesses the problems of the courts, some participants noted that the judiciary has to contend with the absence of a broad-based constituency in Congress, which makes it difficult for the third branch to secure legislative attention for its concerns. For former Assistant Attorney General Maurice Rosenberg, the judiciary has four problems: the problems of province of the courts—what the courts should be doing; the problem of process—the kinds of procedures courts should use; the problem of personnel—how to attract and retain competent judges, secure resources to maintain a healthy judicial system, and prevent the development of a "rampant bureaucracy" that will change the nature of the judiciary; and the problem of structure—the way the court system should be organized.

"These problems," remarked Rosenberg, "have no special constituency. . . . [You] can develop . . . constituencies [against] improvements a lot easier than you can develop . . . constituencies for improvements." Speaking about his own subcommittee of fifteen members, Kastenmeier observed: "If it's a matter of, let's say, an intercircuit tribunal, major reconstruction, major adjustment with respect to the judiciary, I'm lucky to have two members present." Part of the difficulty lies in the nature of Congress. "As tenure grows," Kastenmeier noted, "the attention span has shortened. The proliferation of duties, of subject matter, is so great that it would . . . seem to confound [us]. . . ." That, he continued, is "a sad commentary on the system, but regretfully that's the way it works, and that seems to me part of the challenge we confront today."

A consequence of this lack of congressional attention to the problems of the courts, commented Judge Stephen Breyer, is that the legislative branch does not think systematically about the cumulative effect of legislation on the judicial system. Almost as a matter of course, Congress passes legislation that imposes burdens on the courts, but without any consultation with the judiciary. "We have witnessed in the last decade a tremendous effort by the Congress to pass statutes which throw more and more problems on the backs of the federal judiciary," stated attorney Kenneth Feinberg. Examples abounded throughout the discussion. As an illustration, Mecham offered the case of a child vaccine bill that was tacked on another bill at the very end of the session. "It's going to require the judiciary to go out and hire three or four hundred masters, and train them, and then handle about 10,000 appeals a year . . . and no contact was made with the judiciary at all." (A year later, the judiciary secured some relief through legislation shifting the burden to the Court of Claims.) The addition of such cases, one by one, stretches an already overworked judiciary to the limit. "The cumulative impact" of all this, commented Breyer, suggests treating the federal courts as a "scarce resource." But, echoing Kastenmeier, he stated that "there aren't many people who think systematically, in Congress, about the way in which their legislation is shaping an institution, and is, in major ways, changing the nature of the job, at least for the appellate courts." From his current vantage point as a circuit judge, and reflecting upon his former role as chief counsel of the Senate Judiciary Committee, Breyer declared: "I think to myself, we saw a lot of these bills, and I wish I knew then what I know now. It would have changed a little bit of my attitude."

Scalia remarked that Congress can create more appellate judgeships in the effort to keep up with the added burdens it places on the courts, but it cannot do so "ad infinitum" without destroying the special quality of the third branch. Citing the lack of "awareness" in Congress (as well as the executive and the bar), he continued:

> They don't seem to realize what's happening, that we are seeing the disappearance of what was a distinctive institution of . . . an elite judiciary. . . . It is becoming more and more a bureaucracy, and I think the results will be the quite different results that you get from institutional bureaucratic decisions as opposed to the kind of decisions that the Anglo-Saxon judiciary has been accustomed to coming out with, the decisions of individual bright minds.
>
> So it's that kind of message that I guess I'd like to give to the legislators, to have a look for the long run. Where are we going with the federal judiciary? Can we keep going the way we are without drastically altering what it is? I think that alteration is already in process. It may not even be reversible at this stage.

As for the judiciary's institutional difficulties in presenting its case to Congress, some colloquium participants pointed to the time constraints on judges. "The greatest enemy . . . is time," commented Mecham. "You have judges who are paid to be judges, not to be legislators." When Congress considers legislation that contains language in some obscure part that may have "a devastating impact on the structure of the courts of appeals," Breyer observed, it is too much to expect judges to be aware of those problems:

"They'd have to take an awful lot of time off from what they were doing otherwise, in order to figure out that this word buried in this statute was going to cause this trouble."

In addition, the judiciary lacks effective means for making policy expeditiously. The Judicial Conference is an "unwieldy group in many ways," commented Mecham, although he expected changes in process under Chief Justice Rehnquist. Members of the Judicial Conference "come to town twice a year for two days each, and they have a fantastic agenda. They are lucky to be able to get through it." Judicial monitoring of the legislative process on a daily basis is virtually impossible, so that bills will work their way through Congress without the Judicial Conference having taken a position. In fact, as Mecham predicted, the Judicial Conference has taken some steps since the colloquium to streamline its procedures and increase its effectiveness; examples of such efforts are the revitalization of the Executive Committee and the creation of a small liaison group to help keep track of legislative developments.

Another difficulty for the judiciary, Mecham reflected, is that Congress consists of a "multitude of gateways" that must be attended to. "We not only have the Judiciary committees which historically have played such an important role. We've got to worry about the Appropriation committees . . . the Budget Committees [and] public works committees." Apart from those bodies with which the judiciary must deal routinely, the courts are affected by any legislation that could have a judicial effect. Complicating the judiciary's task, Mecham continued, is the "tremendous turnover in staff on the Hill," which requires an "ongoing effort of the courts" to educate new personnel.

At times, as Leo Levin, then director of the Federal Judicial Center, remarked, courts have been forced to suspend basic constitutional guarantees because of the absence of mechanisms that would enable the legislature and the judiciary to identify and resolve problems expeditiously. Civil jury trials, for example, stopped for a time because the courts—in the attempt to comply with the Gramm-Rudman-Hollings Act—did not have the funds to support them. Yet trial by jury is a fundamental right.

The Uses of Legislative History

The various institutional obstacles within Congress are but one set of legislative problems confronting the judiciary; the courts, according to a common view that emerged at the colloquium, must also grapple with the increasingly complex labyrinth of the legislative process as they attempt to make sense of the statutes they are called upon to interpret. A by-product of the gulf between the judiciary and Congress is that the former has not been able to keep track of and evaluate the changes in the latter. Developments within Congress have critically affected how laws are made, with important ramifications for the judiciary as it seeks to discern legislative intent. For some, court-congressional relations will improve if judges, in their interpretation of legislation, show a greater awareness of the process that shapes statutory meaning. The question, as Levin put it, is "what are the 'legitimate sources' of legislative history?"

That query looms large in those many situations in which a statute is ambiguous, when its plain meaning cannot be gleaned from the words themselves. Should courts, wondered Ross, look to the intent of the author of the bill that becomes law, or should they try to "divine the intent of the higher collective body"? While "Chairman Kastenmeier . . . may have [one particular] view . . . of [the] language . . . he . . . [has] authored, he's not empowered to enact a statute," Ross observed. A bill becomes a law, Starr underscored, "by virtue of the fact that two houses of Congress have passed it." Railsback commented that the person who introduced the original bill may not be a reliable guide in the effort to determine legislative intent; after all, a bill can go "through a rather time-consuming . . . and a rather thorough process, with a lot of input from other people . . . [and] may have only been acceptable to others because of the legislative debate which further interpreted it and refined it."

Whatever the source of wisdom to discern congressional intent, it still remains to identify the body of materials that constitute the legislative record and to afford them due weight. Participants focused especially on the use of committee reports, floor debates, and the *Congressional Record*. Answers varied to Smith's inquiry: "What institutional means are in the Congress to protect the value and verity of judicial history with the knowledge that courts are going to look at it?" The differing perspectives illuminated the problems courts confront in interpreting statutes. The matter of committee reports led to a lively set of exchanges between Scalia and Breyer, joined by Kastenmeier— a unique discussion because it involved a sitting Supreme Court justice, a federal appellate judge, and a key member of Congress. Debate hinged upon differing perspectives about the extent to which committee reports reflected the congressional will.

For Mikva, the committee report is "the most useful document in the legislative history," save for subsequent changes made on the floor. Noting the absence of agreement among judges, he asserted that those who believe committee reports are unreliable because they are written by unelected staff members are "wrong."

Scalia asserted that lawmaking is "a very difficult process," in which a bill cannot be "imposed on the entire polity" without first securing the votes of a majority of the legislators in each chamber. But committee reports, Scalia continued, are not subject to vote; because of the burdens of their work load, most members of Congress do not have time to read them (except perhaps those legislators who are on the committees from which the reports emanate). Such documents thus become devices of committee-staff prescription, used by the staff who write them to construct legislative history. They are not, Scalia remarked, legitimate expressions of the congressional will.

Citing the late Judge Harold Leventhal, Scalia further commented that "the intelligent use of legislative history is like walking into a crowded cocktail party and looking over the heads of the guests to pick out your friends. . . . There's something there for everybody. . . . The amount of hours that lawyers spend, nowadays, combing through legislative history at 100 bucks an hour, is enormous, absolutely enormous." He considered this an irony; legislative history became popular in the 1920s because it offered the promise of controlling "willful judges—the McReynolds and the Sutherlands of the day." Quoting from a 1930 article by Dean James Landis, Scalia noted that such judges allegedly overrode legislative intent by using traditional but outmoded canons of statutory construction. The canons lack a key, thus increasing the discretion of judges who were free to pick and choose among them to further their own policy ends. Legislative history would presumably constrain these judges in ways that judicial canons could not. But for Scalia, the use of that material has had "just the opposite effect." "[If] you read court opinions, you'll find the court will use it when it's helpful and they won't use it when it's not helpful. They'll pick that section that they like. They'll leave out that section that they don't like. I find it difficult to see how it has restrained judicial willfulness."

"Slavish" attention to legislative history, even if conscientiously exercised, cuts against the "creative function" of a judge called upon to reconcile conflicting statutes, Justice Scalia noted. It is the role of the judge to make sense of laws that "rub up against each other."

Supporting a different position with respect to the value of legislative history, Breyer argued that lawmaking in Congress is an "institutional process" and that to understand the meaning of statutes it is appropriate to examine the various dimensions of the legislative record. While agreeing that the judge's task to some degree is to "rationalize the law," he contended that it is also helpful to know how "things work" in the effort "to find . . . what some human being who wrote some words somewhere was getting at." Not particularly concerned about the role of staff, he asserted that they serve senators and representatives and are "part of the process." Nor did he accept Scalia's view of committee reports. To the Supreme Court jurist's query, "You don't really think these people [legislators] know about the committee report, do you?" Breyer responded, "Yes, they do." He argued that interest groups recognize that "what appears in this report is an important part of what later will be considered by the courts." As a consequence, those groups read drafts of those reports "in the greatest detail," and if one lobbyist or representative "finds a sentence that he doesn't like," he will alert the legislators' staffs and say "look at this, this is going to be used against us." That response lead to the following exchange:

SCALIA: Do you think that the members of the Congress who are voting on that law know that?

BREYER: What they know is this. I know if I'm working for Senator "X" who happens to feel that it's fairly important what the AFL-CIO thinks, he's going to ask me if they signed off on this. . . . And before they sign off on it, they read through those things with a fine-tooth comb. . . .

SCALIA: What if your senator is from a state that . . . isn't concerned about what the AFL-CIO—

BREYER: Then he might say, did the AFL-CIO want this, or not? He sees who's supporting it.

SCALIA: Another senator doesn't care.

BREYER: He sees who's supporting it and if he doesn't care, fine, then he's bought the report.

SCALIA: That is not coming to a decision on the particular issue. Most of the congressmen aren't even aware that the issue is there, much less how they want it resolved.

BREYER: It all depends on the issue. . . .

Terming as "outrageous" the position that a committee report could not be considered credible unless it is voted upon by every legislator in each house, Kastenmeier declared:

Very often there is . . . little or no debate on a bill, and the only . . . judicial guidance there is likely to be, will be a . . . single report without a dissent.

Why that should not be given credibility, and validity, . . . I don't know. It probably is the only definitive explanation of the bill outside the language of the bill itself . . . that any court will have to work with. And one can perhaps judge the work product as one will, but it is an attempt to communicate with the courts, and that's what it's all about, in my view . . . as far as this process is concerned.

Kastenmeier's chief counsel, Michael Remington, acknowledged to Scalia that Washington lawyers "not only comb reports for tidbits in the legislative process," but also "spend a lot of time drafting report language . . . and trying to plant it." In one case, "A good law firm proposed two pages of history saying . . . 'The absence of any statutory language in this bill signifies the following congressional findings.' Needless to say, that did not go in the report." Remington defended the report-drafting process by citing a number of safety checks—openness, sharing with outsiders, and striking problems from the report. To those who question the value of such documents because of the role of staff, Kastenmeier and Remington responded: "Should elected representatives give less respect to judicial opinions written in large part by law clerks?"

Thomas Mooney, the minority counsel of the Subcommittee on Courts, Civil Liberties, and the Administration of Justice of the House Judiciary Committee, shared Remington's view and outlined a process with "political" safeguards. A bill, according to his example, is voted out of the subcommittee. Remington, representing Chairman Kastenmeier and other subcommittee members, produces a first draft of the committee report and presents it to him, Mooney, as the Republican counsel. If he identifies a problem, he shows it to his "ranking Republican—now it's Thomas Moorhead." Should Moorhead agree, Mooney will then contact Remington in the effort to resolve the dispute. Assuming that problem is settled, "The report is filed, the bill is reported out of the full committee, the report is then filed with the House of Representatives, becomes final, and then . . . [the ranking Republican] and Chairman Kasten-meier . . . go to the floor of the House as managers. . . . They . . . [make] their statement on the floor. That's legislative history, unless there's a change on the floor."

While expressing support for the integrity of the process, Railsback asserted that it was important that members carefully screen the reports of their committees. A legislator, he remarked, is "very dependent upon staff writing a report on a particular piece of legislation. Sometimes the member is pulled fifteen different ways with different subjects, some of which may interest him or her more than the particular report that's being written, and yet that is part of legislative history."

In expressing his "mild dissent to Justice Scalia," Kastenmeier remarked that the Supreme Court jurist "treats committee reports as Mikva does footnotes, apparently" (an allusion to Judge Mikva's well-known policy of avoiding footnotes in the opinions he drafts). That led Scalia to answer: "Now Congressman, be fair. I didn't say that I would do this. I play the game like everybody else. . . . I'm in a system which has accepted rules and legislative history is used. This is an academic discussion and I'm putting it to you academically. You read my opinions, I sin with the rest of them."

Later, Scalia went on to observe that regardless of what courts might do, administrative agencies "which end up having the first cut at 90 percent of federal law anyway . . . will assuredly use it [committee report]." "What the substantive [congressional] committees have to say constitutes 'marching orders' for the administrative agencies, if they know what's good for them." As a purely academic exercise, Scalia wondered if some thought should be given to whether committee reports, for example, should have perpetual effect, or be binding only as long as the committee has the same composition that it had at the time that it wrote the document. This approach would, in the long run, vest the Congress and committees that are currently sitting with greater influence than would the present judicial use of legislative history that enshrines the views of the original enacting committee.

Apart from committee reports, various participants examined other aspects of the legislative process that bear upon judicial interpretation of statutes. With respect to speeches in the *Congressional Record,* Mikva pointed to one legislative effort to communicate to the courts the parts of legislative history that can be considered legitimate by distinguishing between remarks made by members on the floor and those inserted afterward. For many years, no such differentiation was made so that it was difficult to determine the extent to which statements printed in the *Congressional Record* were part of the legislative debate. To remedy this situation, a "bullet" is now placed before those speeches that were inserted but not delivered in the chamber. But even this device, Mikva acknowledged, has not been particularly effective. "The ingenuity of congressmen is very great, and they found . . . a way to get around" it. If a legislator appears on the floor, declares "Mr. Speaker, I have some remarks to make," leaves without saying more, and then later inserts other remarks in the *Record,* his speech will be published without the bullet.

Even if the bullet were not circumvented, Fisher observed, it might not always be a meaningful guide to legislative history. He would, for example, place more weight on a statement inserted by someone on a committee with responsibility for the bill under discussion than remarks uttered on the floor by a legislator who is not a member of the committee. Another difficulty, Killian noted, lies with the power to revise and extend in both houses. "Even a speech that's delivered on the floor may not be the speech that ends up in the *Congressional Record*"; it becomes a device to construct legislative history for subsequent judicial consumption.

Improvements

Having considered problems of institutional capacity and the uses of legislative history, the colloquium ended with a preliminary inquiry into ways to improve relations between the branches.[4] Accepting Feinberg's view that some tensions between the branches are inevitable, attendees believed that much could be done to ameliorate conditions—or, as Coffin put it, to reverse "a gradual . . . perceptible . . . and unnecessary distancing of the two branches." Some participants suggested change within the judicial branch itself. Others urged a greater role for the Department of Justice, an increased educational effort in both branches about each other's processes, and the borrowing of mechanisms from other experiences that have proved effective in promoting communications. All agreed with former judge Emory Sneeden that one should not expect to "solve all these problems within the next year or two."

With respect to the judiciary, participants suggested that various improvements were possible. Ross supported Coffin's idea that problems in legislation identified in judicial opinions be collected and be made available to Congress. Mecham stated that the courts needed to create an early warning system to monitor from the outset legislative activities bearing upon the judicial system. Moreover, he asserted that it may be desirable to create a "clearing" committee of senior judges who might have the time to keep watch on Congress. The subsequently established liaison group of judges working with the Executive Committee of the Judicial Conference seeks in part to help realize that objective.

Because the problems of the courts have no special constituency in Congress and because the judiciary does not have adequate resources to place its case high on the legislative agenda, it becomes all the more necessary, remarked Rosenberg, to create "institutional arrangements that have low silhouettes, low power bases, but have long-term staying capacity." And the question, he continued, is "What kinds of agencies and institutions are there around now, that are in a position either to be charged up and given more power, or what kind could be created?" Ideally, he said it would be desirable to have a ministry of justice that could take the long view. But short of that, Rosenberg urged the revival of the Office for Improvements and the Administration of Justice in the Department of Justice—a bureau that existed in the Carter administration and was led by Daniel J. Meador and Rosenberg, but was disbanded during the Reagan administration. Because "over half of

4. Frank M. Coffin led this panel. Discussants were L. Ralph Mecham, Hans A. Linde, Leonard Garment, Maurice Rosenberg, Paul D. Carrington, Emory Sneeden, Roger H. Davidson, and Gilbert Y. Steiner.

the business, by volume, in our federal courts, and far more than 50 percent of it in . . . importance, is [the] business of the U.S. Government and its agencies," it makes "a lot of sense for the U.S. government executive branch, Department of Justice, to take an interest in how the courts . . . [are] working."

Breyer put it this way: "The Justice Department is not an alternative to the Administrative Office [of the U.S. Courts], nor an alternative to any kind of feedback. Rather, it should be viewed as . . . a supplement. . . . How can the department be made to take seriously the responsibility of seeing the justice system as a whole and speaking for the institutional interests of the courts as part of that justice system? And . . . how can the department, as part of that task, obtain feedback from the judges as well as from its own lawyers?"

Rosenberg also called for renewed attention to the idea of a three-branch high-level council that takes a long look at the needs of the federal judicial system and works for legislative change—facilitated by its congressional membership.

In view of congressional apathy toward the courts, Carrington suggested that thought be given to devices that do not require the judiciary to secure the attention of several hundred members of the legislative branch. One such successful method is found in the Rules Enabling Act of 1934, in which the general rules of the Supreme Court take effect unless disapproved by Congress within a ninety-day period after they have been reported by the chief justice. Roger Davidson of the Congressional Research Service observed that, in fact, it was not necessary to talk to all members of Congress but only the strategic people in the key committees. So that the Judiciary Committee can better monitor the effect of legislation on the judicial system, Davidson also commented it might make greater use of the rereferral process (by which bills from other committees that have an effect on the courts are sent to the Judiciary Committee).

Several discussants emphasized the need for an educational effort so that judges and legislators understand each other's problems and working environments. That learning process should extend, Mecham observed, to legislative staff as well. To encourage the education in both branches, Ross proposed the integration of staffs—that is, congressional committees should look for people who have worked in the federal court system, and judges should think of individuals who have served on legislative staffs as possible law clerks. In addition, as Mikva recommended, more judges with prior legislative experience should be appointed.

Thinking about the legislative and judicial processes, attorney Leonard Garment remarked that "there is a huge, complex capillary system of transactions and relationships and a flow of information and activities backwards and forwards, and that it is, in that sense, part fact and part mystery, and part substance and part magic." To make sense of those intricacies, he suggested that judges, "just as they are exposed to prisons, be taken on a tour of Congress by those masters of the capillary system of legislation where so much takes place that affects the movement through the arteries."

Several speakers mentioned the importance of informal settings where judges and legislators could discuss concerns. Scalia reflected that "once upon a time, the Supreme Court used to sit in the Capitol . . . and one can imagine . . . the scene of the judges leaving their session and mingling in the corridors with the legislators. . . . I am sure that to some extent the reason that the executive and the legislature get along well enough, despite the inherent conflict that's built into the system, is the fact that they're composed of people who get to know one another, and I think that makes a big difference in any institution."

Apart from considering changes in existing institutions, some of the colloquium participants raised the possibility of borrowing from other experiences and approaches in developing means to improve relations between the branches. Brookings senior fellow Gilbert Y. Steiner commented, "I take it that communication is most likely to be improved if it is possible to develop some kind of a mechanism that involves no preaching by either side, that involves an acceptance of the idea of the coequality of the branches, and that involves acceptance of the notion of a mechanism that has legitimacy." Such a mechanism should provide some opportunity for all of the units within one or another of the branches to be heard. Moreover, it should provide for a relatively open-ended agenda, confining discussions, by and large, to persons who are associated with these two branches—and thus Steiner would not support involving the Department of Justice because it has its own agenda and interests, which could complicate deliberations between the judiciary and Congress. Most important for Steiner, such a device should be a two-way channel in which each branch could express itself to the other. He suggested that a model does exist, which comes from the need to improve communication between relatively coequal agencies and was born not as a consequence of the separation of powers, but rather of the division of powers: the Advisory Commission on Intergovernmental Relations. That body brings together, on a coequal basis, federal, state, and local governments to discuss and examine mutual concerns. Its structure, Steiner commented, may offer a guide to the kind of mechanism that can promote effective communications between the judiciary and Congress.

Borrowing from the states' experience, Linde urged that more thought be given to law revision commissions. Such bodies offer an organized way for the judiciary to present ideas for reform to the legislature. In Louisiana, judges serve as voting members of the revision commission.

Coffin offered a checklist of improvements to be examined at a future session. The list includes judicial communication to the legislature with respect to the burden and workability of legislation; impact statements; mechanisms for transmitting judicial commentary and decisions as to statutes; an ombudsman within Congress to receive complaints about a case, a judge, or the judicial system; devices to clarify legislative history; structural changes within the Judicial Conference and the Administrative Office of the U.S. Courts; and educational seminars and social meetings bringing together participants of each branch. These ideas are among those incorporated and set forth more fully in the last chapter as a blueprint for future research and discussion.

The Continuing Challenge

Robert A. Katzmann

-»»)«<-

In his opening remarks at the colloquium, Judge Frank M. Coffin suggested three specific objectives for the session. The first was to peel off as many misperceptions and erroneous generalities as possible concerning both Congress and the judiciary; the second was to construct the beginnings of an agenda for practical inquiry and implementation; and the third was to initiate an ongoing process to pursue that agenda. "Our hope," he stated, "is that the day's proceedings will impress us as having enough relevance and potential to encourage us to continue to exchange ideas, test, criticize, amend, and finally, recommend and promote within an ever-widening constituency."

That agenda should blend both theory and practice. Were the focus simply an abstract examination of relations between the judiciary and Congress, the work would hardly be done. What is further needed is the linkage of conceptual ideas with pragmatic solutions. The agenda should be faithful to constitutional norms and societal values and respectful of the institutional prerogatives and norms that underlie relationships among the branches. Moreover, any proposals for improvements should be evaluated as to their feasibility—not only whether they can be achieved, but also at what costs. Required is a weighing of advantages and disadvantages, judged in terms of normative views about the way the system should work. Three central themes that constitute the intellectual basis of the inquiry are also at the heart of the agenda for practical improvements. The first delineates the kinds of ground rules for communication and patterns of relationships that are appropriate. The second examines how courts can better understand the legislative process and legislative history, the ways in which Congress can better signal its meaning, and how the judiciary can make the legislature aware of its decisions interpreting statutes. And the third explores the institutional processes and mechanisms that can be devised to improve relations between the branches.

Ground Rules for Communication

The anxiety among judges and legislators about communications stems from uncertainty about the ethical, legal, and prudential boundaries. The canons of judicial conduct provide only limited counsel as to what judges can do; legislators have virtually no formal guidance at all. In the search for a formula governing exchanges between the judiciary and Congress, various questions need to be addressed.

NATURE OF THE ISSUE.   Some agreement must be reached about the kinds of issues that are appropriate for communication and whether the nature of issues affects judicial input. Consider, for instance, two types of legislation. The first, judicial administration or housekeeping, bears upon such things as the structure and procedures of the federal courts, the number of judges, judicial discipline, appropriations, and salaries. The second, general legislation, is concerned with the whole gamut of laws that the judiciary might be called upon to interpret. Between these kinds of legislation, are there any differences in the nature of judicial involvement?

FORMS OF COMMUNICATION.   Communication can be both direct and indirect. The former would include judicial testimony at congressional hearings, personal visits between judges and members of Congress, and telephone discussions between judges and legislators or their staffs. Indirect communication, designed at least in part to reach the congressional audience, would include a judge's speech before some professional groups or university or an article in a law review. Some determination must be made as to the opportunities and problems each form of communication poses and circumstances under which one kind of communication is preferable to another.

MANNER OF REPRESENTATION.   Another important question has to do with who should present the communication and under what auspices. Usually the Judicial Conference transmits the judiciary's positions on legislation. But should individual judges be free to express their views to committees? To individual members? Should there be a clearance procedure for some or all issues? On what basis? In communicating their concerns, should judges seek or accept the support of surrogates in the bar, academia, or the media? Should and can the bar, for instance, have a continuing "honest broker" role? Discussion is needed about what is appropriate in the nature of such surrogate relationships and the kinds of issues that can be handled through surrogates.

INITIATION. The judiciary and Congress have maintained the fiction that the Judicial Conference will not present its views on legislation unless a congressional committee specifically asks for them. In reality, Administrative Office staff members have, on a number of occasions, asked their legislative counterparts to request conference positions on subjects that the judiciary would like to address. The congressional committee has agreed, and then the conference has replied. If the barriers preventing easier interaction between the judiciary and the Congress are overcome, is such a fiction necessary to preserve? In other words, should the judiciary initiate or only respond to a request? Should individual judges be permitted to make proposals?

TIMING. The legislative process involves a number of phases, including initiation, enactment, and oversight. How, if at all, would the nature of judicial involvement change at each phase? What is Congress's responsibility as to the timely consideration of such judicial input?

EXCHANGES BETWEEN JUDGES AND LEGISLATORS. In thinking about appearances before Congress, many judges are concerned about the nature of the questioning. They are anxious about being called on to prejudge issues, provide (in effect) advisory opinions, or offer opinions about the substantive merit of legislation. The tensions between legislators and would-be judges may first surface at the time confirmation is being considered. As Judge Coffin wondered in his *Federalist* essay, "Is it possible to arrive at a consensus on the kinds of questions from legislators and answers from judges that properly serve the interests of the interrogators without entrenching upon the dignity, impartiality, and independence of the judicial nominee?"

CONGRESSIONAL COMMUNICATIONS WITH THE JUDICIARY. Congress communicates with the judiciary when it passes legislation affecting judicial administration or when the Senate considers judicial nominees. It obviously affects the courts whenever it enacts statutes that will ultimately involve judicial interpretation. Moreover, Congress speaks to the judiciary when, in reaction to a court decision, it passes new legislation designed to overturn or to cure a legal deficiency.[1] Beyond such rather formal—and often delayed—

---

1. Legislative overrule can have different meanings. It can imply disagreement with the court, but it need not. Sometimes a court feels constrained by the plain meaning of a statute, but invites change ("overruling") by the legislature. At times, the Supreme Court will simply note that it is for Congress to express its will if it disagrees with the result of a particular case. At other times, the invitation to "overrule" will be more explicit. I am grateful to Professor A. Leo Levin for this observation.

means of communication, it would be worth exploring other ways for Congress to engage in discussions with the judiciary.

JUDGES ON CONGRESSIONALLY MANDATED COMMISSIONS. Also meriting attention is whether and under what circumstances it is appropriate for judges to serve on statutorily mandated commissions.

Understanding the Legislative Process and Legislative History

As I have indicated, the need for an appreciation of the legislative process emerged at the colloquium as an important area for further study. Some believe that improvements in relations between the branches are partly dependent upon a better judicial understanding of that process. Others would contend that what is needed is not so much a better understanding of the legislative process, but a normative framework to guide courts in assessing legislative intent or meaning.

The matter of judicial interpretation is complex; arguably, it has become more complex in the last fifteen years as Congress has changed. One might spend some time pondering what can be done about the legislative fragmentation, the conflicts among committees, the difficulties in making trade-offs, and the lack of deliberation by Congress—all of which contribute to the courts' problems in understanding the legislative process. But there may be more immediate steps that could be taken to clarify statutory meaning and legislative history involving the related matters of statutory drafting, interpretation, and revision. Clarifying statutory meaning has at least three parts. The first is in some sense preventive; that is, it seeks to anticipate potential difficulties and to deal with them before a bill becomes a law. As such, it goes to the heart of the drafting process. The second component focuses on the materials that constitute legislative history and is geared toward finding ways for Congress to signal its meaning more clearly. And the third part entails developing routinized means so that, after the enactment of legislation, courts that have experience with particular statutes can transmit their opinions to Congress, identifying problems for possible legislative consideration.

DRAFTING. The House of Representatives and the Senate have offices of legislative counsel, trained in the nuances of drafting. It would be useful to determine if some way could be found to require that all bills be subject to some central scrutiny of these offices, applying accepted standards, as there is in some states. Might a checklist of common problems be prepared for the benefit of those in Congress who do not use the professional drafting services, which could reduce judicial burdens and at the same time give clearer direction as to legislative intent? Such a checklist would focus the legislators' attention on such matters as constitutional severability, civil statute of limitations, attorneys' fees, private right of action, preemption, and exhaustion of administrative remedies. These issues, when they are not explicitly addressed in the legislation itself, are often left to the courts for resolution. To be sure, in particular cases Congress may deliberately not deal with such matters for political reasons; but in other situations, the legislature might very well choose to do so if made aware of the problem. To improve drafting, periodic seminars involving legislative counsel, staff, and judges might be helpful.

LEGISLATIVE HISTORY. Attention should be paid to the ways in which legislative signals of intent could be made clearer. For example, consider the significance to be attached to committee reports. As described earlier, Justice Antonin Scalia contends that with their heavy work loads, legislators generally do not have time to read these documents (especially if they are not on the committee from which the report emanates). Ultimately, these reports may become important as courts interpret them in the quest to understand the statute. Given all this—and assuming they are to be given weight as courts seek to understand statutory meaning—are there practical means to ensure or make it more likely that committee reports receive positive congressional assent? Are there ways to distinguish between those parts of committee reports that receive such affirmative approval and those that do not? Is it feasible to have the checklist discussed earlier subject to committee approval? Should committee reports have perpetual force, as Justice Scalia wondered, or only be binding as long as the committee has the same composition that it had when it issued the document?

Deserving scrutiny is the question of whether the most important and agreed-upon background and purposes of the legislation can be more sharply identified. Are there ways, as Judge Kenneth Starr queried, for Congress to instruct the courts with respect to the degree of deference it should give to its delegate, the administrative agency? What value should be placed on amicus briefs of legislators seeking to influence a court's view about legislative intent? With respect to the legislative process generally, are there procedures, as Judge Coffin asked, that would help identify the mainstream of understanding where there is such? If not, then how should courts interpret legislative history? What should constitute legislative history?

STATUTORY REVISION. It would be useful to assess as well Judge Coffin's suggestion that judicial criticisms be collected from opinions and rulings and presented for congressional examination. Would it not be worthwhile to identify conflicts among the circuits with respect to legislative meaning, which Congress could resolve?[2]

Mechanisms for Improving Judicial-Congressional Relations

Apart from reaching some understanding about the ground rules for communication and issues relating to statutory construction, interpretation, and revision, it is vital to consider practical ways to improve the mechanisms for interaction between the judiciary and Congress. Such an analysis has at least three components: evaluating structural change within the judiciary and Congress; applying lessons from other approaches; and ascertaining ways to promote ongoing exchanges.

Structural Change within the Judiciary and Congress

In thinking about how the judiciary should provide its views to Congress, it might be helpful to divide the legislative process into its various phases: problem identification, legislative initiation, consideration (or enactment), and postenactment oversight. At each stage, the task is to determine the kind of mechanism within the judiciary—the Administrative Office of the U.S. Courts, the Judicial Conference, the chief justice—that is best suited to achieve the desired end.

Any inquiry about means must include an examination of the Legislative and Public Affairs Office of the Administrative Office of the U.S. Courts: the extent to which it is organized to serve as an early warning system for the Judicial Conference by keeping it informed about legislative developments, anticipating problems, and providing alternative ways to react to events in Congress; how equipped the office is to perform its tasks at the various stages of the legislative process; and the ways the office is organized to forge links with congressional committees and staffs and to offer assistance at hearings or in other contexts. In short, what can be done to reinforce the efforts of an able office as it seeks to deal with the legislative labyrinth?

Also worthy of consideration is how a small policy-planning and evaluation unit soon to be created within the Administrative Office can work with the Judicial Conference committees, offer support for those presenting the

---

2. On this subject, see John Paul Stevens, "Some Thoughts on Judicial Restraint," 66 *Judicature* 177, 183 (1982); Wilfred Feinberg, "Foreword—A National Court of Appeals?" 42 *Brooklyn Law Review* 611, 627 (1976); and Milton Handler, "What To Do with the Supreme Court's Burgeoning Calendars?" 5 *Cardozo Law Review* 249, 275–76 (1984).

judiciary's case in Congress, assist the courts in answering congressional inquiries, and be of special benefit with respect to long-developing legislation.

As for the postenactment stage, if Judge Coffin's suggestion about collecting judicial criticisms for presenting to Congress were adopted, it still remains to determine how and where such a collection point should be created within the federal court system. For instance, should the Administrative Office of the U.S. Courts or the Federal Judicial Center be the locus of activity? It might be useful to categorize the types of problems identified in the opinions and to determine which opinions should be first funneled to the Judicial Conference, the policymaking arm of the federal court system, before transmittal to Congress. As an example of what can be done, the Governance Institute is helping to design a mechanism to transmit statutory opinions of the U.S. Court of Appeals for the D.C. Circuit to Congress and to facilitate legislative consideration.

More broadly, it is important to examine the workings of the Judicial Conference (for which the Legislative and Public Affairs Office labors). The Judicial Conference was not organized to respond to legislative activity on a daily basis. It is now attempting to remedy this weakness through such devices as a legislative liaison group to help the conference's Executive Committee monitor congressional activities. What might be done, if anything, to fortify such efforts? Should there be other changes in committee structure or function?

As a way to make Congress more aware of the problems of the courts, several have suggested that the chief justice deliver a "State of the Judiciary" address to a joint session of the legislature. Is this idea worthy of consideration, or are there other ways in which the chief justice or someone else could communicate the concerns of the federal courts to Congress?

Improvements in relations between the branches could result from changes not only within the judiciary, but also within the legislative branch. In Congress, the Judiciary and Appropriations committees are virtually the only ones with any appreciation of the problems of the courts. Yet the other congressional committees affect the judiciary all the time—for example, whenever they pass legislation that will inevitably involve judicial interpretation or impose burdens on the work load of the courts. The problem is to ascertain how these committees and their legislators and staffs can become more conscious of the problems confronting the judiciary.

One possibility would involve a "tripwire" device that would lead to an analysis of the effect of bills on the judiciary. Required is an examination of the kinds of legislation that lend themselves to "impact statements," taking into account the difficulties in making such forecasts.

Congress would become aware of the judiciary's opinions and suggestions bearing on statutory revision if they were collected on a routine basis, as Judge Coffin proposed, and transmitted to relevant committees. Ascertaining what kind of mechanism should be developed within the judiciary to identify such opinions still leaves unresolved the nature of the legislative role. Deserving further study is how and to whom such recommendations should be conveyed and the ways in which committees or staffs might take action on such suggestions.[3] Preliminary evidence indicates that staffs support the creation of a low-visibility mechanism that would directly transmit judicial opinions and suggestions from the courts to the committees with jurisdiction over the legislation under review.

Focusing on how the judiciary might present its views to Congress is but one part of the equation. Needed as well is an understanding of how the legislature might communicate with the judiciary about the functioning of the courts. As a first step, perhaps the annual reports of activities of the Judiciary committees could be sent to judges' chambers. With respect to complaints about the conduct of a case, a judge, or the workings of the judicial system, is there a need, as Judge Coffin asked, for an ombudsman to receive, assess, transmit, and monitor such complaints? As to legislative reaction to the judiciary's interpretation of statutes, the same mechanism transmitting opinions and suggestions of the courts to Congress could monitor the legislature's responses and make reports available to the third branch.

Short of actual internal structural change, the other two branches might benefit from input by the executive branch. Judge Stephen Breyer and Maurice Rosenberg stated that the Department of Justice can play an important part in the administration of justice.[4] Former Attorney General Edward Levi has suggested that the failure to provide the Department of Justice with a role has deleterious consequences for all three branches.[5] Might it be desirable for other executive departments or agencies, apart from the Department of

3. Remarks of Robert A. Katzmann before the D.C. Circuit Judicial Conference, Williamsburg, Virginia, May 24, 1988. Judge Ruth Bader Ginsburg of the U.S. Court of Appeals for the D.C. Circuit and Peter Huber have advanced the proposal that a standing "second look at the laws" committee be installed in each house (or jointly) to oversee the task of statutory reexamination and repair. Ruth Bader Ginsburg and Peter W. Huber, "Commentary: The Intercircuit Committee," 100 Harvard Law Review 1417, 1429–34 (1984). See also Henry J. Friendly, "The Gap in Lawmaking—Judges Who Can't and Legislators Who Won't," 63 Columbia Law Review 787 (1963).

4. On this point, see also Daniel J. Meador, "Role of the Justice Department in Maintaining an Effective Judiciary," in A. Leo Levin and Russell R. Wheeler, eds., The American Judiciary: Critical Issues (The Annals of the American Academy of Political and Social Science, 1982), pp. 136–51.

5. Letter from Edward H. Levi to Judge Frank M. Coffin, October 22, 1985.

Justice, when preparing legislation for congressional consideration, to include some evaluation of the bill's effect on the judiciary? In that regard, would it make sense for the executive to use a checklist of the kind proposed above for congressional consideration as it sends legislation to Congress?

Learning from Other Approaches

The effort to improve relations between the judiciary and Congress need not be restricted to reforming existing structures within those two branches, but can also draw upon approaches from other experiences. Two, in particular, may have something to offer: law revision commissions in the states and mechanisms to promote cooperation and reduce conflict among federal and state governments.

As Justice Hans Linde observed, many states have law revision commissions that provide for the orderly reassessment of statutes, bringing together representatives of all three branches. Such commissions lead not only to better understanding between the branches, but also perhaps to improved legislative drafting. Might such an approach be useful at the national level?

It might also be profitable, as Gilbert Steiner commented, to study models used in other institutional arenas to promote cooperation and reduce conflict. One such mechanism is the Advisory Commission on Intergovernmental Relations (ACIR). The ACIR was created to monitor the operation of the American federal system and to recommend improvements. It is a permanent national bipartisan body, created by Congress, representing the executive and legislative branches of the federal, state, and local governments and the public. Would there not be merit in delving deeper into the ACIR experience (or other such mechanisms) to see if it might serve as a guide?

Promoting Ongoing Exchanges

Several attendees remarked that the mere process of interaction between representatives and personnel of each branch was important. Concentrating only on institutional mechanisms may obscure the fact that human beings populate institutions, and that the conflicts between organizations may be reduced if the people within them were to know one another and to secure a better appreciation of each other's problems and responsibilities. Other kinds of exchanges might be appropriate.

For instance, as part of their orientation, new members of Congress and their staffs could take part in seminars on the judicial process, perhaps given by those who work in the federal court system. Similarly, new judges, staff attorneys, and law clerks could benefit from workshops on congressional lawmaking.

Also meriting discussion is the value of holding ongoing colloquia, perhaps through a university or research institution, that would bring together judges, members of Congress, and personnel within each branch for dinners, lectures, and discussions. Perhaps a society could be created, consisting of judges, legislators, and even executive officials, which would sponsor such activities.

Conclusion

The core problems of judicial-congressional relations are long-standing. No one should have any illusions about the ease with which they can be addressed. Some issues may be intractable. At the very least, heightened understanding should benefit each branch, and policymaking, too.

In an exchange about the colloquium with Representative Robert Kastenmeier, at an oversight hearing of the Subcommittee on Courts, Civil Liberties, and the Administration of Justice of the House Judiciary Committee, A. Leo Levin, then director of the Federal Judicial Center, remarked: "I think there is a tremendous potential to begin early on a very small basis, one that is not terribly intrusive. I think there is a lot more that can be done, and my hope is that something will be done to facilitate the working together of the different branches of government."[6]

Under the auspices of the Governance Institute the next stage of activity is under way: the creation of working groups consisting of judges, legislators, key persons in the legislative, judicial, and executive branches, and members of the private bar. Over the next few years, each group will have the task of examining in depth, with the purpose of facilitating practical results, one of three critical areas that give rise to this work.[7] The objective is to assist those in the judiciary and Congress who would seek to ameliorate the current state of affairs between the branches.

Little more than sixty-five years ago, Benjamin Cardozo, reflecting upon the experience in his home state of New York, lamented that "legislature and courts move in proud and silent isolation." As a consequence, "On the one side, the judges, left to fight against anachronism and injustice by methods of judge-made law, are distracted by the conflicting promptings of justice and logic, of consistency and mercy, and the output of their labors bears the tokens of the strain. On the other side, the legislature, informed only casually

6. *Oversight of the Judicial Branch,* Hearings before the Subcommittee on Courts, Civil Liberties, and the Administration of Justice of the House Committee on the Judiciary, 100 Cong. 1 sess. (Government Printing Office, 1987), p. 47.

7. These activities will be undertaken in tandem with the book I am writing for the Brookings Institution on relations between the judiciary and Congress.

and intermittently of the needs and problems of the court, without . . . systematic advice as to the workings of one rule or another, patches the fabric here and there, and mars often when it would mend."[8] The same could be said of the national legislature and judiciary. In New York, Cardozo's plea led to the creation of a law revision commission. Determining the shape of possible structural improvements in the effort to improve relations between the federal courts and Congress is a part of the continuing challenge.

These working groups represent a commitment to address a significant area of institutional stress. The salient features of the effort lie in identifying several smaller parts of the problem, developing in advance explorations of concrete proposals, assembling a small but representative group to reflect upon the proposals, and making recommendations of the actions deemed the most useful. These ventures constitute the beginning of a process. As a community of interest takes on depth and continuity, one may hope for insights and resolutions as yet unforeseen.

8. Benjamin Cardozo, "A Ministry of Justice," 35 *Harvard Law Review* 113, 114 (1921).

Contributors

-›››X‹‹‹-

PATRICK S. ATIYAH is professor of English Law at St. John's College, Oxford University, and was visiting professor of law at Duke University School of Law at the time of the conference. His books include *The Rise and Fall of Freedom of Contract; Promises, Morals and Law;* and *Form and Substance in Anglo-American Law: A Comparative Study in Legal Reasoning, Legal Theory, and Legal Institutions* (with Robert S. Summers).

FRANK M. COFFIN is a U.S. circuit judge, sitting on the Court of Appeals for the First Circuit. He served as chief judge from 1972 to 1983. He is chairman of the Committee on the Judicial Branch of the Judicial Conference of the United States. Judge Coffin has also served in the legislative and executive branches, as a member of Congress from Maine and as deputy administrator of the Agency for International Development. His books include *The Ways of a Judge: Reflections from the Appellate Bench* and *A Lexicon of Oral Advocacy.*

ROGER H. DAVIDSON is professor of government and politics at the University of Maryland. He was formerly a senior specialist in American government and public administration at the Congressional Research Service. He is the author or coauthor of numerous articles and books, including *The Role of the Congressman; Congress Against Itself;* and *Congress and its Members.*

ROBERT W. KASTENMEIER has been a member of Congress from Wisconsin since 1959. He is chair of the Subcommittee on Courts, Civil Liberties, and the Administration of Justice of the House Committee on the Judiciary, and also serves on the Subcommittee on Civil and Constitutional Rights of the House Judiciary Committee, the Subcommittee on Legislation of the House Permanent Select Committee on Intelligence, and the Subcommittee on Program of Budget Authorization of the House Permanent Select Committee on Intelligence. Representative Kastenmeier has written several articles on court reform.

ROBERT A. KATZMANN, formerly a senior fellow and now a visiting fellow in the Brookings Governmental Studies program, is president of the Governance Institute. A lawyer and a political scientist, he is directing the project on judicial-congressional relations at the invitation of the U.S. Judicial Conference Committee on the Judicial Branch. He is the author of *Regulatory Bureaucracy: The Federal Trade Commission and Antitrust Policy* and *Institutional Disability: The Saga of Transportation Policy for the Disabled,* and coeditor of *Managing Appeals in Federal Court.* Katzmann has also written on regulation, the administrative process, antitrust policy, institutional reform litigation, and court reform for a variety of journals. He is an adjunct professor of law and of public policy at Georgetown University.

HANS A. LINDE is a justice of the Oregon Supreme Court. He served as a law clerk to U.S. Supreme Court Justice William O. Douglas, legislative assistant to Senator Richard L. Neuberger of Oregon, a professor of law at the University of Oregon Law School, and as a member of the Administrative Conference of the United States. He is the author of numerous articles in scholarly journals. With George Bunn, Fredericka Paff, and W. Lawrence Church, he wrote a casebook, *Legislative and Administrative Processes.*

MAEVA MARCUS is director of the Documentary History Project of the Supreme Court. She holds a Ph.D. in history and is the author of numerous articles. She wrote *Truman and the Steel Seizure Case: The Limits of Presidential Power* and coedited *The Documentary History of the Supreme Court of the United States, 1789–1800.*

MICHAEL J. REMINGTON is chief counsel of the Subcommittee on Courts, Civil Liberties, and the Administration of Justice of the House Committee on the Judiciary. He has been a trial attorney in the Department of Justice and the deputy legislative affairs officer of the Administrative Office of the U.S. Courts. Remington has written several articles on the administration of justice.

EMILY FIELD VAN TASSEL was formerly an associate editor of the *Documentary History of the Supreme Court, 1789–1800.* She is currently a Ph.D. candidate at the University of Chicago and is an adjunct professor of law at the Georgetown University Law Center.

Conference Participants

with their affiliation at the time of the conference

➤➤✕◄◄

THOMAS E. BAKER
Supreme Court of the United States

JUDGE STEPHEN BREYER
U.S. Court of Appeals for the First Circuit

WILLIAM R. BURCHILL, JR.
Administrative Office of the U.S. Courts

DEAN PAUL B. CARRINGTON
Duke University School of Law

WARREN I. CIKINS
The Brookings Institution

JUDGE FRANK M. COFFIN
U.S. Court of Appeals for the First Circuit

SHARI COMINS
Latham and Watkins

ROGER H. DAVIDSON
Congressional Research Service

JUDGE WARREN EGINTON
U.S. District Court, Connecticut

WILLIAM ELDRIDGE
Federal Judicial Center

KENNETH FEINBERG
Kaye, Scholer, Fierman, Hays and Handler

LOUIS FISHER
Congressional Research Service

LEONARD GARMENT
Dickstein, Shapiro and Morin

LINDA GREENHOUSE
New York Times

HAYDEN GREGORY
Subcommittee on Crime
House Committee on the Judiciary

STEPHEN HESS
The Brookings Institution

JUDGE IRVING HILL
U.S. District Court
Central District of California

JEFFREY W. KAMPELMAN
Shaw, Pittman, Potts and Trowbridge

REP. ROBERT W. KASTENMEIER
Subcommittee on Courts, Civil Liberties,
and the Administration of Justice
House Committee on the Judiciary

ROBERT A. KATZMANN
The Governance Institute and
Brookings Institution

WILLIAM C. KELLY, JR.
Latham and Watkins

JOHNNY H. KILLIAN
Congressional Research Service

A. LEO LEVIN
Federal Judicial Center

JUSTICE HANS A. LINDE
Oregon State Supreme Court

BRUCE K. MACLAURY
The Brookings Institution

ROBERT MALLETT
Kaye, Scholer, Fierman, Hays and Handler

193

THOMAS MANN
American Political Science Association

MAEVA MARCUS
Documentary History Project
Supreme Court of the United States

FRANCIS J. MC NAMARA, JR.
Cummings and Lockwood

L. RALPH MECHAM
Administrative Office of the U.S. Courts

JUDGE ABNER J. MIKVA
U.S. Court of Appeals for the D.C. Circuit

THOMAS MOONEY
Subcommittee on Courts, Civil Liberties,
*   and the Administration of Justice*
House Committee on the Judiciary

PAUL E. PETERSON
The Brookings Institution

THOMAS RAILSBACK
Blum, Nash and Railsback

KIMBERLY REED
University of Virginia School of Law

A. JAMES REICHLEY
The Brookings Institution

MICHAEL REMINGTON
Subcommittee on Courts, Civil Liberties,
*   and the Administration of Justice*
House Committee on the Judiciary

PROFESSOR MAURICE ROSENBERG
Columbia University School of Law

STEVEN R. ROSS
Office of the Clerk
U.S. House of Representatives

JUSTICE ANTONIN SCALIA
Supreme Court of the United States

CHESTERFIELD H. SMITH
Holland and Knight

EMORY SNEEDEN
McNair Law Firm, P.A.

SYLVAN SOBEL
Federal Judicial Center

JUDGE KENNETH STARR
U.S. Court of Appeals for the D.C. Circuit

GILBERT Y. STEINER
The Brookings Institution

EMILY FIELD VAN TASSEL
Documentary History Project
Supreme Court of the United States

WILLIAM WELLER
Administrative Office of the U.S. Courts

LAURIE WESTLEY
Senate Committee on the Judiciary

RUSSELL WHEELER
Federal Judicial Center

BRAD WILSON
Supreme Court of the United States

Index

→>>X<<←